W9-CZU-300

THE GOLDEN AGE
OF
AMERICAN ILLUSTRATION
F. R. GRUGER
AND HIS CIRCLE

MY GREATEST DISCOVERY by ALBERT PAYSON TERHUNE
American Magazine, June, 1929, Page 28

THE GOLDEN AGE
OF
AMERICAN ILLUSTRATION
F. R. GRUGER
AND HIS CIRCLE

By Bennard B. Perlman

Introduction by F. R. Gruger, Jr.

North Light Publishers, Westport, Connecticut

Published by NORTH LIGHT PUBLISHERS, a
division of FLETCHER ART SERVICES, INC.,
37 Franklin Street, Westport, Conn. 06880.

Distributed to the trade by Van Nostrand
Reinhold Company, a division of Litton
Educational Publishing, Inc. 450 W. 33rd Street,
New York, N.Y. 10001

Manufactured in U.S.A.
First Printing 1978

Library of Congress Cataloging in Publication
Data

Perlman, Bennard B.
  The golden age of American illustration.

  1. Gruger, F. R. — Friends and associates.
2. Illustrators — United States — Biography.
I. Title.
NC975.5.G78P47   741′.092′4   [B]   77-99224
ISBN 0-89134-011-4

Designed by Walt Reed
Printed and bound by The Book Press

THE WITCH DOCTOR OF ROSY RIDGE by McKINLEY KANTOR
The Saturday Evening Post
April 15, 1939

Contents

SOMETHING NEW by P. G. WODEHOUSE
Illustration for *The Saturday Evening Post,* July 10, 1915, Page 16

Dedicated to the Golden Age of American Illustration, to F.R. Gruger and all the artists whose creative abilities helped make the literature and events of the period come alive.

Foreword

During the late nineteenth and early twentieth centuries many of the country's leading portraitists, landscapists, muralists and even abstractionists were also producing illustrations for newspapers, magazines and books: Winslow Homer, Frederic Remington, Joseph Pennell, Thomas Eakins, John Twachtman, Childe Hassam, John Sloan, William J. Glackens, Everett Shinn, George B. Luks, George Bellows, Maurice Prendergast, Lyonel Feininger and Arthur G. Dove, among others.

The vast majority of the artist-illustrators eventually abandoned their dual roles, preferring instead to concentrate on painting, sculpture or printmaking. One who did not was F.R. Gruger.

For forty-five years, from 1898 until 1943, that signature appeared on some six thousand illustrations, which earned for Frederic Rodrigo Gruger the longest career, and a prominent place, in the limited front rank of American illustrators.

The first and last of his illustrations were created for *The Saturday Evening Post,* which reproduced more than half of his life-time production; the remainder appeared in some thirty of the leading magazines of the period.

Gruger illustrated stories by more than four hundred authors, from Bret Hart and Theodore Dreiser to F. Scott Fitzgerald and William Faulkner.

The Golden Age of American Illustration dawned with the decade of the 1880s. Using the artwork in English periodicals as their standard of excellence, American artists such as Edwin Austin Abbey, A.B. Frost and Howard Pyle began producing illustrations to accompany articles in *Harper's, Scribner's* and *Century.* Abbey was the acknowledged master of English historical drawing, Pyle of the American past, and Frost the best illustrator of rural America. Abbey and Frost were natives of Philadelphia and had attended the Pennsylvania Academy of the Fine Arts there. F.R. Gruger, also a Philadelphian and Academy-trained, became their successor.

During Gruger's student days he was a classmate of Sloan, Glackens, Shinn and Maxfield Parrish. In the years that followed he lived and worked in New York, and numbered among his friends and acquaintances such artists as J.C. Leyendecker, Franklin Booth, James Montgomery Flagg, Norman Rockwell, Arthur William Brown, Dudley Gloyne Summers, Edgar F. Wittmack, Henry Raleigh, Neysa McMein and John R. Neill, all of whom were similarly part of the Golden Age of American Illustration.

The era began to tarnish and fade in the 1930s, when the Depression saw many magazines fail. Others had eliminated illustrations for reasons of economy. The story-telling drama and appeal of such original artwork was also challenged by an increasing use of photographs.

For five decades the Golden Age flourished because of a desire to heighten the literary experience through visual interpretation, and the availability of a host of talented illustrators with perception, experience and skill. This, then, is their story, and the chronicle of one artist in particular who helped make it happen.

Bennard B. Perlman
Baltimore
February, 1978

"He had blundered upon the watchman in the cabin."
THE CUTTING OUT OF THE "HEAVENLY HOME" by NORMAN DUNCAN
Ainslee's Magazine, July 1902
This was one of the very early half-tone illustrations made by FRG for the magazines.

Acknowledgments

Although Frederic Rodrigo Gruger has been recognized by *Time* Magazine as the "dean of U.S. magazine illustrators,"[1] the artist's aversion to publicity limited the number of articles in print about him. When I began this project some three years ago, it was therefore most fortunate that I could count on the full cooperation of F.R. Gruger, Jr. "Ted" Gruger has proven to be far more than a reservoir of facts and anecdotes about his father and the period; he has become a research colleague, delving into the books and magazines of the era with devotion and enthusiasm.

He has also provided me with access to extensive family records, including his father's library, correspondence between F.R. Gruger and members of his family, diaries, sketches and hundreds of photographs and motion pictures taken by the artist. The wealth of information gathered on the following pages attests in part to his memory for detail. We have spent many hours together poring over documents, taping conversations and seeking answers to questions long left unresolved. In short, without such aid and encouragement this volume could not have been written.

The author is likewise indebted to F.R. Gruger's daughter, Elizabeth G. Van Buren, and his cousin, John A. Frank who have been most cooperative and generous with their time.

The origins of this book actually reach back some twenty years, to a time when the author began collecting information for another volume, *The Immortal Eight: American Painting from Eakins to the Armory Show, 1870 to 1913*. In this connection I had one telephone conversation with F.R. Gruger himself, on September 8, 1952, just six months prior to his death. During June and July, 1956, the writer was taken by Ted Gruger to interview his mother and sister at the latter's home in Brielle, New Jersey. For these associations and recollections I am most grateful.

Others in the 1950s who provided material for this book include: Everett Shinn, Maxfield Parrish, Edward W. Redfield, Dorothy Grafly, Margery Ryerson and Mrs. John (Helen) Sloan. The last, a long-time friend, has given untiringly of her wise counsel and has aided in the reading of the manuscript prior to publication.

Foremost among those who welcomed my inquiries and responded to the limits of their memories and abilities are F.R. Gruger's peers, the illustrators themselves: Dudley Gloyne Summers, Frank C. Bensing, Carl Roberts, Harold Von Schmidt, Everett Raymond Kinstler, Norman Rockwell, William Reusswig, Paul Bransom, Donald Teague, Raeburn L. Van Buren, Adolph Treidler.

And Harold N. Anderson, Harry Beckhoff, John Falter, Mario Cooper, John J. Floherty, Jr., Peter Helck, Stevan Dohanos, Garrett Price, Leonard Holton, Henry Pitz, Thomas Fogarty, Jr., Dow Walling and Tom Lovell.

I wish also to thank Mrs. John R. (Margaret) Neill, Mrs. Edgar Franklin (Maud) Wittmack, Bill Zerbo, Walt Reed, W.T. (Pete) Martin, Ben Hibbs, Arthur William Brown, Charles T. Henry, Coy L. Ludwig, Fred M. Meyer, Mrs. Oliver Cromwell Curtiss, Ruth Plumly Thomson and Ray Powell.

F.R. Gruger's library, his papers and a portion of his collection of illustrations have been donated to the University of Oregon at Eugene. Two of the University librarians, Edward Kemp and Martin Schmitt, have been especially helpful during the research period and have contributed invaluable service in reviewing the manuscript. Similarly, Milton Hopkins, PhD, editor and author, offered many worthy suggestions after a careful reading of the text.

And, finally, a note of appreciation to the individuals and institutions whose kind assistance has made writing this book such a joy: Thomas N. Armstrong, III, former director of The Pennsylvania Academy of Fine Arts; Arpi Ermoyan, the New York Society of Illustrators; Lawrence Campbell, the Art Students League; Janet Shafer of Pratt Institute; Elsa Long, The School of the Art Institute of Chicago; Helen L. Carlock, The Encyclopedia Britannica; Wendel L. Woodham, The United States Naval Academy; Ruth Candliss of the Miss America Pageant; and numerous staff members of the Enoch Pratt Free Library and the George Peabody Library of Baltimore, The Library of Congress, Free Library of Philadelphia, The Philadelphia Museum of Art, New York Public Library, Yale University Library, Brooklyn Museum and the Delaware Art Museum.

B. P.

March 30, 1953 issue.

Introduction

Automobiles were scarce and fascinating when I reached the age of seven. We would run to the porch or front lawn to see one go by at the dizzy speed of 18 mph, announced well in advance by its unmistakable clatter. It is not surprising, therefore, that my first recollection of my father at work was standing beside his rocking chair (he always used one, for by rocking back he could view his work from a greater distance) and watching him finish a pen-and-ink drawing of an automobile which had run head-on into a tree.[1] This was very interesting of itself, but even more so was the fact that the rear wheels were rotating while the front wheels were still. My curiosity was answered by a lucid explanation—my first introduction to the field of mechanical engineering.

This disposition of father's to explain clearly and simply from an astonishingly broad fund of knowledge was to become a major element in the education of my sisters and of me, and a constant encouragement to the development of our interests. An unobtrusive guidance and a ready companionship went hand in hand with his generosity in providing materially for his family.

He was good-natured, optimistic and positive, while at the same time modest and socially unaggressive. But he liked people and was intensely interested in and observant of them. In return he was genuinely liked by those who got to know him, for he was a gentleman with some Victorian qualities whose knowledgeable conversation was illuminated by a real sense of humor. "FR," as he was often called by his friends, seemed content to achieve what prominence he could through his work, but he never relaxed the effort to make it speak eloquently, to which persistence some of his last illustrations bear witness. I believe he considered competitiveness as somewhat sordid and inherently wasteful. On his return from Philadelphia one day he told me of an incident when he stopped in at the *Post* to see Mr. Lorimer and the Art Director, Mrs. Riddell. In the course of the conversation she mentioned "his competitors." He replied: "I compete with no one. I do my own work to the best of my ability and I believe the other illustrators do the same."

Quality was always his goal. Not that he was a perfectionist in the popular sense, but he did endlessly strive to do the best job of which he was capable in the time he had. I have known him to work weeks and redo a drawing many times to surmount a problem which seemed to defy solution. On the other hand there were compensating experiences when drawings would be finished quickly and with little effort. Many a time he said to me as a youngster, when no doubt I deserved the admonition: "Remember, there is no such thing as 'good enough.' Whatever you do, do the best you can."

From years, literally, of study of the magazines while seeking the facts of his record, I have the sincere impression that F.R. Gruger dealt with a greater range of subject matter than any other illustrator. Each had range, of course, but most got to be favored by certain types of stories which were then fed to them with somewhat inhibiting regularity. FRG, on the other hand, was sent manuscripts of an extraordinary variety—mostly "period" or non-contemporary stories, or when contemporary, of foreign, unusual locales. Among the originals I have, which make up less than 15 percent of his output, are pictures set in Mesopotamia, Rome, Medieval Europe, Elizabethan England, Colonial America, Civil War and modern times. There are stories of American Indians and Blacks, of Orientals, Arabs, Mayas and Incas, as well as tales involving ships and the sea, animals, mostly horses and their accoutrements, and rural American life. Because of this variety, very many aspects of architecture, furniture, costume and equipment were treated in authentic detail. His work depicts instances of war from the Crusades to World War I; home life from the hovel to the palace; gardens, landscapes, forests, clouds; country and city scenes; and illustrates stories of mystery and of love in an imaginative and individual way, in the latter rarely relying on the pictorially trite embrace.

Through all of this the human figure predominates; active, expressive and in character —and all created without the use of models. His extraordinary ability to depict character and his fine compositions are the aspects of his work which were given recognition so often during his career. I do not know of a single instance where he relied on caricature. Understanding the facial anatomy of the various races, he could depict them unmistakably without exaggeration. One feels that he deeply respected the dignity of the people he drew; and by identifying with them, developed an understanding and sympathy which made them particular individuals expressing themselves with characteristic gesture and their own personal behavior.

These aspects of father's illustrations are built into compositions of line and tone which are always balanced and fluid. Precise tonal values and accurate linear perspective combine to create an astonishing effect of the third dimension and of atmosphere in the literal sense.

FRG was a friend and admirer of many of his contemporaries and had a collection of about forty original subjects given him by perhaps thirty different artists.[2] Names I got to know very well, of men he particularly admired, were: Walter Biggs, Reginald Birch, Franklin Booth, Arthur William Brown, Pruett Carter, Charles E. Chambers, Dean Cornwell, Harvey Dunn, James Montgomery Flagg, Charles Dana Gibson, Arthur I. Keller, J.C. Leyendecker,

Wallace Morgan, H.J. Mowat, John R. Neill, Norman Price, Henry Raleigh, F. Walter Taylor and N.C. Wyeth.[3]

His imagination was not limited to graphic art for he was creative in the three-dimensional world as well, playing a prominent part in the design and detail of the houses he built, in his gardens and their architectural features and the landscaping about his homes. A good deal of our furniture was designed by him and built to his specifications. Similarly, many of our toys were designed and made to his order, happily in the days when plastics were not even a glint in the chemist's eye. In optics he created several accessories and two special purpose lenses which he had built by Carl Zeiss. He was keenly interested in photography and as early as 1907 was making color plates by the Lumiere process. He never used photography directly in his work, but took hundreds of photographs for pleasure and as reference material. Later 16 m/m motion pictures attracted his interest, resulting in the exposure of thousands of feet of film. With a 4″ refractor telescope and a binocular microscope he inspired in us an interest in the heavens and in the realm of the minute.

Father was cautious and would not take unnecessary risks. He was not tempted by gambling, and alcohol gave him bad headaches. He would not take part in sports involving physical risk. Similarly, although dexterous and endowed with mechanical aptitude, FRG would do no mechanical work about the house. His attitude was that he used his hands to make pictures and thus was able to pay others to do the chores. He enjoyed the respect and cooperation of the local artisans, however, because he respected them, was able to explain clearly what he wanted done, to make technical sketches and to inspire a desire to excel.

Although father would sometimes discuss politics with mother his conversation was normally free from the subjects of political affairs, business and finance. At the dinner table he would be really interested in our activities, in current events and would often tell us about the story he was illustrating. Otherwise his conversation ranged over as wide a field of subjects as his book collection. (In looking back I sometimes wonder how one who had to do so much reading in connection with his work, found the time and urge to do so much more.)

The fact that FRG did not commute to work and had no visible means of support led the townspeople in Avon, N.J., to believe at first that we lived on mother's money. Being a Nineteenth Century Methodist minister's daughter, mother's contributions, although manifold, were not heavily weighted with packets of bonds.

My appreciation of this book about my father does not stem primarily from the belief that he was a fine artist, but rather from the knowledge that he was a fine and unusually whole person.

I think his goals in life were two-fold: to excel, not competitively, but from a belief in intrinsic merit, in his profession of Illustration; and to provide his family with a full, interesting and rewarding life. Though he attained these goals, he would have been the first to point out that they could have proven illusory had he not had the good fortune to marry a woman of comparable integrity whose mature affection spelled unfailing support.

Frederic R. Gruger, Jr.
Bellerose, N.Y.

notes

[1] "Millington's Motor Mystery," see page 57.

[2] The majority of these, together with FRG's papers and a large selection of his original drawings, have been given to the Library of the University of Oregon; and other of his and his contemporaries' work to the Sanford Low Collection of American Illustration of the New Britain Museum of American Art.

[3] Others whose careers paralleled FRG's are: Paul Bransom, Charles Livingston Bull, Anton Otto Fisher, Thomas Fogarty, Herbert Johnson, W.H.D. Koerner, Charles D. Mitchell, May Wilson Preston and James M. Preston, F.E. Schoonover, H.J. Soulen, Clarence Underwood and George Wright.

Chapter 1

When America celebrated the one hundredth anniversary of its Independence in the form of the Philadelphia Centennial Exposition, the event was heralded as the "greatest spectacle ever presented to the vision of the Western World."

Carriages, horsecars and special trains from Washington, Baltimore, New York and Boston jammed the routes leading to the gently rolling slopes of Fairmont Park. There some two hundred buildings had been erected just for the occasion, including one which covered four times the ground of St. Peter's in Rome.

The Exposition's grandiose Machinery Hall quickly became the focal point of attention, a tribute to America's mechanical genius and coming of age. Here were to be found an assemblage of working models to awe, instruct and amuse the spectator; inventions such as the Corliss steam engine and the self-binding reaper, the telephone and the continuous-web printing press.

In the ornate and imposing Memorial Hall was housed the country's first national art exhibition: fifteen rooms of American painting, a thousand canvases calculated to dazzle the viewer. The Exposition emphasized "biggest" and "best," for here, too, was displayed the largest ceramic piece ever produced, a colossal statuary rising twenty-one feet.

The City of Philadelphia had been decked out in red, white and blue bunting for the grand opening on May 10, 1876, a day announced by the ringing of the Liberty Bell in Independence Hall and the sound of all the bells of Philadelphia joining in a merry chorus. President Ulysses S. Grant was in attendance that day, as were some 186,671 other individuals, a crowd described by the New York *Herald* as the largest ever assembled on the American continent.[1] Little wonder, then, that the official Centennial handbook raised the rhetorical question:

> What better method of celebrating our Country's birth to freedom than by a grand exhibition...What better place in which to hold such an exhibition is there than Philadelphia?[2]

Actually, the Centennial Exposition opened three weeks later than first planned; its inaugural was supposed to have coincided with the anniversary of the Battle of Lexington. The one Centennial event in the city which did correspond with the earlier date was the formal dedication of the new and elegant building of the Pennsylvania Academy of the Fine Arts at Broad and Cherry Streets.

The Pennsylvania Academy, established in 1805, was venerated as the country's oldest art institution. It was indeed appropriate that the completion of this new edifice should have been associated with the Centennial year, for the Academy had originally been constituted in the very room that witnessed the signing of the Declaration of Independence. If Independence Hall marked the birthplace of American freedom, it could also be considered an incubator for American art.

The symbolic link had become a reality when one of the signers of the Declaration of Independence, George Clymer, was elected the first president of the Pennsylvania Academy.

From the outset, America's eminent artists were associated with the Academy in Philadelphia, which sought "to promote the cultivation of the fine arts (and) to unfold, enlighten and invigorate the talents of our countrymen." Charles Willson Peale, the person most responsible for its founding, was a distinguished painter, originator of the nation's first museum and patriarch of its first great family of artists. William Rush, one of the art school's original directors, has been called the first native American sculptor. George Caleb Bingham, William Harnett and Mary Cassatt studied there; in fact, the proud boast of the Pennsylvania Academy is that throughout the first one and one-quarter centuries of its existence, virtually every significant figure in American art had been somehow associated with the institution.[3]

The effect of the Centennial celebration was to further Philadelphia's preeminence in the field of American art for several decades to come. As a result, the Pennsylvania Academy's quarters at Broad and Cherry Streets served as an increasingly powerful esthetic magnet, attracting prospective young artists from metropolitan Philadelphia and beyond.

For instance, by the years 1892 and 1893 there labored, in a single classroom, a coterie of art students whose contributions to the fields of illustration and painting would be recognized within a decade: John Sloan, William J. Glackens, F.R. Gruger, J.J. Gould, Everett Shinn, Florence Scovel, James Preston, Elmer Schofield, Edward W. Davis, Maxfield Parrish, Joseph Laub, Guernsey Moore and J. Horace Rudy.

Florence Scovel hailed from Camden, New Jersey; Everett Shinn was born downstate in Woodstown. John Sloan came from Lock Haven, Pennsylvania and James Preston from the northwest Philadelphia suburb of Roxborough. And Gruger, Glackens, Schofield, Parrish and Moore all called Philadelphia home.

Frederic Rodrigo Gruger was born in Philadelphia on August 2, 1871. His father, John Peter Gruger, was of remote German descent; his mother, Rebecca Rodrigo Gruger, of Spanish lineage. Her family had fled from the political unrest in Europe in 1848, settling first in Cincinnati and then in Philadelphia, where Rebecca's father ran an artificial flower manufacturing concern.

F.R. Gruger's paternal ancestors came to this country from Hesse, Germany, in 1735. Two brothers, both well-to-do farmers, left their native land as political refugees and emigrated to Middletown, Berk's County, Pennsylvania. For over a century the family continued to live there and in Womelsdorf, Columbia and Lancaster, Pennsylvania, all within a forty-mile radius.[4]

Frederic Rodrigo Gruger was the seventh generation in this country and was named for an Uncle Frederic, who fought in the Civil War. By 1879 the family moved from Philadelphia to Lancaster, and FRG lived there from the time he was eight years old until his nineteenth birthday, as he once recalled in a letter:

> Cousin Walter was about my age and my chief crony in the 1880s. Vacation time meant a long visit with grandparents, cousins, uncles and aunts who all lived in one big house just where the pavement ended and the dusty road to the real country began.
>
> In the back yard were chicken pens. Collecting the household eggs was Walter's privilege which he shared with me on a competitive basis. Whichever got dressed and downstairs first of a morning grabbed the basket and went for the eggs.
>
> One mean and rainy morning our competition became a slow race. Being the better dawdler I followed down and went into the back parlor where my grandfather sat reading. I stood at a window that looked down the garden along the wet and slippery boardwalk with leaves plastered on planks smeared with squashed tomatoes. And there, down by the smokehouse, was Walter coming along under a dripping hat, collar up and basket huddled under his coat. A dismal picture. But when he slipped and fell, the day didn't seem so bad and I set up a great noise of laughter and danced about...being ten years old.
>
> Grandfather turned a page and said quietly, "Go see if he's hurt and what eggs are broken."
>
> After a few pleasurable moments I returned to announce that "five eggs are bust and Walter skinned his knee."
>
> Grandfather nodded. "Get a dime out of your money box," he said, "go up to Mrs. Bender's and buy five eggs."
>
> "But, Grandpa, *I* didn't break 'em."
>
> "No?"
>
> "No, I didn't. I was in *here*."
>
> "So you were. But *you* had all the fun...go buy the eggs!"[5]

F.R. Gruger's father became associated with a family named Howell, owners of a marble yard in Lancaster.

John Gruger, father of Frederic Rodrigo Gruger

Eventually he and Frank Howell became partners in the enterprise, and the firm operated under the name of Howell & Gruger. The stone contractors produced marble linings for the interiors of buildings, as well as architectural details such as friezes, cornices, window lintels and sills. The company supplied some of the stonework for the Philadelphia City Hall.

Howell & Gruger also supplied much of the stone for the new Lancaster High School while F.R. Gruger was a student there. He got to know the operation of the marble yard quite thoroughly, and displayed an aptitude for sketching designs for the stonework. Young Gruger worked for his father during school vacations, and on other occasions was sometimes called out of class to help direct the setting of stones.

One summer FRG was made foreman of a gang working on the high school. He was on the third or fourth floor, when without warning the guy wire that held a hoist gave way, and the forms fell directly toward him. He stepped out onto a rather flimsy scaffold, put there to hold mason's tools. The boards bounced up and down with his weight, but fortunately held. As he looked down at the ground, he saw his father running to catch him if he fell.

To accelerate the slow and laborious task of cutting stone with wire and sand, John Gruger looked for a steam saw that would do the job. After considerable discussion

Young FRG Jr. and his grandmother

between father and son, the youngster made a complete set of drawings for the kind of engine necessary to operate the saw, then located a steam engine of the type required. After the steam saw was installed, FRG was responsible for its operation.

During his student days at Lancaster High, FRG did well with very little effort. What he lacked in exact knowledge he made up for in logic. When a history teacher asked him to date a certain event, he replied that he didn't know, but that it was about the same time that such-and-such was going on in another country. The instructor commended him for his reply, for it showed that he had acquired an understanding of history, even if he had failed to memorize a date.

FRG spent a great deal of time reading outside of school. He had a sizable collection of books stored in a mausoleum in the local cemetery. On pleasant days he would sometimes play hookey, take a few of his favorite volumes, and sit in the graveyard and read. He did not have the fear other youngsters would have had of such an environment because his father's marble works produced tombstones, and he might have drawn the designs for some of them. [6]

FRG was constantly drawing and from his earliest remembrance it was quite clear to him that he wanted to become an artist:

> My father and my uncle were excellent pen draughtsmen. On my left hand is a blue tattoo mark gained at the age of three by grabbing my father's ink-filled pen, a sort of innoculation, perhaps. [7]

FRG's father was an amateur sculptor, and would occasionally carve a small head from the marble yard scrap. He also created jigsaw puzzles by mounting art reproductions on thin wood. But he resisted his son's professed interest in an art career, and suggested he learn a trade. Rejecting this notion, FRG decided to join the navy. He took the examinations for admission to the Naval Academy in Annapolis, and had a sponsor for his appointment there. When he approached his father and proudly announced: "Behold, a future admiral!" the idea was immediately rejected. "One thing I will not give my consent to is your going into the military service," John Gruger stated firmly. Perhaps by a process of elimination, this made a career in art an acceptable alternative.

FRG's real exposure to art began when he became acquainted with William Arnell, a stationer, who took an interest in him. Gruger was only twelve years old at the time:

> On the south side of East King Street in Lancaster stood Fondersmith's Stationery Store, immaculate, perfect of its kind, a small Brentano's. William T. Arnell was in charge of the picture department. He was a tall man, slender, fragile, who died in his twenties. He was my first teacher; by no means the least of those to whose criticism and advice I listened. [8]

In Arnell's stock were excellent reproductions of the works of the Old Masters, the best Victorian painters and many lesser artists. "He used them in an effort to develop what appreciation and understanding a twelve year old boy might gain from them," FRG recalled.

Arnell introduced him to the pen drawings of Edwin Austin Abbey, Charles Reinhart and Charles Keene, and encouraged him to make line for line copies of them. Abbey's technique and subject matter proved especially appealing to FRG, who soon began collecting Abbey reproductions. A worn red fiber folder of his marked "Edwin Abbey" attests to a continuing interest in the artist, who was then regarded as the best of the English or American illustrators. Abbey's fine line pen-and-ink work, his costumed courtiers and medieval settings were challenging tasks for the teenager, but FRG soon became adept at duplicating Abbey's illustrations for such classics as *She Stoops to Conquer* and the *Merry Wives of Windsor*.

The fact that Edwin Austin Abbey was a native Philadelphian who had studied at the Pennsylvania

FORD. "Hang her, witch!"
Merry Wives of Windsor — Act IV., Scene II, by William Shakespere

Illustration by Edwin Austin Abbey

Academy was not lost on the aspiring artist.

While working under William Arnell's guidance, FRG learned of James S. Earle & Sons picture gallery in Philadelphia through announcements of exhibitions. When an exhibit of original Abbey drawings was held there in 1890, FRG went to the showrooms at 816 Chestnut Street, carrying with him one of his copies. He was pleased to discover that the original of the drawing he had made was in the show and further, that he had so well estimated the dimensions of the work that the original and copy were virtually identical in size.

While FRG was making the comparison, Mr. Earle observed what appeared to be an Abbey drawing in his hands and the boy was accused of stealing one of the pictures. FRG became the center of attention, all the more so when he explained what had happened. Mr. Earle, obviously impressed by the youthful talent, suggested that he enroll in classes at the Academy.

In the fall of 1890, F.R. Gruger took Earle's advice.

notes for chapter 1

[1] Based on the population of the country at that time, this number would be equivalent to a crowd of about 925,000 persons today.

[2] "Contributions to the International Exposition, Philadelphia," p. 153

[3] "Who's Who in Philadelphia," *Time* Magazine, February 7, 1955, p. 67

[4] Peter Kruger, F.R. Gruger's great grandfather, was a wagonmaker. FRG's grandfather, Adam Peter Gruger, was a manufacturer of wagons, carriages and whips, who would amuse himself by weaving designs on his fingers with colored threads. He would then apply the patterns to whip handles. The family surname, originally Kruger, had been changed arbitrarily by Adam Peter because many of the Krugers had identical given names, causing constant confusion.

Henry Cruger, whose branch of the family adopted yet another spelling, had been a prosperous Philadelphia merchant during the Revolutionary War, at which time he contributed funds and merchandise to aid Washington's Army at Valley Forge. In recognition of that public service, a small pastel portrait of him by James Sharples was hung on the first floor landing in Independence Hall.

[5] Letter sent by FRG to "Life in These United States," *Reader's Digest* (undated).

[6] Despite his erratic attendance, FRG maintained an above-average record. For one two-month period, he ranked second among the twenty-four students in his class. The top pupil achieved a grade of ninety-one, followed by FRG with an eighty-four, Hiram D. Mc-Caskey with eighty-three and Joseph R.T. Gray, Jr. with eighty-two. The McCaskey and Gray youths were Fred's closest friends. Hiram McCaskey's father, Dr. John P. McCaskey, was principal of the high school and a great influence on FRG. He took a special interest in the students, and was credited with being one of the first educators to introduce supplementary school activities, which included the early promotion of gymnastics. Dr. McCaskey subsequently became mayor of Lancaster. Joseph R.T. Gray, Jr., FRG's other schoolboy chum, would one day become his brother-in-law.

[7] "F.R. Gruger," *American Artists*, n.p.

[8] Ibid.

MISTRESS QUICKLY. "Marry, this is the short and the long of it; you have brought her into such a canaries, as 'tis wonderful."
Merry Wives of Windsor — Act II., Scene II, by William Shakespere

Illustration by Edwin Austin Abbey

Thomas Anshutz — *Steelworkers . . . Noontime* (1890)
Private Collection, New York (or N. Y.)

Robert Henri — *Night, Café Terrace* (1899)

Charles Grafly — *Hugh H. Breckenridge* (no date)
Courtesy of The Pennsylvania Academy of the Fine Arts

18

Chapter 2

When F.R. Gruger matriculated at the Pennsylvania Academy in the fall of 1890, he began his studies in what was called the Antique Class, where students drew from plaster casts, a solid tradition at the Academy. The practice had prevailed in the city since 1784, when a plaster cast of Venus arrived from Europe, and was soon being drawn by the students of Charles Willson Peale. In 1806, within a year of the Academy's founding, the U.S. Minister to France, Philadelphian Nicholas Biddle, persuaded Napolean to send to this country casts of classical statues acquired by France.[1]

The Antique Class at the Academy was scheduled from 9:00 a.m. to noon, and from 1:00 to 3:30 p.m. daily. A decade earlier it was mandatory that the beginner remain in the Antique Class for six months, but the system was changed by Thomas Eakins during his tenure as the school's director, from 1882 to 1886. FRG found the new arrangement to his liking, for it provided that when a student could control a drawing, and had demonstrated some knowledge of anatomy, he was recommended to the Life Class, where students drew from the nude model. A student's instructor might elect to send him back for a couple of months of additional drawing from the Antique, where more fundamentals could be acquired.

FRG entered the Academy with considerable facility for pen drawing, but had virtually no experience with charcoal, the medium employed almost exclusively that first year. In his second year he enrolled in the Composition Class, another area in which he possessed little background.

> When I was a student we all were greatly interested in the Composition classes although, I seem to remember, none of us knew what it was all about when we went into the first session.
> We soon found out. We had an exceedingly good instructor who explained fundamental picture structure...After we had got along fairly well with that part of it, we went into another class where it was explained to us how the function of structure applied to the meaning of the picture. To the story.[2]

The Composition Class instructor, Henry J. Thouron, sought to stimulate the creativity of his students. He would draw a rectangular area, then locate within it a few freehand lines and a dot. "Now I want a picture where this dot is the lobe of a man's ear and these lines are incorporated," he would advise. All of the elements would have to become part of the composition; *that* was the challenge. Each student then evolved an original picture where the design was controlled by the novice artist, rather than by

happenstance.[3]

Not all in the class were equally stimulated by this approach. Maxfield Parrish once complained: "Think of giving the composition class as subject 'The Signing of the Declaration of Independence'..."[4]

While FRG also studied at the Pennsylvania Academy with Robert Vonnoh, James P. Kelly and Thomas Anshutz, he always credited Anshutz with providing his greatest insight into composition and art.

By the fall of 1892 FRG was working full-time as a newspaper artist, so he relinquished his daytime studies at the Academy in favor of evening classes with Anshutz. There he met William Glackens, John Sloan, Joseph Laub and James Preston, all similarly employed in various newspaper art departments. They, however, were enrolling in an Academy class for the first time.

Thomas P. Anshutz, himself a Pennsylvania Academy alumnus, was a born teacher. He refused to impose a given technique upon the class but allowed each member to solve the problems of drawing and working from casts. Like his own teacher, Thomas Eakins, he taught anatomy by carefully modeling each muscle in clay, then placing the forms upon a skeleton. A nude model would be posed nearby, so that the comparative muscles could then be viewed and easily understood.

Tom Anshutz was at once a teacher and a friend. His students considered him one of the crowd, and called themselves "Tommyites" and "Smudgers," the latter a reference to their method of blending charcoal in their drawings.[5]

During the first evening of the Anshutz class several Academy alumni dropped in. Charles Grafly, a sculptor, had been a student there from 1884 to 1888, having studied under both Eakins and Anshutz. He had recently returned from Paris, where one of his life-size female figures had received honorable mention in the Salon of 1891. Equally impressive to the students was the fact that a Grafly sculpture entitled *Daedalus* had just been purchased for the permanent collection of the Pennsylvania Academy.

Grafly brought with him another former Academy student, Robert Henri, an Anshutz alumnus who had begun teaching classes in anatomy, portraiture and drawing from the Antique at the nearby School of Design for Women. FRG related:

> (Henri) was in Paris when I first went to the Pennsylvania Academy of Fine Arts. I heard him spoken of and I realized his return was somewhat eagerly anticipated. When he did come home I, along with everyone else, fell under the spell of his winning personality...[6]

Party in Charles Grafly's studio — Philadelphia, late 1892. This photo was taken after the show, "Annie Rooneyo". John Sloan met Robert Henri at this party.
Identifiable in the photo are Henri, in lower left center, wearing a stove pipe hat, seated to the left of Edward Redfield who has a ring in his nose. Sloan is in the center, rear, under a large pistol. Gruger is apparently not in this photo.

John Sloan Collection, Delaware Art Museum

Henri spoke that evening in the Academy classroom of the paintings he had seen in Europe, and then proceeded to make a charcoal drawing of the female nude who was posing before the group. FRG drew also. "That first evening," he recalled, "when I did a charcoal sketch of the model, I sat directly opposite Henri, so he got into the picture too." [7]

A few weeks later Charles Grafly held a party at his studio on the southwest corner of Twenty-second and Arch Streets, to which he invited many of the currently-enrolled Academy students, along with those of his European traveling companions who had returned from abroad. The Grafly affair was strictly stag, with nearly forty Academy alumni and students in attendance. Some of the older men appeared in costume, usual in those days when artists gathered to entertain themselves. Host Charles Grafly combined a flowing black artist's cravat with fur-covered cowboy chaps while Edward W. Redfield came dressed as a bearded sheik with an oversized ring through his nose. Hugh Breckenridge was enveloped in a striped shawl, Elmer Schofield sported a bib and fake beard, and Henri a battered top hat and the long ruffled cuffs of a French gentleman. Those more conservatively dressed, among them many of the Anshutz students, included Glackens, Sloan, Gruger, Davis, James Preston, Charles Williamson, John Weygandt, Charles Young and William Gosewisch.

The Grafly party, the first social get-together of so large and significant a contingent from the Academy, would lead to other such studio gatherings, through which a sense of camaraderie developed.

Despite the seriousness of their studies at the art school, the students found time for frivolity. Although smoking, for instance, was traditionally forbidden in the Life Class, a sign announcing "Smoking Permitted" appeared on the bulletin board one day. As a result the students had to peer at the model through a thickening atmosphere. The Academy's grand staircase, with its soaring space and Victorian, wrought-iron decoration, was a natural location for horseplay, which included racing down the stairway on drawing boards. FRG was crowned speed champion in that event.

After a semester with Anshutz, the group learned that their teacher was leaving for Europe in mid-year. The spring term began with a replacement who proved to be unsatisfactory to many in the class. There was a general feeling of boredom at having to draw continually from the Antique. In addition to the instructional problem, tuition was a growing concern, for the Academy fee of five dollars a month became an increasing hardship in a year of financial crisis.

In February, 1893, Sloan and Joe Laub, who shared a third floor studio at 705 Walnut Street, discussed a cooperative scheme. Their idea spread among the former Anshutz students. A photographer's quarters were rented at 112-114 North Ninth Street, and there on March 15 the Charcoal Club was born. Equipment consisted of a half dozen easels and chairs, model's stand and a large table borrowed from Sloan's studio. They also installed Welsbach lights, a decided improvement over the dimly-lit Academy classrooms.

On April 8 the Philadelphia *Times* reported on this latest addition to Philadelphia's art organizations:

Under the skylight in a room formerly occupied by a crayon photographer, the club holds its nightly sessions. Composed as it is of members engaged in industrial artwork, the meetings are devoted to practice and mutual criticism of immediate practical value.

On three evenings Tuesday, Thursday and Friday of each week a paid model is posed. The remaining nights are given up to sketch work. Compositions are submitted each Monday evening when all of the members of the Club sit in judgment on the results. Criticisms are freely given and the interchange of ideas kindles and sustains a lively interest. The successful competitor is chosen by a vote of the Club.

Three subjects thus far have been assigned for competition: Dawn, Spring and Ophelia. For the best composition of the latter, the award was made last Monday evening to Robert Henri...

Within the first month of its existence, the Charcoal Club had a membership of twenty-seven; by May it had thirty-eight. Henri served as president of the group, Sloan was secretary and Joe Laub treasurer. Among the other regular members were Gruger, Glackens, Shinn, Davis, J. Horace Rudy, Albert Adolph, Vernon Howe Bailey, William Gosewisch, Harry Rotter, W.E. Worden and Carl Lundstrom.

About the Charcoal Club, FRG once observed:

We had a bit of a composition class among ourselves, as advanced students. We had no teacher. We put up our studies and all of us had a crack at them. It was a good class. Robert Henri used to come in, occasionally, and John Sloan and William Glackens and Everett Shinn. Well, the idea that any mark on paper had power came up. We talked about that. Plenty. Then one of the students went up to the sheet of charcoal paper that was always ready, just in case. He drew a rectangle and put a dot in it. The dynamic dot, someone called it. We talked for an hour about that dot. Then the same lad drew very lightly the diagonals and diameters and put a dot where they all crossed in the center. You'd be surprised at the number of things we found to say about that. Why was the first dot the dynamic dot and the second one completely static... [8]

Club members worked in pen-and-ink as well as charcoal, and the majority of their studies were portraits. Above all, they sketched with a kind of carefree abandon which was not likely to be tolerated in the Academy classes. One of FRG's efforts, a six-inch high charcoal

Early Gruger figure sketch

drawing, depicts a standing nude model, relaxed with knees slightly bent and an arm thrust forward. The figure is dramatically lit by the glow of the Welsbach lights. There is no degree of detail or polish, and the paper's texture is revealed through roughly blended tones of gray.

Harrison Morris, director of the Academy, kept a wary eye on the Charcoal Club. Its membership had grown to almost twice the number attending his evening class. Yet by summer there were signs that the new enterprise would not flourish. Members began to drop out. "Cooperative schemes at two dollars per month won't stand hot weather," John Sloan philosophized. On September 14, 1893 the final class was held, and the Charcoal Club passed into limbo. Not even the cooling breezes of autumn revived it.

As a parting gesture, Sloan made a charcoal drawing of four anguished artists stuffed into the rear of a wagon. "The Charcoal Club is on the Wain," read the caption.

The Pennsylvania Academy eagerly welcomed back its errant students, and even purchased the group's easels, chairs and Welsbach fixtures. Thomas Anshutz was teaching again at the Academy that fall, and some of the group enrolled in his evening class once more.

Meanwhile, during the summer a nucleus of the artists from the ill-fated Charcoal Club had begun to transform the dying weekly Life Class into a lively discussion group which met on Tuesday evenings at Henri's studio. An air of companionship permeated these informal gatherings, and 806 Walnut Street soon became a veritable haven for a group of illustrators, painters and sculptors.

Robert Henri's studio was in a made-over loft building, a four story structure with bay windows on each floor. His quarters were on the upper level, where a sky-light had been built. An audience of up to two dozen would assemble to hear Henri's inspired, impromptu lectures. This was his domain, and he would hold forth in a captivating manner.

The weekly meetings were at first undirected talks, but Henri gradually assumed the role of moderator. On one occasion he would voice opposition to the Academy's exhibition policy, which appeared to overlook the work of the newspaper artists who were studying there. On another he regretted the general lack of interest in the Academy classes, pointing to this indifference as indicative of the contradictory art worlds of Philadelphia and Paris. Many of his biting comments and witticisms had their origin in William Morris Hunt's *Talks on Art*, both volumes of which Henri possessed. Hunt's observations were incorporated into Henri's own thoughts:

> The highest light on the face is usually on the spot which would get wet first if you were out in the rain...
> You think it an insult to put a shadow upon a face! The Lord doesn't think so! [9]

Henri selected other portions of Hunt's discourses as more serious food for thought:

> Some people have expressed themselves as discouraged in their expectation of finding any art in America, and have "long since ceased to hope!" Let us remember that art...has always existed, in all nations, and the tradition will probably not die here. [10]

FRG remarked:

> Henri pretended no superiority. He made us feel that he was just an older student who by good fortune had enjoyed great advantages, advantages which he shared freely...[11]

FRG was a regular at Henri's Tuesday evenings, as were Sloan, Glackens, Davis, Preston, Grafly, Redfield, Schofield, Breckenridge and Calder. [12]

Henri's Tuesday evenings had a marked effect upon most of the newspaper artists and Academy students who attended. The younger men were receptive to Henri's philosophy. Some, like John Sloan, would readily admit the influence: "Henri could make anyone want to be an artist...", he said. Others acknowledged Henri's contribution in thought-provoking silence: on more than one occasion, FRG walked home from the art talks with William Glackens and noted that not a word passed between them.

There were also lighter moments at 806. "If we threw a party in the studio, we got a keg of beer or some wine and cheese and crackers," Sloan recalled. Once he drew up a menu card listing frankfurters, black bread and beer on tap, with each item written in German to help simulate a rathskeller atmosphere. At other times the crowd produced amateur theatricals and Henri's studio was transformed into a little theatre. Charles S. Williamson, an Academy alumnus teaching at Gerard College, was an amateur lyricist of the Gilbert and Sullivan variety. He produced comedies given such titles as *Annie Rooneyo* and *The Widow Cloonan's Curse*.

The audience was composed primarily of Academy students. The first row sat on newspapers arranged on the floor, the second row on chairs and benches. Back row seats consisted of window shutters placed across carpenter's saw-horses. "The audience was provided with beer and crackers, and there was more time devoted to intermissions than the play itself," observed Sloan. [13]

George duMaurier's *Trilby* was published in 1894, and Williamson seized upon it as a natural for the 806 players since the heroine was an artist's model. DuMaurier himself was a well-known illustrator whose ink drawings in *Punch* were a great inspiration to newspaper artists.

The appeal of the farce, called *Twillbe*, was so general that the production was moved from the confines of 806 Walnut Street to the lecture room of the Pennsylvania Academy. Billed as the "Third Grand Christmas Effusion of the P.A.F.A. Students," *Twillbe* was staged on December 29, 1894 before a typically high-spirited, year's end crowd. Sloan had spent weeks creating the sets, Ed Davis supervised the choreography, and Henri and Glackens helped with costumes and make-up.

The cast consisted of Henri, Sloan, Glackens, Davis, Williamson, Shinn, Laub, Preston, Frank A. Taylor and Dennis Kelly. The heroine, played by John Sloan, had enormous feet instead of the delicate little ones for which Trilby was famous. Sloan sang *Sweet Alice Ben Bolt* in his best falsetto. Henri was the villain, Svengali, appropriately bitten to death by New Jersey mosquitoes in the final act.

A mock boxing match photographed in 1895 at 806 Walnut Street. Standing, from left: James Preston, John Sloan, Everett Shinn and F. R. Gruger (holding cigarette). "Boxer" on the left is George Luks. Sloan Collection, Delaware Art Museum

Much of the fun was impromptu. When Sloan, as Twillbe, jumped on a table at the sight of a mouse, his false bosom fell on the floor. With a magnificent gesture, Henri kicked the padding into the wings, and the play was completed with a flat-chested heroine.

FRG attended most of the theatricals, but was never a member of the cast. Less demonstrative than the others, he was content to enjoy the hilarity from a seat in the audience or from backstage. When he did participate in the antics at 806, it was more than likely in a tableau for the benefit of an amateur photographer. On one such occasion George Luks, stripped to the waist and wearing a pair of boxing gloves, crouched low against another mock pugilist. Behind them stood a dozen of the artists, properly attired in overcoats and derby hats as if at ringside, among them Gruger, Sloan, Preston and Shinn.

The role was somewhat symbolic, for it was typical of FRG during his lifetime to avoid the spotlight except through his work.

John Sloan as "Twillbe," Photo from Sloan Collection, Delaware Art Museum

notes for chapter 2

[1] Fraser, p. 146

[2] FRG teaching notes, c. 1946

[3] Conversation with F.R. Gruger, Jr., May 16, 1973

[4] Letter to the author, December 18, 1957

[5] Denny, p. 15

[6] Renwick, p. 32B (Bibliography)

[7] Conversation with F.R. Gruger, September 8, 1952

[8] FRG teaching notes, c. 1946

[9] Perlman, p. 61 (Bibliography)

[10] Ibid.

[11] Renwick, op. cit. (Bibliography)

[12] A. Sterling Calder's father had created the statue of William Penn for the city hall, and his son, Alexander Calder, would one day create the mobile.

[13] John Sloan notes

Above and left.
The pen and ink drawings by F. R. Gruger reproduced here, exemplify the dual role of newspaper artist-reporter at the turn of the century. These were made for the Philadelphia *Public Ledger* and published on March 4th and 5th, 1897, to cover the Inauguration of President McKinley.

Opposing attorneys are depicted during a courtroom trial.

Chapter 3

During the fall of 1892, while Gruger, Sloan, Glackens, Preston, Davis and Laub were enrolled in the evening Antique Class at the Pennsylvania Academy, they were also working full-time in the art departments of several Philadelphia newspapers. Their job was to illustrate the news.

These were the days before the press photographer. Newspapers contained no photographic supplements. The artist was assigned to translate into visual images what the news reporter put into words. Both artist and reporter were sent out together on assignments to cover conventions, murder trials, fires and anything else which might prove to be newsworthy.

Although newspaper illustrations appeared in this country as early as the 1830s, their use did not become popular until 1884, the year the New York *World* blossomed forth as a picture paper. Once the *World*'s circulation increased, the editor planned to withdraw the pictures. However, when this was done sales dropped off so dramatically that illustrations had to be reinstated.[1]

By 1891 nearly every New York City daily had pictures, but in Philadelphia the idea was just taking hold. Initially the artist's job was simply to make a pen-and-ink rendering over a photographic image or silverprint, converting it to a line drawing using waterproof ink. Then the photographic image was bleached out, and a zinc line cut made of the remaining artwork.

It was in this way that events such as the Cherokee Strip land rush of 1893 were pictured by young artists who had never ventured west of the Ohio River.

Sometimes as many as three men would cooperate on a single large drawing. The artwork would be created in parts and then fitted together: there was no place for stylistic differences among the artists in such a group effort. A four-column drawing took about two hours to produce, and the photo-engraver would try to hurry along the process by placing one hand on the drawing and holding a pocket watch in the other.

Initially the newspaper editors were opposed to the use of illustrations, for it meant more work in arranging the pages, greater care on the part of the pressmen and less space for the reporter. The compositor also complained, for each drawing reproduced in the paper meant less type for him to set, with a resultant loss of pay. Yet despite these objections, the illustrated newspaper became increasingly popular, since readers could grasp the impact of an event more quickly from a drawing than through a printed description.

F.R. Gruger secured his first newspaper job early in 1891:

> Someone on the old *Record* suggested that it would be a good stunt for the Sunday paper to invite several of the art students to make drawings for it of the prize winning pictures in the current Academy show. Fortunately, I was one of those chosen...I didn't know enough to realize that I had been given a tough job. I just did it.
> The engraver who made the plates sent for me. I did not delay. He was very gracious...and gave me several to render. I must have done them passably because I was given quite a few more to do...[2]

The painting which FRG was assigned to draw was *The Brook* by Charles H. Davis. It had just been purchased by the Pennsylvania Academy from the Sixty-first Annual Exhibition, held in the Academy galleries from January 29 to March 6, 1891.

FRG's sketch measured only two and one-half by four inches and the lines in it were crisply drawn. The years of copying Edwin Abbey's illustrations contributed to his success with pen-and-ink at this juncture.

As a result of FRG's drawings in the *Record*, he received an invitation to join the art staff of the Philadelphia *Item*, a weekly containing serialized stories, a society column and one headed "News, Chat and Gossip of a Special Interest to the Ladies." FRG drew decorative headings for such regular columns as "Farm and Garden;" one week he would depict a girl standing beside a well, the next a woman wearing an apron with the words "Farm and Garden" lettered neatly across the front. Most of the *Item* art staff, including C.J. Taylor and Frank Dougherty, were in the habit of signing their drawings, but Gruger inscribed his with the initial "G" within a quarter-inch square.

By July, 1891 FRG had left the *Item* for the *Press,* becoming the first of the group to go to that publication. Eventually, Sloan, Glackens, Shinn, Luks and Davis would all be on the *Press* art staff, though they never all worked there simultaneously.

FRG drew for the Sunday edition. His illustrations appeared regularly, and in increasing numbers during the summer months. For the July 19, 1891 issue, he created four pen-and-ink drawings to illustrate E.J. Edwards' *Peggy: A Tale of the Revolution,* and on August 2 there were eighteen FRG sketches, including a portrait of

Thomas Gray and the church at Stoke Pogis, to accompany the printing of Gray's *Elegy*.

The Philadelphia *Press* artists still worked exclusively from photographs during the first six months of Gruger's tenure on the paper. Occasionally front page drawings were featured, but most of the illustrations appeared on pages two and three, and were architectural in nature. Sometimes the caption under the drawing would carry the words "From a photograph."

On January 26, 1892 the *Press* featured its first news illustration created by an artist on the spot, a depiction of President Benjamin Harrison addressing Congress. Beneath the drawing appears the words "Sketched from the gallery by a staff artist of the Press" and this editor's note:

> THE PRESS Staff Artist left this city for Washington at 7:20 a.m. yesterday, made the sketches for the above illustration, from the gallery of the House, during the reading of the message, reached THE PRESS office at 7 p.m., and finished the illustrations in time for this issue.

In its February 9 issue, the *Press* contained another artistic scoop: drawings of the ruins of the Hotel Royal in New York City where twelve persons had died and fifty-four were reported missing. The credit line read: "Sketched yesterday by a staff artist of 'The Press'."

Before the end of the year all of the other papers in the city had followed the lead of the Philadelphia *Press*. There was an increased demand for artwork in the dailies. Glackens now joined FRG on the *Press*, while Sloan and Laub began working for the *Inquirer,* where Ed Davis was also employed.

The drawings of a newspaper artist had to be transcribed accurately and rapidly. Quick sketches were made at the scene and each artist developed his own artistic shorthand. As Everett Shinn explained:

> If a fire was to be covered then a marginal notation..."eight stories and seven across," representing widows. A quick note of some detail of a cornice or architectural peculiarity was drawn in more carefully. More crosses where fire blazed in windows. Marks indicated fire engines, scaling ladders, hydrants, hose and other apparatus...[3]

Then the race was on against the clock and the competing dailies. Sometimes there were attempts to elaborate on a drawing while being jogged in a bouncing hansom cab

Early barber chair. One of the hundreds of background sketches of settings, props, people and their gestures recorded in FRG's sketchbooks.

on the way back to the paper. Upon arrival there was a mad dash to the drawing table, scribbled notations were rapidly assembled and the penciled hieroglyphics translated into a finished drawing.

Soon the photo-engraver's chemically stained hand reached for the artwork, and a seemingly unsympathetic voice would warn: "Two minutes to the deadline." The sketch, with ink still wet, was whisked off to the newspaper's only camera, there to be photocopied as the first step in the reproduction process.[4]

The artist-reporter's mind had to be a veritable sponge, able to soak up details at a glance. On one occasion, FRG was dispatched to cover a train wreck on the outskirts of Philadelphia. After publication of his drawings, he was visited by the owner of a house near the crash scene. The man had come to congratulate FRG for the fidelity of detail with which his building was depicted.

In order to sharpen their memories, the artists drew constantly. FRG filled hundreds of six by nine-inch pages with figures in an unending variety of stances: gesturing during a street conversation, poised with hat and coat in hand, a shirt-sleeved workman sitting on steps. Some of the drawings were mere fragments: a high back chair, a sofa, the artist's rolltop desk and studio clutter, the wheel

FRG as a newspaper artist, at his drawing board.

assembly of a railroad boxcar, the disarray of his bedroom, a muscular arm, a clenched fist, clasped hands. A good many of the figure sketches, carefully shaded in pencil, are no more than two inches square, approximating the width of a newspaper column.

FRG made several drawings of his newspaper office. In one an artist sits in a swivel chair sketching while another leans back to appraise a drawing. A third man sits at an oval table reading the paper. Another drawing shows a fellow artist wearing a bowler hat, a folded newspaper in his lap. In the background, a pull-down light illuminates the face of a staffer who sits reading a paper.

The artist-reporters would often draw by themselves in the large classroom at the Academy before leaving for work on the newspapers. As an added pastime they played memory games, repeatedly testing one another with the routines they had discovered in Horace de Boisbaudran's book, *Training of the Memory in Art*. "Guess how many steps there are from here to there?" one of them would challenge. "How many tables are in the next room?" Or the group would congregate outside of the Press Building at Chestnut and Seventh to observe the passing parade of humanity, noting the swing of an arm or the shuffle of a leg.

After a year on the *Press*, F.R. Gruger changed newspapers once more:

> William Glackens joined the staff of the *Press* about the same time I did...One midnight we climbed down from the lunch counter at Thompson's Spa and met Mr. J.F.A. Jackson who told us that the *Ledger* was...(to be illustrated), that he was in charge of the art department, that he wanted us; would we come along? Yes, we could! We liked Jo Jackson right away...[5]

Jackson elaborated:

> When I was called to take charge of the proposed department there were two artists I wanted on the *Ledger*. You (FRG) were the one and Glackens was the other. I knew neither of you, but I did know your names and got someone to help me make the contact...I felt perfectly happy when you said you would come...You came quickly, but Glackens wanted to go south in a freight car, or something, with Redfield, so he did not turn up for some time...
> I had to convince the powers that be that "boiler-tint" cuts[6] were inartistic and passe.

The SARAH J. FIELD PRIZE, an Etruscan Vase in perfect condition was awarded to F. R. Gruger December 2, 1895 for a painting in the student's exhibition at The Pennsylvania Academy of The Fine Arts.

> Perhaps I never convinced them, but I knew the *Ledger* had the best newspaper artists...[7]

Glackens became associated with that paper late in 1892, and remained there until July 1894 when he returned to the *Press.* FRG continued for seven more years after Glackens' departure, becoming the *Ledger*'s premier artist.

Joseph Jackson, just three years Gruger's senior and himself a former Academy student, was now FRG's closest associate on the paper. Each year, beginning in 1892 and continuing for a decade, Jackson presented him with a book on art or architecture for Christmas, with a fitting inscription. The first was *The Life and Letters of Charles Samuel Keene,* one of the pen-and-ink artists of *Punch,* of whose work FRG was particularly fond.

On December 3, 1895 the *Public Ledger* contained a small article headed "The Field Prize Awarded." It was about one of their own staff artists:

> Frederic R. Gruger was yesterday awarded the Sarah J. Field prize, consisting of a Greek vase, by a committee consisting of Miss Blanche Dillaye, Mr. Joseph DeCamp and Mr. E.W. Redfield, for one of his paintings in the students' exhibition at the Academy of the Fine Arts.

Subsequently, the Academy curator forwarded "the certificate of Mr. Thomas B. Clarke for the genuineness of the Antique Vase awarded to you...:"

Description
Krater from Nola, Italy.
This fine specimen of the best period of Greek Art (4th Century B.C.) was found by Signor Doria of Santa Maria di Capua who was a well known digger and collector. At his death it, with other items, came into the possession of his nephew Commandatore Galozzie from whom it was purchased by Henry de Morgan in 1892.
The rim of the vase is decorated with a border of Laurel leaves. At the base of the picture decorating the vase runs a Greek border—On the boot is a victory marching to the right toward an Ephebe.[8] Both figures are draped. On the back is an Ephebe standing—The glaze is most brilliant. Dimensions—Height 10″ Diameter 9-1/2. Athenian Red Figured Greek Pottery.

FRG placed the trophy on a bookshelf in his studio. The Sarah J. Field prize seemed a fitting conclusion to FRG's years at the Academy, for the summer term of 1895 was his last.

Earlier in 1895 FRG and Ed Davis had joined in a business venture. Pooling their talents as designers and illustrators, they established a commercial art studio at 1510 Chestnut Street. Gruger still worked for the *Ledger,* and Davis was the assistant art editor to Frank Crane on the *Press.* But both men sought additional income: FRG because of his recent engagement to his childhood sweetheart, Florence Gray; and Davis, due to the birth of a son.[9]

The cooperative arrangement was listed as "Davis & Gruger, artists" in Gopsill's *Philadelphia City Directory.* The impetus for the firm came from a manufacturing company which approached FRG while he was still attending the Academy, requesting that he produce pen-and-ink illustrations of their line of men's clothing. As a result Davis & Gruger made illustrations primarily for Whitaker & VanHagen, an advertising firm at 925 Chestnut Street.

FRG also produced other types of advertising designs: "The poster received today is the best yet. It's a corker," acknowledged George Whitaker in May, 1896. The 1890s was the decade of a poster craze which swept America. Among others of the group, Maxfield Parrish was producing posters for Columbia Bicycle, Hornby's Oatmeal and the Welsbach Light; and John Sloan, one of the innovators of this art form, had been designing advertising placards for the Bradley Coal Company and creating magazine covers in a poster style for several years.

By the time FRG and Ed Davis were established in their studio on Chestnut Street, virtually all of the other newspaper artists were similarly renting space nearby. Most of the studios were located in four or five-story walk-ups, originally office buildings. But as the business center of the city shifted away from Independence Square and Washington Square, the commercial structures became vacant. Subdivided into smaller spaces, they were outfitted with flimsy partitions and rented cheaply, the artist tenants adding skylights.

John Sloan — *Night on the Boardwalk* (1894) Early poster-style drawing for the Philadelphia *Inquirer* Sloan Collection, Delaware Art Museum

Edward Penfield — Poster Calendar, 1897

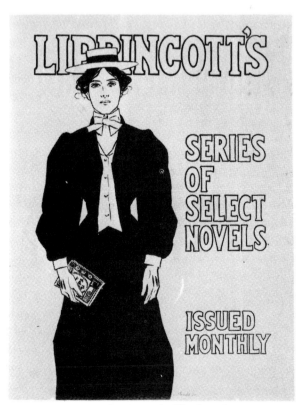

Maxfield Parrish — advertisement for Columbia Bicycles, 1896 Courtesy of Coy Ludwig Photo: Cornell University Library

J. J. Gould — magazine poster for Lippincott's

William J. Glackens: pen and ink, 8″x12″.   From F. R. Gruger's personal collection

During the next few years there was a constant reshuffling of artists' studios. In 1892 Sloan initially shared a third floor room at 705 Walnut which looked out across Independence Square, with J. Horace Rudy, a designer, and then with Joe Laub, a fellow artist on the *Inquirer.* The following year Sloan and Laub had relocated in 806 Walnut Street as successors to Henri, who had left for Europe. Edward Redfield was in Room 12 of the same building. When Henri returned, he, Laub and Sloan shared the space, and the Tuesday evening gatherings commenced. But the next year, 1894, Henri moved to 1717 Chestnut Street while Glackens released his studio at 724 to George Luks, in order to share the one with Henri.

The 1717 Chestnut Street address was considered one of the finest studio buildings in the city. It was also one of the largest, and housed the Studio Society, an association of a dozen women artists who used the premises for painting and conducting art classes.

When Gruger and Davis dissolved their partnership, FRG relocated in the 1717 building, briefly sharing the studio with Glackens. Gruger and Glackens possessed similar temperaments. They were both good listeners who shunned incessant chatter, and they were hard workers on the newspapers. Referring to their years together on the *Press* and the *Ledger*, FRG once remarked:

> I learned to draw the hard way. I worked at it. So did William Glackens...When the rest of the (newspaper) staff had gone home at eleven

o'clock at night we really got down to work. We labored on pictorial problems. Valuable hours.[10]

Even after Glackens left the *Ledger* to return to the *Press,* the two men socialized frequently, for the *Press* building was located at Chestnut and Seventh, the *Ledger* at Chestnut and Sixth.

FRG continued to work for the *Public Ledger.* The drawing tables were arranged in a row along the double windows of Room 408, so that the light would stream in over the artists' shoulders from the Chestnut Street side. Above each drawing board a light hung by a cord from the high ceiling, a circular shade shielding the artists' eyes from the glare of the bulb. Each artist was supplied with a two-foot square taboret, the top of which functioned as a repository for pens, ink, sketches and a glass of beer or ale.

As the pace quickened prior to the daily deadline, tables became cluttered with papers, books and bottles of glue with large rubber stoppers. There was an atmosphere of noisy confusion and the pall of smoke from many pipes, the movement of men in shirtsleeves and vests, some wearing straw hats or derbies. Amid this sense of tension and apparent disorder, the artists worked undisturbed, their faces shielded by translucent green visors:

> Then, one day, an enthusiastic reporter came rushing into our department announcing that one of the *Ledger*'s advertisers paid the incredible sum of six hundred dollars a day for his half

"Good morning", Minnie O'Reilly said. "I have come to be a reporter, please. I have always thought I would like the life." "My Gawd!", murmured Larry Black.
DIAMONDS by GRACE SARTWELL MASON
Hearst's International, May 1923, Page 32/3.

In a letter postmarked February 14, 1923 to his wife and daughters who were spending several weeks in Algiers, FRG said: "The drawing I finished to-day is of the interior of a newspaper office of the late Nineties — about the time I went to the *Ledger*. So it should be authentic and it is."

page of space. I wonder that I had enough sense at that time to take the hint. Nevertheless it seems that I grasped the idea of many pages in the *Ledger*, free of charge, whereon to show my wares and I labored my very hardest on my newspaper pictures that they might be my best.[11]

Art editor Joseph Jackson sent FRG out regularly to cover important court cases, and sometimes to Congressional committee rooms in Washington. "This is quite a strenuous life," Gruger once remarked, pointing out that he was occasionally forced to sleep sitting up on the train back to Philadelphia.

It was understood that an artist doing such drawings was present simply as a recorder of the scene; his sole function was to put down on paper what he saw, and forget what he heard. FRG, of course, could not help but overhear committee discussions while in Washington. He became politically disillusioned when he heard a group of government officials discuss how they might prevent certain news from becoming public knowledge prior to the close of the stock market in New York, thus allowing the insiders to profit. As a result of such experiences, FRG refrained from voting in any election for many years.

On the evening of January 26, 1897 a major fire erupted in a business block across from the Philadelphia City Hall. The next day the *Ledger*'s front page told and a four-column drawing illustrated the story.

FRG had been called upon to cover that story, but had politely refused. The editors were extremely annoyed. However, Gruger felt that there comes a time when one's personal life must take precedence. For January 26 was, after all, his wedding day.

notes for chapter 3

[1] Smith, p. 52

[2] "F.R. Gruger," *op. cit.* (Bibliography)

[3] Shinn, Unpublished Autobiography (Bibliography)

[4] Ibid.

[5] "F.R. Gruger," *op. cit.* (Bibliography)

[6] A type of stock drawing distributed to newspapers by syndicates.

[7] Letter to FRG from Jo Jackson, April 14, 1939

[8] A young man.

[9] Stuart Davis would one day earn his own reputation in the annals of American Art.

[10] FRG teaching notes, c. 1946

[11] "F.R. Gruger," *op. cit.* (Bibliography)

Florence and Frederic Gruger at the time of their marriage, 1897

Chapter 4

The marriage of Florence Felton Gray to Frederic Rodrigo Gruger took place in the Madison Street Methodist Episcopal Church in Chester, Pennsylvania, where the ceremony was performed by the father of the bride. The event was duly reported on January 27, 1897 by the Chester newspaper:

> The large auditorium, as well as the choir gallery...was filled last evening with invited guests, who attended the wedding of Miss Florence Gray...of this city. The ceremony was performed by the bride's father, Dr. J.R.T. Gray, pastor of the Madison Street M.E. Church...

The Gray family, like the Grugers, came from Philadelphia. Florence Gray's father had served with the rank of major in the Civil War, after which he studied for the ministry. His ancestors had originally settled in Georgia, after emigrating from England.

FRG had known Florence Gray since she was ten or twelve years old, when both families were living in Lancaster:

> I always observed and I have before mentioned it— that from a little girl you were reserved, and had an ideal above that of other girls...

he once wrote during their courtship.

Because Dr. Gray was a Methodist minister, he was sent from one parish to another. The family had lived in Frankfort and Easton, Pennsylvania, as well as Philadelphia, Lancaster and Chester. It was in Lancaster during the 1880s that FRG and Florence's brother, Joseph Gray, Jr., were high school classmates and the closest of friends.

F.R. Gruger had been an attentive suitor. When the Gray family lived in Frankfort during 1890 and 1891, he regularly bicycled the seven miles there and back. After their move to Chester the following year, he cycled twenty-five miles round trip. Sloan, Glackens and Laub went bicycling in Fairmont Park and to the city's outskirts, but FRG would often forsake their company for that of Florence and her brother.

He mailed some of his newspaper drawings to Florence. On March 18, 1891 he sent her the original sketch of Charles H. Davis' painting, *The Brook,* which had been drawn for the Philadelphia *Record* just shortly before. On August 14 he wrote:

> Enclosed are my drawings in *The Press* of last Sunday, and the one preceding. They are few and like all my work are so bad that I sincerely hope you cast them from thee when thou hast perused them.

FRG also sent affectionate letters. On his birthday in 1891, Fred carefully scribed an entire missive on parchment, enclosing a note:

> This letter is as nearly like an old letter which I saw out at ye Philadelphia Library as I could make it, it had had a frail piece of parchment enclosed as has this. 'twas written in ye seventeenth century.

When FRG visited the Grays he would sometimes stop off at Graham's Florist Shop on Chestnut Street to purchase a bouquet. Due to the strict attitudes of Florence's parents, certain types of entertainment were taboo: card-playing was out of the question, as were theatres; both were considered immoral. But the couple did go bicycling together, took walks, played croquet and went boating on the streams around Chester and in Fairmont Park. And sometimes Florence would just look on for what seemed like hours as FRG and her brother, standing on opposite sides of the street, threw a baseball back and forth with rhythmic monotony.

The Gray family customarily spent the summers at Gap, Pennsylvania, where they had a home and FRG would be welcomed there as a guest of the family. They also visited Atlantic City, already a sizable resort, and Ocean Grove and Ocean City, both Methodist-sponsored developments.

Florence's strict upbringing prevented the couple from wandering too far afield unchaperoned, even for the day. In March 1895 FRG invited Florence to accompany him on a visit to New York; she agreed only after being assured that his cousin Katherine would be going along.

FRG's primary purpose in making the trip was to review an exhibition of paintings by Edouard Manet at the Durand-Ruel Galleries on Fifth Avenue. Henri had been extolling the praises of Manet's brushwork and chiaroscuro to the newspaper artists, and had talked up the show. Manet, who had died in 1883, was represented by twenty-nine works, including such masterpieces as *La Bonne Pipe*, the *Gare St. Lazare* and *Concert aux Tuileries.*

Katherine Gruger wrote along the bottom of her exhibition catalog:

> ...spent Friday, March 15, 1895 in New York City. Snowed or hailed all day. I left Chester at 8:55 A.M. Arrived home at midnight. Had fine time. Ferries to Brooklyn—across Brooklyn bridge in cars—walked, rode up Broadway to

Durand-Ruel Galleries—visited stores—Sterns, Clark's restaurant—rode elevated, road to Metropolitan Museum—walked down Sixth Ave.— around Tombs—Clark's supper—home.

The following July, FRG wrote a formal note to Dr. Gray, asking for permission to become engaged to his daughter. The Reverend replied:

> I have not even seen Mrs. Gray since receiving your letter. As she is equally interested in Florence's happiness and welfare, I feel that I ought to talk your proposal over with her. I believe, however, that she will agree with me that if Florence has given her consent, there is no reason why we should not do the same.
> To you, personally, I have no objection, believing you to be of upright character, and possessing ability to make your way in the world...

After the engagement was announced, FRG invited Florence to travel with him and a group from the Academy on a two-week canal boat trip. When she was unable to accept, he embarked on the excursion without her. More than a dozen men and women went along, including Guernsey Moore, J.J. Gould, John Justice, Frank Walter Taylor, Edward Russell and Elizabeth Shippen Green. The mule-drawn canal boat was provided with living quarters and made a round trip through Pennsylvania and New York State as far as Newburgh.

Five weeks after F.R. Gruger and Florence Gray were married, FRG would once again take a trip without her, this time on business. The *Public Ledger* had dispatched him to Washington to cover the inauguration of President McKinley. Gruger's drawings were many and varied. In the March 4, 1897 issue, five two-and three-column pen-and-inks appeared in the sixteen pages of the *Ledger*, providing a broad view of the preparations. The captions read: "Scenes in Washington on the Eve of the Inaugural," "The President's Reviewing Stand at the White House," "The East Room Where the New President will be Received" and "Interior of the Pension Building, Decorated for the Inaugural Ball."

FRG also drew a portrait of Mrs. Nancy Allison McKinley, the eighty-seven year old mother of William McKinley, who would witness the inauguration of her son.

Two of FRG's drawings were printed in the March 5 edition. "Parade Passing the President's Reviewing Stand" and "The Crowd in Front of the Capitol" were each reproduced a full five columns wide. The latter pen-and-ink sketch was an ambitious undertaking, a composition of the people massed in front of the east facade of the

Excursion aboard the canal boat

Capitol, witnessing President McKinley's Inaugural Address. Top hats and derbies are raised on high, a young child clutches his father's arm and a fashionably dressed lady stands on a chair to view the proceedings.

The figures are natural and life-like, each skillfully outlined in ink and then given form through the use of parallel line shading. Gone are the somewhat stilted, decorative people who appeared in FRG's earliest newspaper drawings six and one-half years before. The intervening period of study, observation and practice had developed an artist considered one of the best in his field.

William Glackens was also on hand for the presidential inauguration, covering the event for the New York *Herald*. Glackens had settled in Manhattan after returning from Europe the year before, and had begun working for the *Herald* less than three months earlier.

It was becoming increasingly apparent to Gruger and Glackens that the days of the artist-reporter were numbered. Four years before the art editor of the *Herald* had suggested to its owner that halftone reproductions could be printed in the paper from photographs. This idea was deemed preposterous, and the art editor was fired. Now, however, in 1897, halftones were being printed on high speed presses by the rival New York *Tribune*.

The artist-reporter's role was not immediately eliminated by the appearance of the first newspaper photographs because without full-time photographers on their staffs, the papers initially depended upon freelance work. Even when there were regular staff cameramen, artists were often assigned to cover important events with them, in case the photographers missed. The camera was not yet infallible. And sometimes the photograph was simply ruined in developing, in which case an artist would be required to produce a sketch of the subject.

William Glackens — Illustration for "Our War With Spain" by Richard H. Titherington, *Munsey's Magazine,* April, 1899.

The use of the halftone process by newspapers also made it possible, for the first time, to reproduce drawings with gray shaded areas created by pencil or watercolor wash, tones halfway between the black ink lines and the white of the paper. FRG would soon create the first such halftone drawings to appear on the pages of the *Public Ledger.*

On February 15, 1898 the Battleship *Maine* blew up in Havana harbor and by April the United States and Spain were at war. Within two weeks Glackens was dispatched to Cuba by *McClure's Magazine,* for which he had previously served as a free-lance artist. Harry Dart, the *Herald*'s art editor, soon followed. With the ranks of its art staff thinned, the New York paper looked to Philadelphia for help. As a result, FRG was loaned to the *Herald* by the *Ledger,* and by spring he and Florence had taken up residence in a brownstone boarding house on west Twenty-fourth Street, in an area known as London Terrace, from which the present apartment complex took its name.

FRG worked each day in the Herald Building on Herald Square, for during his tenure on the paper he was assigned to the office, making illustrations for stories filed by reporters. Composite pictures of Manila Bay and other important locations were created and sometimes drawings were produced in advance of some war action, then had to be scrapped because a particular battle never took place.

Frank Crane, the former art editor of the Philadelphia *Press,* was also now on the *Herald* staff, and in July, 1898, he found a job there for John Sloan. It was like old times, for Everett Shinn and George Luks were in New York as well. But the reunion was shortlived. Sloan, unhappy on the New York paper, returned to the Philadelphia *Press* by October, and when the war was over, the Grugers also left Manhattan, for Florence was expecting her first child and

George Luks — Drawing in the Philadelphia *Evening Bulletin,* February, 1896, an incident in the Spanish-American War. Caption: "In Hot Pursuit of a Scout . . . An insurgent scout has been overtaken by Spanish troops in a rocky defile near Guara. They fire upon him, and THE BULLETIN artist in Cuba sketches him as he falls from the saddle."

wished to be near her family when the baby arrived. On November 5, 1898 Elizabeth Rodrigo Gruger was born in Philadelphia.

In 1899 FRG produced his last major work as an artist-reporter. It involved the America's Cup Race for yachting supremacy. In the fall of that year, the English challenger *Shamrock* was scheduled to race against the American yacht *Columbia* in the waters off Long Island. The challenge was a major topic of conversation for weeks prior to the race. Newspapers featured stories about preparations, measurements of the boats and the departure from England of Sir Thomas Lipton, owner of the *Shamrock*.

By coincidence or design, Admiral George Dewey had just arrived in New York harbor aboard his flagship *Olympia*, and on September 28 the *Public Ledger* contained an FRG drawing captioned: "Admiral Dewey returning to his Flagship after his official visit to the officers of the fleet." As FRG became involved with preparations to cover the America's Cup Race, he was unable to sketch additional events surrounding Admiral Dewey's triumphant arrival. On October 2, 1899, when the *Ledger* carried a five-column drawing captioned: "The Land Parade in New York—Tenth Pennsylvania Regiment Passing in Review Before Admiral Dewey," the drawing was by William Glackens.

One of the *Ledger*'s chief concerns with the coverage of the forthcoming race between the *Columbia* and the *Shamrock* was how to get hold of FRG's drawings. It had been arranged for him to view the contest from the deck of the New York *Herald*'s press boat, which would follow at a discreet distance. But his sketches were valueless unless they arrived in Philadelphia in time to appear in the next day's paper. The solution: Carrier pigeons.

It is not clear whether the paper or FRG hit upon the plan. Carrier pigeons had, after all, been used by the paper previously. As early as the 1840s a carrier pigeon express had been established by a Boston firm to service the *Public Ledger*, the New York *Sun* and the Baltimore *Sun*. The firm had several hundred birds, and would release some from ships as they approached within fifty miles of Boston harbor, providing the papers with important foreign news.[1]

On the other hand, FRG might have suggested the idea himself, for while working for the *Weekly Item* back in 1891, he had produced six one-column illustrations for a story entitled "Homing Pigeons. How the Fleet Winged Birds May be Kept and Trained."

It was determined that FRG's drawings would be made on thin, tissue-like paper about six inches square, placed in a capsule, and flown by carrier pigeon from the ship to Philadelphia. The fragile drawing surface of the

paper would not allow for much in the way of detail or shading, but at least the *Ledger* would scoop the other Philadelphia papers.

FRG's cup race drawings first appeared on the pages of the *Public Ledger* on October 6, 1899. During the first week there were four attempts to hold the race, but light winds prevented either boat from finishing within the prescribed time. Gruger turned to drawing the press boats. Two sketches were reproduced under the captions: "The Steamships *Ponce* and *La Grand Duchess* Following the Yacht Race." Beneath the drawings was an explanation:

> It is from These Boats that the Frequent Bulletins of the Races are Transmitted by Wireless Telegraphy to the New York *Herald*, and Immediately Repeated to the *Ledger* over its Private Wire, Giving the First Accurate Accounts of These Events.

On October 11, the *Ledger* reported that fog and lack of wind had caused still another postponement, and reproduced two FRG drawings depicting "The Yachts at Moorings in the Horseshoe at Sandy Hook."

Following this fourth failure to run the race, he was recalled to Philadelphia. There the *Ledger* assigned him to the opening of an International Commercial Congress. Among FRG's drawings in the October 16 *Ledger* was one showing that paper's impressive display at the exposition. It featured a public demonstration of Ottmar Mergenthaler's linotype machine, first used by newspapers to set type mechanically just thirteen years before.

FRG was back in New York by the sixteenth for the first successful contest between *Columbia* and *Shamrock*. The next day his drawing of *Columbia* winning the race appeared in the *Ledger*. On October 18 the *Columbia* won again; the *Shamrock* topmast broke midway through the contest.

Finally, on October 21, 1899 the *Public Ledger* announced triumphantly in a two-column headline: "America's Cup Remains Here." The article concerning the *Columbia*'s third straight victory was accompanied by a four-column Gruger drawing on page one and another on an inside page. Like all of the works he had sketched during the preceding three weeks, these were signed, "F.R. Gruger, New York."

This country's yachting achievement was considered of such major news value that word of the Boer War in South Africa was given a subordinate position in the paper.

FRG continued to work on the *Ledger* for another few years, during which time there were fewer calls for on-the-

PHILADELPHIA, SATURDAY, OCTOBER 21, 1899.

COLUMBIA WINNING YESTERDAY'S RACE

F. R. Gruger's drawing of the America's Cup Race, the final victory of *Columbia* over Lord Lipton's *Shamrock*.

GREAT BATTLE RAGED IN NATAL

FOUR KILLED BY DYNAMITE

INGHAM AND NEWITT ARE FOUND GUILTY

Drawings for Christmas Supplement, *Public Ledger,* 1901

spot sketching. His grand finale as a newspaperman occurred in the *Public Ledger*'s Christmas supplement for 1901, in which were reproduced no less than thirty-four of his drawings, all of them illustrations for short stories, such as "A Christmas Duel" by Guy Boothby, "Christmas at Valley Forge" by Roland Ringwalt and "Christmas Plays in Olden Times" by his friend and former art editor, Joseph Jackson.

For one decade, the 1890s, the artist-reporter had been in vogue. Ten years saw the rise and fall of a profession—one which necessity brought into being and invention eliminated from the American scene, but which served as art apprenticeship to several who were destined to contribute significantly to the field of American illustration.

note for Chapter 4

[1]Lee, p. 490

The Saturday Evening Post, April 1, 1899

The Saturday Evening Post, October 3, 1903

The Saturday Evening Post, October 28, 1905

These three early *Post* covers show the gradual refinement of the masthead lettering, as well as the transition from a cover with story and illustration to a story-related subject, to an independent cover design. The two upper cover illustrations were done by FRG, the lower by his friend Guernsey Moore.

Chapter 5

When FRG returned to Philadelphia in the fall of 1898, after having served on the art staff of the New York *Herald*, he was informed by Guernsey Moore, a former classmate, that the art editor of *The Saturday Evening Post* desired to see him.

The old Post Building was located at Fifth and Arch Streets, just three blocks from the *Ledger*. It seemed somehow symbolic that Benjamin Franklin, generally credited with founding the magazine in 1729, should be buried directly across the street. Gruger made his way to the fourth floor of the aging structure. The art editor who had been impressed with FRG's newspaper work offered him a story to illustrate: "The Mystery Connected with Mrs. Jessop" by E. Rentoul Esler.

When the November 5, 1898 issue of *The Saturday Evening Post* appeared, F.R. Gruger was represented by four drawings. The date was doubly significant as the beginning of his career as a magazine illustrator and as the day his daughter was born.

The *Post* was in the process of reorganization, having been purchased in a near bankrupt state the year before by Cyrus H.K. Curtis. Curtis had founded the *Ladies' Home Journal* in Philadelphia two decades earlier; his publishing empire would include acquisition of the *Public Ledger* by 1913.

The Golden Age of American Illustration was at hand, with its origins rooted in Civil War days, when Winslow Homer covered the conflict for *Harper's Weekly*. During the last third of the Nineteenth Century, this publication and *Harper's Monthly* featured the work of nearly every major illustrator. Charles Parsons, art editor of Harper's periodicals from 1863 to 1889, began or promoted the careers of such artists as Edwin Austin Abbey, Arthur Burdett Frost, Charles Stanley Reinhart, William Allen Rogers, Albert Sterner, Edward W. Kemble, Frederick Dielman, Howard Pyle, Frederick S. Church and Frederic Remington.

Prior to the 1890s *Harper's Monthly*, *Scribner's* and *Century* were the leading American magazines. These were the old, well-established publications which catered to the educated, upper class. At twenty-five and thirty-five cents an issue, they were too expensive for the general public. During the 1890s a number of new, popularly priced monthlies were begun, such as *McClure's, Munsey's* and *Cosmopolitan*. Set to sell at ten cents, they were especially appealing to the large middle class.

Into this crowded field of monthlies came *The Saturday Evening Post*, appearing weekly and selling for five cents. Under Curtis' skillfull management and the editorial policies of George Horace Lorimer, the circulation of *The Saturday Evening Post* soared from sixteen hundred copies in 1897 to two million by 1920. [2]

When FRG began illustrating for the *Post* toward the end of 1898, it was a sixteen-page tabloid. There were virtually no illustrations, only minor decorative spots at the start or conclusion of an article. Nor did the magazine have a distinctive cover; articles began on the front page. The logotype at the top of page one was the epitome of conservative taste, displaying a classical motif which included pilasters, volutes and garlands, and the title of the magazine was spelled out in a Roman type face.

All of this was about to change. George Horace Lorimer, the *Post*'s new editor, sought to alter the magazine's entire format. Soon after F.R. Gruger produced his first illustrations for the November 5, 1898 issue, he was given an assignment to work with Guernsey Moore on the redesign of the magazine. Since FRG had relinquished his studio on Chestnut Street when he was sent to the New York *Herald* earlier in the year, he sat at his drawing board in the *Ledger* art department and tackled the job. J.J. Gould and James Preston assisted.

> ...Guernsey Moore designed the type and the whole physical appearance of the book, and I rather fancy that J.J. Gould gave him more help than the rest of us. [3]

FRG stated, modestly minimizing his own role. Gould's contribution had been largely that of a critic.

On January 21, 1899 a new *Saturday Evening Post* logotype was incorporated into the cover design. The magazine's name appeared in an italicized type style based on colonial designs, providing a simplified look to the page. But the magazine was still printed in black and white. It was to be serveral months before full-page, poster-type, two-color drawings would provide the *Post* with a totally new look, one which would become a familiar trademark for decades.

Four of FRG's drawings appeared on the cover of *The Saturday Evening Post* during January, March and April, 1899. At the time the art editor chose the cover illustration from the lead story. During that year FRG created forty-three drawings for the magazine, eight of which were in pencil or charcoal, and reproduced as halftones.

The Saturday Evening Post was luring artists away from the Philadelphia papers, despite the assertion, reported in an article written in 1900, that "...Newspapers today pay an artist a third more for his work than the magazines and weeklies pay him." John Sloan was still employed by the *Press* but would begin a two year association with *The Saturday Evening Post* in 1905. Glackens, starting in 1902, created nearly three hundred *Post* draw-

May Wilson Preston models for her husband, James Preston. Both were very popular illustrators.

Portrait sketch of John R. Neill by FRG

ings over the next ten years. Sloan wrote to Robert Henri that "Jimmy Preston has dropped newspaper work and is doing work for *The Saturday Evening Post*..." By 1899 illustrations by Gruger, Preston, Gould and Guernsey Moore were appearing on the pages of the *Post*, together with those of a host of other artists: A.I. Keller, Will Crawford, Howard Chandler Christy, George Gibbs, B. Martin Justice, Gustave VerBeek, Henry Hutt, Frank X. Leyendecker, Elizabeth Shippen Green, Charlotte Harding and Harrison Fisher.

Early that year Everett Shinn, having relocated in New York, was appointed art editor of *Ainslee's Magazine*. Shinn had shuttled back and forth among the art departments of the New York *Herald*, *Journal* and the *World*, occasionally working alongside Glackens or George Luks. Now he produced a number of magazine cover designs and short story illustrations for *Ainslee's*, as did Florence Scovel, a former Pennsylvania Academy classmate whom he had recently married. Shinn also invited Gruger, Glackens, Sloan, Preston and Moore to contribute to *Ainslee's*, and their drawings began appearing in the March, 1899 issue. After only a year, however, Shinn was replaced as art editor, and from among the group of artists his successor retained only Gruger. FRG's illustrations continued in *Ainslee's* each month until September, 1902, when the magazine announced a new editorial policy that eliminated pictures.

During FRG's three-year association with *Ainslee's*, he had illustrated two dozen stories, employing a flat-pattern approach with solid gray backgrounds behind his figures, thereby successfully utilizing the new halftone process.

Earlier in 1902, another project was commenced on which the old Philadelphia gang could collaborate. Glackens was approached to illustrate an ambitious edition of the novels of Charles Paul de Kock, a minor French author, contemporary of Balzac, who wrote racy stories about Parisian life. When Glackens learned that the planned publication was to involve fifty volumes, he called in his friends. Ultimately, nineteen illustators participated in the enterprise for the Frederick J. Quimby Company of Boston.

In addition to Glackens, the contributors included Gruger, Sloan, Luks, Preston, Ernest Fuhr and Albert Sterner. FRG produced a dozen pen-and-ink and halftone compositions, with one of the latter appearing as a hand-colored frontispiece. His artwork was created for volumes one and two of *The Gogo Family* and *M. Martin's Donkey*.

By 1902 FRG's illustrations were on the pages of *Scribner's, McClure's, Success* and *Leslie's Popular Monthly Magazine*, although the number of assignments now being sent him by *The Saturday Evening Post* exceeded those from the other four publications combined.

FRG was a favorite of the *Post*'s new editor. Lorimer, a former Boston *Post* reporter, had been hired as the magazine's new literary editor. Publisher Curtis placed him in charge when he went abroad in search of a new editor-in-chief, but was so pleased with the appearance and content of the magazine in his absence that he cabled Lorimer to place his name on the masthead as editor. It first appears there in the June 3, 1899 issue.

Lorimer was only three years older than FRG, and the two men shared a mutual respect for each other. Prior to

George Horace Lorimer as sketched by James Montgomery Flagg.

"When John L. Sullivan went through the stock yards, it just simply shut down the plant." One of FRG's illustrations for Lorimer's *Letters from a Self-Made Merchant to his Son.*

his appointment as editor-in-chief, Lorimer had written an article for the Christmas, 1898 issue, illustrated by Charles Louis Hinton. But shortly thereafter he made known his own preference for FRG's work, and for many years the names of Lorimer and Gruger appeared together as author and artist. The journalist's most famous work, "Letters from a Self-Made Merchant to his Son," was illustrated by FRG in the *Post* beginning with the October 5, 1901 issue, and continuing in eight installments over the next year. Lorimer dictated the stories to his secretary, sometimes with FRG in attendance:

> Occasionally he (Lorimer) would send for me and I'd sit beside his desk in an ancient red leather chair and listen while he told the story to his secretary who tapped it on her typewriter...[4]

The author seemed to be stimulated by an audience. He would interrupt his dictation to elaborate on the story or discuss it with Gruger. Every so often Lorimer repeated an incident in order to emphasize it to the artist. But FRG made only mental notes during these sessions. Afterward, in his studio, he created sketches for future use. The years of memory training as an artist-reporter made this procedure possible. Gruger's original drawings for "Letters from a Self-Made Merchant to his Son" were requested by the author, who hung them in the library of his estate at Wyncote, on the outskirts of Philadelphia.

On the thirtieth anniversary of Lorimer's assuming the editorship of *The Saturday Evening Post*, he wrote to FRG:

> ...there are only a few of us left, and among all

the old timers and the new ones, too, no one has contributed more to the success of the weekly than you have.[5]

By 1899 FRG had embarked upon his career as a magazine illustrator in earnest. He rented a studio in a six-story building at 1020 Chestnut Street. J.J. Gould's studio was there, too, and he and Guernsey Moore became close friends of Gruger, replacing the camaraderie of Glackens, Shinn and Luks, who by now were all in New York. Gould and Moore demonstrated their congeniality toward FRG by each designing a bookplate for his growing library.

Gruger also met other artists in the block, notably John R. Neill, who shared a studio at 1010 Chestnut Street. Like FRG, he was Academy-trained and a newspaper artist. Neill's first job had been as a cub reporter for the Philadelphia *Inquirer*, but when he began submitting little sketches with each of his stories, the editor endorsed the art.

Neill was always more successful at illustrating fairy tales and mythological stories. Realism was not his forte. His fanciful ink drawings caught the eye of Frank K. Riley, a Chicago publisher, who visited him with an offer to illustrate a book by L. Frank Baum called *The Marvelous Land of Oz*.

Baum's first literary effort, *Mother Goose in Prose*, had been published in 1897 with illustrations by Maxfield Parrish, a "first" for him too. Then Baum's *Wonderful Wizard of Oz* appeared three years later, with artist W.W. Denslow's visualizations of Dorothy and her friends. When Denslow declined doing a second *Oz* story, John R. Neill was asked to take his place.

John R. Neill, pen and ink illustration, 16 by 13¾ inches.

L. Frank Baum was the perfect writer for Neill's imaginative pen-and-inks. Neill would illustrate another dozen *Oz* volumes by Baum, creating with him an artist-author team somewhat like that of Sir John Tenniel and Lewis Carroll.

F.R. Gruger saw less of Neill after 1901, when FRG moved his studio to 729 Walnut Street, and his home from Philadelphia to his brother-in-law's house in Chester. Joseph R.T. Gray, Jr., with whom he had graduated from Lancaster High School, was an M.D., having studied at the Hahnemann Medical College in Philadelphia and at Johns Hopkins in Baltimore. Dr. Gray had married Rachel Blakeley, but in 1901 Mrs. Gray died in childbirth, and Fred and Florence Gruger moved in with him, providing companionship and helping with housekeeping.

The Grugers' own dauther was two and one-half years old at the time, and within another year, on January 21, 1902, Frederic Rodrigo Gruger, Jr. was born. Soon it would become necessary for FRG to find a home of his own.

F.R. and Florence Gruger might have considered a move to New York, weighing its advantages with the difficulty of meeting *The Saturday Evening Post*'s weekly deadlines from a distance of ninety miles. FRG was doing more and more work for the *Post*, from forty-two illustrations in 1901 to eighty-five in 1902 to one hundred and thirty-seven in 1903. He must have wondered whether his favored position with the magazine and his income would be in jeopardy by a move away from Philadelphia.

FRG's father-in-law, Reverend J.R.T. Gray, solved the dilemma. He had purchased a small tract of land in Avon-by-the-Sea, New Jersey, from a member of his congregation who was selling lots there. Since Dr. Gray already owned a summer place in Gap, Pennsylvania, he made a gift of the Avon lot to his daughter and son-in-law. They visited the seaside resort and decided to build a summer home.

Avon-by-the-Sea was a developing community on the Jersey coast. It had originally been intended as a town for factory workers who were to produce a brand of cigars named "Key East," but when the enterprise failed to materialize, the area was promoted as a summer resort. It is just south of Asbury Park and Ocean Grove, both originally founded as Methodist camp grounds some thirty years earlier.

Construction of the Grugers' home in Avon was begun in 1904. It was planned as a large, three-story, Tudor-type house with oak paneling in the living and dining room, six bedrooms on the second floor and a studio comprising the entire third floor. The structure was designed by William L. Price, a Philadelphia architect and friend of FRG's, who had designed the Traymore Hotel in Atlantic City.

In 1904 Avon-by-the-Sea was a community about one-half mile square, laid out along the lines of Philadelphia, with streets and alleys arranged geometrically along two perpendicular axes. All seven miles of its sidewalks were of flagstone. A half mile boardwalk was built in Avon during the 1890s, about the same time that its more famous counterpart was being constructed in Atlantic City.

During the summer of 1904, the Grugers rented a house in Avon while their own home was under construction. When they arrived in the seaside resort that first year, FRG and Florence brought with them another addition to their family, a month-old infant daughter named Dorothy.

Florence Gruger and the three children enjoyed the outdoors while FRG spent the best part of each day at his drawing board. By now his work was appearing in another Curtis publication, the *Ladies' Home Journal,* as well as *Century Magazine.*

A year earlier, one of Gruger's drawings had caught the attention of Alexander Drake, art editor for *Century,* who invited the artist to visit him in New York. FRG did, and was given a story to illustrate:

> ...When I took the drawings in to him...he said they were too "newspapery" so I made them all over again. "Better," he said, "but not good enough yet; have another try." So I did. That time they were accepted. [6]

The Avon house. Gruger's studio occupied the entire third floor.

Some artists might have been justifiably annoyed at having to draw three sets of illustrations in order to please an art editor, but FRG was grateful to Drake: "His criticism and advice was priceless...."

Toward the end of 1903 FRG had made several trips to New York in connection with work for *Century, Leslie's* and *McClure's.* He was in the habit of visiting William Glackens and James Preston, and would dine with them at Mouquin's. Once Glackens had his fiancee, Edith Dimock, travel down from Hartford for the day, with Gruger serving as chaperon.

On New Year's Eve Glackens, confined to bed with the grippe, wrote to her:

> I am going to have dinner sent over from Shanley's tonight...You must understand that you have an invitation. I suppose Bill (FRG) will be the only guest, and probably he won't turn up...Tomorrow night Bill and I are having our New Year's dinner chez Preston...[7]

On February 16, 1904 William J. Glackens and Edith Dimock were married in Hartford. Glackens, at age thirty-four, was the last of the Philadelphia gang to marry. His fellow artists looked on the event as the fall of the final eligible bachelor in their midst. A special Pullman car was reserved to transport family and friends from Philadelphia and New York to the ceremony. Included in the entourage were Everett and Florence Shinn, George Luks, May Wilson Preston and FRG. Mrs. Gruger did not make the trip because she was in her sixth month of pregnancy. Gruger, Shinn and Luks were among the ushers at the wedding.

In the fall of 1905, The Century Company approached FRG with an ambitious project to produce a group of drawings to accompany Anne Warner's "Seeing France with Uncle John," which was scheduled to appear in *Century Magazine* the following year. The commission would require Gruger to make a trip abroad to research and sketch the subjects described by the author.

FRG accepted the assignment with mixed emotions, realizing that it would take him away from the family for several months. After completing his commitments to the other magazines, he left Avon on November 29, 1905, stayed the night with James and May Wilson Preston in New York, and embarked the following day for Europe aboard the S.S. *Noordam.*

On this, his first voyage, FRG saw the ocean with an artist's eye. He wrote his wife:

> I only wish you could see the ocean out here. From the shore at Avon we get no idea of it at all. I feel that I never saw it before. The great waves and deep valleys roll by as the ship bows and rolls through them...you would never tire of their endless variety of color, of everything about the sea. It is the most wonderful thing I ever saw and wish you could have seen the moon burst through the great, black masses of cloud and edge them all with silver, bathing the sea in a light that cannot be imagined...

He wrote lengthy letters to Florence, describing his adventures and also his longing to be reunited with her:

> My thoughts of you are those delights upon which I shall live until I see you again seated by the fire with all the kids about you, and know that I am home...
> Tomorrow I will have been away from you, and that means home, for just a month...I do not think I shall ever come over here again without you. I miss you dreadfully...

On December 12, 1905 FRG wrote from Holland:

> I got out early and took a dash all alone into Germany to see an old, old farm house and a queer little, red tiled town...
> Yesterday the "doctor"[8] and I went to Haarlem, we went into the old palace where are the Frans Hals portraits—I thought I knew Frans Hals but I found that nothing I had seen gave me an idea of what this man could do— The human story told by those few great works was touching in the extreme...
> We went down to the great museum of Haarlem a most wonderful place and as we passed the door of the picture gallery, caught sight of an Israels[9] painting and made a bee line for it closely followed by the Dr. I was telling him about it

when the curator, who was with us, bowed profoundly and said to me—"You are an artist, is it?" I modestly refrained from denying the same and he beckoned us to an inner room, where after arranging a rack and two chairs he brought *us* a large portfolio containing sixty original sketches by Michaelangelo. He kindly allowed us to take them out one by one and examine them, some of the sheets were drawn upon both sides, studies, sketches, wonderful. We came upon many having his writing, his signature, little memoranda and one old sheet contained his first draft of the dome of the great Cathedral at Rome—these things take a fierce hold upon me—my hand trembled as I looked upon the thought of a mind so far back, among the piled up years...

FRG was equally awed by the architecture and history he discovered at every turn:

> We were going to see the Great Church on the Market place...up a narrow stair then through a doorway into the vast transept. I looked for the first time upon an ancient church of old historical association. I could not keep my hat on. We passed down the aisle and saw embedded in the wall a cannon ball, a relic of the Spanish siege...the nearly forgotten story of the old struggle of these people came into mind as I saw those records of struggle and hope...

In Amsterdam Gruger found comfortable quarters at the Victoria Hotel and wrote home on December 13:

> We visited the Rijksmuseum today and were filled with pictures. Frans Hals by the bunch, Rembrandt and a lot more old fellows...We saw a gown that belonged to Madame Pompadour, a beautiful thing and a lot of painted fans, all silently eloquent pages of the long history of men and women...
> ...and saw Rubens' *Descent from the Cross*...it is a wonder...I could not get away from it. It has a marvelous power to hold one.

On December 15, 1905 FRG arrived in Paris. He settled at the American Art Association, a building on the Notre Dame des Champs which catered to students of art, architecture and literature. He had arranged to rendezvous with John Weygandt, a former Academy colleague and a staff artist with the *Public Ledger:*

December 15, 1905

...I have been very kindly received by the

members of the club (the American Art Association), and was astonished to find myself perfectly well known.
I found John Weygandt without trouble and he brought me here and introduced me as Mr. Gruger. Several men arose and one of them said "Not F.R.?" Then they showed me some of my drawings upon the wall and, of course, I, as usual, felt embarrassed. I wish I didn't under those circumstances...
Work is going forward all along the line and I will share Weygie's studio. It is all right, but doesn't compare to mine at home...

December 16, 1905

Yesterday morning I ran into the Luxembourg (Museum) for an hour and found one of old Henri's paintings[10] in a very complimentary position...

December 19, 1905

You should see the palace of the Louvre, it is a marvelous building, vast. Oh my! that was magnificent Royalty—for sure. You could tuck the City Hall of Philadelphia away in one corner of the court and forget it, except of course the great tower of the City Hall, which would reach far above anything in the vicinity...

On December 23 FRG and Weygandt, who spoke fluent French, left Paris on a trip through Normandy, stopping first at Rouen:

December 25, 1905

...the great Cathedral is all that is claimed for it, many parts have fallen to decay and workmen are replacing some of the exquisite Gothic carving...I shall never forget Christmas morning in the Cathedral of Rouen...
We stood for a few minutes on the slab that marks the site of the ancient burning of poor Joan (d'Arc)—One feels the sadness of the poor girl's fate, when one stands there and reads the simple statement that here she was burned, the buildings that witnessed the tragedy are no longer there, except in some of the small streets adjacent an ancient house remains, wearily leaning against a younger and more robust neighbor...

December 29, 1905

This (Saint Lo) is the land of the Middle Ages

for sure, it is the land of the candle and the bed warmer, of wood fires in your bedroom, of dusk at half past three and darkness at four...

January 1, 1906

I had a letter from *Century* telling me there is a strike on among the printers and asking me to hustle the first installment. It will leave in a day or two...

January 8, 1906

Work has not gone as well as I hoped—I was willing and did my best—The drawings I have made are much in advance of the work I did previously in the U.S. but the light is so very poor that I have a great deal of trouble. Some days it is almost impossible to work at all. Dark until late in the morning and at three o'clock—I mean too dark to see my work...I have decided to cut Italy out and save that money towards your passage over here, for I will sure bring you to see the sights...

FRG and John Weygandt also visited Mont Saint Michel and Beauvais before ending their journey. "Now for Paris and to finish up the drawings and then home," FRG wrote his wife. On January 22, Gruger set sail for New York. He had observed, sketched and gathered sufficient data to allow for the completion of his drawings back in Avon. Gruger executed both pen-and-ink and wash drawings for *Century Magazine,* works which were authentic in every detail. In one of his letters he had confided:

I can tell you one thing...the woman who wrote the story was never here. The yarn is full of inaccuracies, impossibilities, in fact. I know, for I went and looked...

Not long after his return FRG fell ill with pneumonia and pericarditis, an inflammation of the sac around the heart. Because the afflictions followed so closely his return from Europe, the local gossips in Avon rumored that he had contracted "ship's disease." His recovery was to take six weeks, with recuperation requiring a wheel chair.

By the summer of 1906 FRG's health was restored, but during his illness art editors had stopped forwarding stories to him, for fear their deadlines could not be met. No work was forthcoming during the first half of the year from the *Ladies' Home Journal, Everybody's, Munsey's* or *McClure's.* Even *The Saturday Evening Post* had stopped its steady flow of manuscripts. His illustrations appeared only through the April 14 issue. Finally, the *Post*

The Ruins of the Abbey of Jumièges. *Century Magazine,* June, 1906. From the Cabinet of American Illustration, Library of Congress, Washington, D.C.

of August 25, 1906 contained four drawings which once again included the familiar "F.R. Gruger" signature. The famine was over, and FRG began the long road back, gradually regaining the momentum of his illustrating career.

notes for chapter 5

[1] Peterson, p. 3

[2] Ibid., p. 10

[3] Renwick, p. 14 (Bibliography)

[4] Renwick, p. 15 (Bibliography)

[5] Letter to FRG from Lorimer, April 25, 1929

[6] Renwick, p. 16 (Bibliography)

[7] Glackens, *William Glackens and the Ashcan School,* p. 46

[8] "Doctor" was a young clergyman he had met named Harrington.

[9] Jozef Israels (1824-1911), a popular Dutch painter.

[10] In the summer of 1899, Henri, in Paris, submitted a painting entitled *La Neige* (The Snow) to the annual Salon. The work was subsequently purchased by the French government and hung in the Luxembourg museum.

Frowning, Bristling More, He Said: "Read On! It's Incredible. Have You Come to What
He Did About the Bonds?"

CHILD'S PLAY by JAMES GOULD COZZENS,
The Saturday Evening Post, February 13, 1937, Page 17.

Note:
FRG incorporated in this illustration a corner of the pergola and a portion of the
fence which surrounded the garden at his
Avon home, both of which he designed.

Chapter 6

The Avon house was designed for summer use only, but after the first season the Grugers decided to have a steam heating system installed, so that they could live there the year 'round.

Like other resort towns, Avon was oriented toward summer occupancy. There was a handful of permanent residents, local artisans and merchants, who lived along Main Street, parallel to the ocean. The rest of the homes were largely uninhabited during the off season, with as few as four families living in them.

Beginning with the winter of 1906-7 and continuing until that of 1911-12, solitary and leisurely Avon-by-the-Sea would become the Gruger family's home. Their life in the three-story house at 316 Woodland Avenue would be interrupted only by two winters spent in Lansdowne, Pa.

The activities of F.R. and Florence and their three children changed with the seasons. The youngsters spent almost the entire summer on the beach with their friends. FRG, who enjoyed swimming, would join them on weekends. The family also owned a canoe, which they carried the few short blocks to Sylvan Lake or to Shark River at the other end of town.

There was an extensive walled-in English garden with many flower beds, flagstone walks, a formal pool and a large vine-covered pergola. During the growing season Florence brought freshly-cut flowers into the house daily. It was one of her principal interests. The Grugers subsequently purchased an adjoining lot, on which they cultivated a vegetable garden and maintained a playground for the youngsters.

FRG bought the children a pony and a small carriage, and had a stable built adjacent to the house. For several years this was a source of fun and activity.

When cold weather set in, the family moved indoors. For entertainment, the children would turn on a Victrola, or gather around the piano where their father played his favorite Chopin or melodies they could sing. FRG's piano playing was an almost nightly after-dinner ritual while they were still young.

Florence often read to the children, drawn up before the living room fireplace, while their father peeled apples and shelled nuts for them. She was especially fond of James Fenimore Cooper's writings and similar stories of adventure and exploration. After Elizabeth and Fred, Jr. were old enough to read for themselves, the recitation continued for little Dorothy's sake. The sessions were eagerly awaited by the youngsters as a Sunday afternoon pastime, particularly in bad weather. FRG also treated them to a variation of the newspaper artists' memory game, as Elizabeth recalled:

> Things would be put on a table for so many minutes and then he'd cover them up and see who could remember more of them. We would be given so much time to look at the objects. We'd have friends in and play. You'd be surprised how many you do remember. [1]

Their father did not participate in any strenuous physical activity with them because he wished to avoid risking even a slight injury to his hands. A stiff wrist or a bruised finger could seriously handicap his drawing ability.

The youngsters had an unusual collection of toys, including a steam train that FRG had bought while in Europe for his son's fourth birthday, and later, a scale model of a stationary steam engine:

> ...we filled her up with hot water and burned alcohol underneath the boiler with the result that in a few moments the flywheel was spinning around merrily and each small part behaving perfectly. All of us children had a good time

the father confessed.

Although FRG was often in his studio, under pressure to complete a set of illustrations for an impending deadline, he could usually find time for his family, as Ted (FRG, Jr.) explained:

> Father would always come to the breakfast and dinner table with the entire family. He was an interesting talker at dinner and conversed a great deal, discussing things he had read, and ideas he had.

Elizabeth added:

> Dad was lots of fun. He showed a marvelous sense of humor at our meals, dinners particularly. Father always claimed that if you laugh it was very good for your digestion. We would have hilarious meals, just enjoy ourselves. They were never quiet and sedate. He just loved a good time.

The family usually had beef dishes, which FRG preferred. He used to cook steaks on the fireplace, and make home-made bread and popovers. Desserts regularly consisted of fresh fruit, cut up. When the Reverend Gray visited them, grace was said as a matter of courtesy, but otherwise omitted. FRG was not a religious person in any sense, though his parents were Dutch Reform and his in-laws Methodist. He was, however, a student of the Bible, which he respected as literature.

When FRG went into the third floor studio of the Avon house, the family knew he was unavailable, and short of the house catching fire or one of the children suffering a serious accident, he expected his wife to deal with all of the normal daily routines. "When the door was closed to his studio, we knew he was busy and we just never went up those stairs," Elizabeth remarked. But Ted confesses: "I used to go up a lot and sit on the landing at the top of the stairs, in front of his closed door, and look at books."

The eighteen by thirty-five-foot studio provided a serene and spacious work area. There was a fireplace located in an alcove, as well as built-in cabinets of his own design. A semi-circular niche housed a plaster cast of one of Rodin's sculptures, a recumbent figure. The work space contained his drawing table, which could be tilted or rotated, elevated or lowered. There was also a rolltop desk, a couch, two other tables which he had had built, and bookcases for his research library.

FRG wore a smock, but only in the studio. He never affected the style of a bohemian artist. His suits were tailor-made and he dressed like a conservative banker, always wearing a coat, tie and vest. Gruger was of medium height, a handsome man with deep-set eyes, heavy brows and a firm mouth and chin. Although his physiognomy appeared resolute, there was a little quirk at the corner of his mouth which made him seem about to smile, which he did easily. He wore glasses to correct his farsightedness and astigmatism, and always sat in a rocking chair at his drawing board, rocking back to view his work at a greater distance. A small antique cabinet served as his taboret, on which he kept his brushes, pencils and erasers. A pipe or Lucky Strike cigarette was also a regular fixture.

FRG's early newspaper drawings had been in pen-and-ink, a technique necessitated in those days by the limitations of reproduction. Among his influences then were American artists Abbey, Frost and William Thomas Smedley, an Academy-trained illustrator from West Chester, Pennsylvania; plus Leech, Keene, Gavarni and duMaurier, all of whom worked either for the English humor magazine *Punch* or for the French *Charivari*. Abbey's illustrations of the comedies and tragedies of Shakespeare were printed in *Harper's Monthly* over a period of thirteen years, allowing for a continuous exposure. But of greater significance was the large number of books with drawings by these and other contemporary artists on the shelves of FRG's bookcases. His collection included John Leech's *Pictures of Life and Character;* four volumes, in French, of the work of Gavarni; *Our People* sketched by Charles Keene and *English Society at Home* by George duMaurier.

George du Maurier

Gavarni (Guillaume Sulpice Chevallier)

Gavarni's illustrations, especially the early ones, are single figures; to appreciate them one must read the captions. Keene, a realist, drew his characters in an environment; duMaurier's drawings were more elegant, Leech's more imaginative. Although English periodicals such as *Punch* were widely distributed in this country, the English and French illustrators also became known through the issuance of their drawings in book form and in American magazines.

FRG was aware of contemporary Americans as well, and had in his collection volumes illustrated by Joseph Pennell, Howard Pyle, Maxfield Parrish and Charles Dana Gibson.

Arthur Burdett Frost

Charles Samuel Keene

William Thomas Smedley

John Leech

" 'Sometimes I fetch a nag up and gallop around
and shoot' "

MOTHERING ON PERILOUS, V-THE BOY THAT FIT
THE MARSHAL
by LUCY FURMAN
The Century Magazine, April 1911, Page 858

When the halftone came into greater use, FRG expanded his technique. First he used charcoal, then conté crayon and finally the Wolff pencil. While he continued to work on occasion in pen-and-ink for *The Saturday Evening Post* until 1907, and for *Century* and *McClure's* as late as 1912 the majority of his illustrations after 1904 were tonal. The medium most closely associated with his name was known as Wolff's Carbon Drawing Pencil, made in England. The Wolff pencil is ideal because it produces a full range of values, and provides a rich, velvety black.

FRG used several pencils of varying degrees, sketching initially with a hard pencil, then using a softer one for the large areas of darks. His favorite was the softest, a BBB. Of equal importance to him were water color washes using lamp black.

As a result of the visit to Europe in 1905-6, FRG learned to admire particularly the work of Rubens, Rembrandt, Velasquez and Tintoretto. These artists were all represented in the books in his library. Their use of dramatic foreshortening, light and dark organization and the juxtaposition of compositional elements had a lasting appeal to FRG's sense of pictorial construction.

A T-square hung from the top of his drawing board, which he used as a hand rest to prevent the drawing from being smudged. It also gave him a check on his vertical lines.

FRG produced his illustrations on an unusual surface:

> There was a cheap cardboard used for mounting silverprints. We (FRG and Glackens) worked on that (on the *Ledger*). No one cared how much we used. It was known as railroad blank. Conté crayon worked well on it, so did watercolor. I continued always to use it until long years after, it came to be known as Gruger Board...[2]

The cardboard's soft surface was particularly receptive to his media. His combination of wash and Wolff pencil on Gruger Board soon became widely imitated.

FRG's procedure in developing an illustration was simple and direct. Although thumbnail sketches were sometimes made beforehand, he usually worked on the final illustration from the start. Typically, his compositions stressed environment, creating an authentic setting for the figures.

First he would very sketchily indicate the principal masses of darks and lights in the composition, usually through the use of washes of lamp black and water, using Winsor & Newton camel's hair brushes numbers two, three and four. Brush sizes were small; FRG's illustrations, despite their monumental appearance, rarely exceeded twenty-four inches in either dimension.

Once the tonal masses had been laid down in wash, the drawing was developed out of the tonal background by means of the Wolff pencil. Landscapes or interiors with period furnishings gradually emerged. The soft, compressed carbon pencil could be sharpened to a fine point for detail, or the side of the point used to obtain additional tone. The lamp black of the wash and the carbon black of the Wolff pencil matched each other compatibly and FRG would often use a Ruby eraser as a stump to smooth the strokes into a tonal blend with the underlying wash. When sharpened to a point, the eraser could be used to pick out light areas and highlights. This combination of mediums was very malleable and allowed FRG to make changes or refinements readily. If displeased with the beginning, he would turn the drawing over and begin again; the working surface of Gruger Board was identical on both sides. Perhaps thirty percent of his illustrations have partially completed works on the reverse side.

When the drawing was finally completed, he would spray it with fixative. He usually matted or mounted the artwork, then placed a protective piece of tissue and a kraft paper cover on top.

FRG had little difficulty drawing structures because of his thorough understanding of perspective and of building construction. His figures were pure creations; he

In these two unfinished versions of the same subject, Gruger's method of working can be clearly seen. Over a lightly indicated pencil drawing, the tonal masses were laid down in broad washes of black watercolor. The drawing was developed over this in Wolff pencil, made of compressed carbon, which could produce values ranging from light grey to a dense black. Tones could also be blended, or even completely removed, with a Ruby eraser. This permitted FRG great flexibility, and figures were often erased and shifted in pose or scale as the rendering progressed.

worked neither from posed models nor from photographs of them. Drawings of people, especially heads, represented his greatest problem. Part of this was due to his persistence in attempting to achieve the proper characterization. Erasure after erasure of an area would finally wear thin the surface of the illustration board, whereupon he would recommence the entire composition. FRG was not in the habit of patching his artwork by cutting out an unsatisfactory area and inlaying a redrawn portion. "I've made many a drawing over a dozen times," he once admitted, "until every editor I ever knew...lost his patience."

The pressure of constantly working against a deadline, coupled with the eye strain associated with creating detailed drawings, resulted in violent headaches, occasionally so dreadful that FRG was unable to draw for several days at a time.

He had the ability to produce compositions which drew the spectator into the situation. Details were often implied, rather than being supplied by the artist. According to a fellow illustrator, Harry Beckhoff:

> When Gruger laid out his pictures, he sort of designed the shade for them. He just showed the edge of a table and the edge of a chair and didn't draw the rest of the thing at all, but it would look great.[3]

This illusion of reality by implication was one of FRG's greatest strengths. As his daughter Elizabeth once explained:

> Father never broke up any dramatic form with too much detail. My sister once told me an example of this. Someone was talking to her about one of father's drawings, one in which a cupboard filled with specific pieces of china and glass was important to the story, and this person said that it amazed him that anyone could draw all of this detail and keep within the composition. My sister didn't remember the drawing and looked it up out of curiosity and was very entertained to find that not one piece of china or glass was drawn. Dad had used a few highlights necessary to the composition and they, together with the imagination of the beholder, had supplied the detail.

FRG was always conscientious about researching illustrations, and his information on historical detail reveals itself again and again. He would expend long hours and much effort to create drawings which would ring true, even when the required background information was unavailable. On one occasion his artwork involved a story about the Crusades, and dealt with those Europeans who stayed

CRUSADE by DONN BYRNE
The Saturday Evening Post, 1927

on and lived among the Saracens. Several interior views were so convincingly executed by him that, after the story was published, a museum curator wrote asking where he had found examples of the furniture depicted since, to the best of the curator's knowledge, there was none extant. Of course, there was none. FRG simply designed the furnishings himself.

On another occasion he was provided with a story which dealt with an invention for making diamonds artificially. He had placed in the background of the illustra-

"You Have Been a Prisoner in Damascus, Sir Miles?" the Grand Master asked.

tion just the bare suggestion of some sort of machine which was supposed to exert great heat and pressure in the diamond-making process. Soon a letter arrived from the inventor who had seen Gruger's drawing and, simply from the very sketchy suggestion, concluded that the artist must have the technical knowledge for constructing such a machine. And once the U.S.Navy contacted FRG after he drew the interior of a submarine, accusing him of having obtained classified information.

FRG maintained a library of over three hundred volumes to aid in his quest for accurate resource material. Many of the books were collected for the illustrations alone. The artist's library ranged from a copy of *Godey's Lady's Book* to the *Report of the William Pepper Peruvian Expedition of 1896*, from *Italian Furniture and Interiors* to *The Yerkes Collection of Oriental Carpets*. Others dealt with the subjects of astronomical instruments, arms and armor, Pre-Columbian art, the history of dance and ships of the seventeenth to nineteenth centuries.

The books provided specific details to supplement the

They Knelt Slowly. All of Them But One. The Muscles of His Neck Were Tense; His Hot Eyes Wavered Between Defiance and a Superstitious Fear.

Miniature Model Representing a Temple.
From *Maya Architecture* by George Oakley Totten

THE HOUSE OF DARKNESS by C. E. SCOGGINS
The Saturday Evening Post, January 3, 1931, Page 18

artist's fertile imagination. For example, when Gruger illustrated C.E. Scoggins' "House of Darkness," he needed to depict an entrance to a Mayan temple. The artist discovered an architectural plan for just such a structure in George Oakley Totten's *Maya Architecture.* It shows the front and side elevations of a "Miniature Model in Terra Cotta Representing a Temple." FRG's illustration, like the Mayan model, depicts the building's entrance in the form of an animal head, its open jaws constituting the doorway. This representation was original, yet based upon archaeological fact.

His reputation for artistic veracity led to commissions to illustrate stories about far-off lands and exotic cultures. He carefully researched Oriental architecture, furniture and decoration, utilizing the knowledge thus gained in such serials as J.P. Marquand's "Ming Yellow" and "No Hero." His convincing creations of the Oriental gave form to Marquand's "Mr. Moto" and Earl Derr Biggers' "Charlie Chan."

The artist was especially adept at representing the Negro with dignity, as in his illustrations for Stephen Vincent Benet's "Freedom's a Hard Bought Thing." Similarly, his portrayal of the American Indian is true-to-life and devoid of caricature in such stories as Walter D. Edmonds' "Drums Along the Mohawk."

In addition to his library, FRG developed an extensive collection of photographs and clippings filed for reference purposes.

Sometimes it was the uniform or costume that fascinated him: A German officer astride a horse, a Moroccan sultan, an Italian king, a Sioux Indian, a Russian czar. FRG was interested in literary figures and well-known personalities whose pictures he culled from many sources.

The majority of the magazine clippings date from 1906, 1907 or 1908, although there are some from as early as 1897. The collection contained pictures by many artists as well, including George du Maurier, Dante Gabriel Rossetti, Puvis de Chavannes, Camille Corot, and of his friends Glackens, Shinn, Sloan, Henri, Grafly and W. Elmer Schofield.

A third body of resource material involved a set of 26 photograph albums with hundreds of pictures neatly clipped and pasted on their mat black pages. Each volume was catalogued and numbered on the spine. Number one was devoted to paintings, number two to tables, number three to gardens, and so on. Others feature sofas, beds and entrance doorways of every period. In one album FRG had mounted his own photographs of trees of all varieties and filmed at all times of the year.

In the near-isolation of Avon-by-the-Sea, such an extensive set of research materials was almost a necessity.

Without it, Gruger would have been at a loss to illustrate such stories as "Spoiling the Egyptians," "A Message for Mikado" or "Java Head."

FRG's studio was his hideaway, a retreat from the daily activities in the household. But one day, when Ted was almost seven, he quietly ventured into the sanctuary while his father was working. There was FRG at the north end of the studio, seated at his drawing board under the sizable four-sash windows, with reference tables and taboret nearby. The youngster was captivated, not only by the work of art before his eyes, but by the subject matter as well:

> I was standing beside the chair looking at this picture. It was of an automobile which had hit head on into a tree, the rear wheels were rotating and sending out a cloud of dust and the front wheels were stationary. That intrigued me. Of course, we didn't know much about automobiles in those days. We'd run to the front of the house to see an automobile go by, it was that rare. I wanted to know why the rear wheels were going around and the front ones weren't so father explained to me that they were the ones that received the power from the engine.

The completed drawing, for "Millington's Motor Mystery" by Ellis Parker Butler, appeared in the November, 1909 issue of *Century Magazine*.

It was not long after creating this illustration that FRG purchased his first automobile, a 1910 Mitchell. The car was full of brass lamps, brass rods and brass carriage lights, and young Ted's job was to keep them well polished. The stable for the children's pony was converted into a garage, and a pit was constructed in the floor so that a mechanic could work underneath. FRG had a gas and oil pump installed, with a fifty gallon gasoline tank placed underground.

The Grugers often went for a Sunday drive, stopping at a clearing in the woods to have a picnic lunch. They explored much of New Jersey, over the flat, sandy roads, and sometimes drove to see J.J. Gould, who lived in Swarthmore, Pennsylvania, or relatives around Philadelphia. In those days it was necessary to change license plates when entering another state, so as they crossed the bridge leaving Trenton, FRG brought the car to a halt, located a screw driver in the tool box and affixed the Pennsylvania plates.

Automobiling was a real adventure then, as Ted remembers:

> When it rained the roads were turned to liquid mud and the side curtains offered little protection, so that everyone got drenched.

Once we had to stop and go into a farmhouse and ask for shelter until the storm abated.
Engines had to be cranked, a hazard because a backfire sometimes broke an arm. Father cranked with his left arm, in order not to jeopardize the use of his drawing hand.
We never went out, it seemed, but that we got a puncture. Tires were very hard to change because they were held on with a steel ring which, first of all, had to be pried off. The tire also had to be pried off and resisted like a powerful rubber band. The tube was then extracted, pumped up and placed in a pan of water to locate the leak. After patching, it was replaced in the shoe which somehow was got back on the rim. Then came an exhausting hand-pumping operation. The whole procedure took about an hour.

Despite the annoyances, the Grugers enjoyed their outings by auto. Traveling by car could be—indeed had to be—done at a leisurely pace. The Model T Ford had just been introduced in October, 1908 so there was still very little traffic on the roads. Yet the automobile was already making its impact on other facets of American life: Charles Dana Gibson's pale-faced Gibson Girl was being replaced by a sun-tanned, outdoor type as women took up driving.

America was having its first taste of freedom that comes from mobility. For Fred and Florence Gruger, the car would provide more accessibility to friends, increasing the number of visits to and from their somewhat isolated position in Avon.

notes for chapter 6

[1] Conversation with Elizabeth Gruger Van Buren, May 15, 1973

[2] FRG teaching notes, c. 1946. A New York art supply company sold some 300,000 sheets of Gruger board between 1920 and 1953. However, when FRG died, his name was dropped. The board, still available, is now simply referred to as "mount board."

[3] Conversation with the author, November 28, 1972

"I ran the nose of the machine into a tree, and threw on the high speed suddenly."

MILLINGTON'S MOTOR MYSTERY by ELLIS PARKER BUTLER
The Century Magazine, November, 1909, Page 122

"I am no mere Knight of Wits, as you may take it. In fact I am Lord of The Fair Acres of Arcady".

FREE AIR by SINCLAIR LEWIS
The Saturday Evening Post, June 21st, 1919, Page 22.

FRG at the wheel of his 1910 Mitchell. Young Ted is a passenger in the rear seat.

Two compositional sketches in Wolff pencil. Size of originals, approximately 5 by 4 inches.

Gesture sketch in pencil, exact size.

" 'Stand up you little, lazy Josephine and drink too,' cried Therese Tallien. 'No, don't rise like a snake undulating its coils, but spring like a panther. Health to Barras'. They drank, Josephine sipping and smiling at her friend's frenetic enthusiasm. 'To General Buonaparte! And may his star lead him high and far!' "

"THE THUNDERER" by E. BARRINGTON
Harper's Bazaar, September 1926, page 67

Chapter 7

The Gruger family's touring car simplified delivery of *Saturday Evening Post* illustrations to Philadelphia. In those days the *Post* was the one magazine which adhered to a strict deadline. If an artist received a story but was unable to complete the work in time, it was understood that the manuscript would be returned immediately, so that it could be reassigned.

Except for reasons of illness, FRG never turned down a *Post* story. He assumed—probably correctly—that each one was selected for him as part of the editorial policy of the magazine. But other illustrators were not equally conscientious. Glackens admitted disliking illustration. He often tore up his drawings in disgust as he redrew the same subject again and again. By 1915 he would abandon the profession altogether, thereafter devoting himself entirely to painting.

Sloan, on the other hand, was discouraged by the often poor quality of writing given him. Both Glackens and Sloan had received stories by important authors, but instead of being asked to illustrate the great novels of men like Theodore Dreiser and Stephen Crane, they were assigned their pot boilers such as *A Traveler at Forty* and *Great Battles of the World*.

FRG received both short stories and serials from the *Post*. For the first installment of a serial, three illustrations were required, after which two drawings were included each week except for the final part, which rated only a single picture. Sometimes he would send along an extra spot drawing or vignette, either feeling it was required or simply creating it on impulse. These extras were normally used, although he was not compensated for them.

Until about 1915, illustrations in the *Post* were relatively small and there were anywhere from four to eight in a story. This probably was in imitation of the policy of the monthly magazines, such as *Century, McClure's* and *Scribner's*. About the time of the First World War the small format monthlies phased out illustrations, and shortly thereafter ceased publication altogether. The larger weekly and monthly magazines reduced the number of their illustrations, but increased their size, introducing the full-page and then the double-page spread.

Occasionally FRG provided a suggested layout to the *Post*, indicating how his pictures should be placed in relation to the type. The art editor might or might not follow his advice. But the magazine never supplied him with layouts, nor did it indicate the size or shape of his pictures.

Text from *The Saturday Eveing Post* always arrived in galley proofs. FRG's approach was to read the galley through once, making marginal notations of situations which he thought offered opportunities for illustration. The *Post*'s policy allowed the artist complete freedom of choice in selecting what portions of a story to illustrate. But this was not true with all magazines, as Ted pointed out:

> If Father received a manuscipt from an editor with passages marked for illustration, he would send it back and ask for a fresh one. Of course, for any magazine for which he was in the habit of working that was unnecessary, because they were aware of his feeling. It might happen only once with any given magazine, but it was known to happen. He felt that he could not necessarily do a satisfactory job if someone else specified what was to be illustrated, rather than his choosing after having studied the story.

One of the art editors for *Pictoral Review* was in the habit of sending the artists rough sketches of the compositions he wanted drawn. FRG illustrated only four stories for that publication. On the other hand, some illustrators used to submit pencil miniatures of rough ideas first, seeking approval before proceeding with the finished product. But F.R. Gruger sent the magazines only his completed artwork.

FRG usually read the story twice. If a particular person was to be featured in an illustration, he would read back to assemble any details the author had provided about facial features, physical characteristics or dress, taking careful note of furniture and surroundings. After having made a preliminary study, he might put the text aside for a period to allow the ideas to incubate in his mind, permitting other picture-worthy possibilities a chance to surface. By the time he began drawing, he had a very clear mental picture of what his illustration was to be, and could begin the final composition.

FRG regularly worked from about 9 a.m. to 7 p.m. daily, and sometimes as late as 11 o'clock. He would refresh himself with tea at 4:30 every afternoon from a handsome service of Royal Copenhagen China which he kept in the studio for that purpose. On occasion he would destroy a drawing at 6 o'clock in the eveing that was due in Philadelphia at 10 o'clock the next morning. He would then draw through the night, invigorated by cups of tea, and sometimes work to 8 a.m. With the engine of the car running outside, he would add the final touches to the drawing, place a protective cover on top and give it to Ted or Dorothy, who would rush it to Philadelphia.

In the artist's first years on the *Post*, illustrations were occasionally joint efforts. FRG and James Preston created a series of subjects for Albert J. Beveridge's "The White Invasion of China," which appeared in the magazine throughout November and December, 1901. Together they

"Maggie Hawks, will you come down out of there this instant!" Parthy whirled on Andy. "There! That's what it comes to, minute she sets foot on this sink of iniquity. Play acting."

SHOW BOAT by EDNA FERBER
Woman's Home Companion, May, 1926, Page 22

produced a total of ten drawings. There were also times when an illustrator filled in for a friend. In October, 1903 *The Saturday Evening Post* contained three halftone illustrations FRG had drawn for an installment of "The Boss" by Alfred Henry Lewis. Earlier parts of this serial had been illustrated by William Glackens, so Gruger modified his style to harmonize with the artwork that had already appeared. Glackens, perhaps in Hartford at the time, courting his future wife Edith, resumed the serial in the next installment.

Two years later Glackens reciprocated. In the December 30, 1905 issue of the *Post*, William Allen White's "A-Babbled O'Green Fields" was accompanied by two FRG drawings and one by Glackens who, in this case, appears to have altered *his* style to correspond with Gruger's. Once FRG produced five of eight installments for a serial in *Harper's Bazaar*, which circumstances forced him to relinquish. The remaining illustrations were done by Everett Shinn. After doing three parts of Edna Ferber's "Show Boat" for *Woman's Home Companion*, he

was laid up with illness. R.F. James and Henry Raleigh did the final three.

Early in 1910, *The Saturday Evening Post* sent F.R. Gruger a galley for a story, a ten-parter, planned to begin in April. It was "The Varmint" by Owen Johnson. It was the beginning of a long and interesting association.

Johnson's first novels were based on his own prep school experiences at Lawrenceville, New Jersey. At the select academy there, he had met characters who became the prototypes for the Tennessee Shad, the Prodigious Hickey, Doc Macnooder and John Humperdink Stover. Johnson's tale of boarding school life and schoolboy pranks would soon delight the *Post* readership, as would FRG's illustrations, beginning with the very first characterization of Dink Stover setting out from the Trenton railroad station for Lawrenceville.

Owen Johnson described the Tennessee Shad as a lanky lad walking with "a stiff-jointed lope of his bony body." FRG had his real-life counterpart on hand, as Elizabeth recalled:

She read it. She looked up. The last shadow had vanished of that gay mood in which she had entered. "Let me see. Tennessee. Trains."

One of the illustrations for the serial by Henry Raleigh, made during FRG's illness.

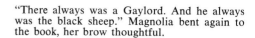

"There always was a Gaylord. And he always was the black sheep." Magnolia bent again to the book, her brow thoughtful.

SHOW BOAT by EDNA FERBER.
Woman's Home Companion, July, 1926, Page 23

This contribution was by R. F. James. For continuity, he and Raleigh both imitated Gruger's style.

The Tennessee Shad
by OWEN JOHNSON
Originally published around 1910;
Reprinted as part of *The Lawrenceville Stories* in 1967 by Simon and Schuster.

The Tennessee Shad stuffed into a wheelbarrow that Skinner was trundling.

Gene Moore was studying to be an illustrator, and he came down and spent a year at Avon and lived at a boarding house a couple of streets over. He used to come over and Dad let him work at one end of the studio. And he's the one who posed for the Tennessee Shad. He was a tall, lean, lanky critter and he was very funny. Father said nobody but he could get into the poses that the Tennessee Shad was supposed to be in. He was on the couch one time, I don't know what the pose was to be, it had been described by Owen Johnson. "Take that pose for me" Father said, and he did. He just twisted himself like a pretzel.

Even in such an instance as this, FRG did not resort to using a model in the conventional sense, for the pose was not kept for any length of time. He would simply sit and look for a couple of minutes, and then say, "O.K., thanks." He rarely drew on such occasions.

"The Varmint" ran in *The Saturday Evening Post* in ten installments, from April 9 through June 11, 1910. The next year Dink Stover, the hero, appeared on the pages of *McClure's Magazine* with the experiences of his college days, entitled "Stover at Yale."[1]

Owen Johnson provided passages which FRG translated into strikingly real images, of Dink Stover "curled up on his window-seat, rolling tobacco clouds among the fog of smokers in the room," "flinging himself at a football tackling dummy" and "his solemn departure from the field following the Yale-Princeton game."

The adventures of "Stover at Yale" unfolded in *McClure's* from October, 1911 to May, 1912. In preparation for creating the illustrations Johnson, himself a Yale alumnus, had taken Gruger to New Haven. The artist was provided a thorough tour, which included the dormitory buildings, dining halls and the athletic field, locations where the action in "Stover" takes place. Many Yale students at that time lived near the campus in private homes remodelled into rooming houses or make-shift dormitories. According to F.R. Gruger, Jr.:

"The period of duns sets in and the house became a place of mystery and signals."

McClure's Magazine, January 1912, Page 311

Illustrations for STOVER AT YALE
by OWEN JOHNSON, 1900

Given to The Yale University Library
by F. R. Gruger, Jr., 1923 S

McClure's Magazine, January 1912, Page 306

"Stover went to the window; 'They're running around Pierson Hall like a lot of ants', he said."

Owen Johnson and Father went through those erstwhile private homes. I'm sure some of the interiors Father drew were in such places. They are well described in "Stover at Yale." Other settings were in dormitories with the typical window seat, fireplace, etc. From this trip he brought away impressions of the kind of decoration and furnishing the students had in their rooms. So with Owen Johnson as guide he got an excellent idea of the social, athletic and academic life of the students of that day.

I am not sure whether a similar trip was made to Lawrenceville in connection with "The Varmint" and "The Tennessee Shad." In any case Lawrenceville was not far from Avon. I remember being shown the school once myself.

When the first installment of "Stover at Yale" appeared in *McClure's* in October, 1911 the Grugers were preparing to close their Avon house and spend the winter in Bermuda. The previous month Florence and a neighbor had left from New York and spent eight days in Bermuda, at which time Florence located the house they would rent. FRG, who had been suffering from rheumatism ever since his illness in 1906, determined that going to a warmer climate would help. Bermuda had been suggested by a fellow illustrator, Gustave VerBeek, a friend of Mark Twain and of his biographer, Albert Bigelow Paine, both of whom had lived in Bermuda.

Paine had just completed his major literary work, *Mark Twain, A Biography: The Personal and Literary Life of Samuel Langhorne Clemens,* to be published by Harper's in 1912.

The Grugers embarked for Bermuda on December 30, 1911 on the Royal Mail Steam Packet *Tagus,* and soon took up residence in their rented home, "Abergyle," on Spanish Point. The family was informed that the house had once served as an inn, a statement substantiated by ten-year old Ted, who later recalled:

> I subsequently, in poking around, found a room, which had been sealed up, full of empty bottles. A lot of those old bottles were odd shapes and very crude looking. "Abergyle" was supposed to be a couple of hundred years old and to have been an inn at one time.
> The house was large, with a driveway. It had four big rooms upstairs and two downstairs. No bathroom. The rooms measured about twenty by thirty. There were high ceilings. We slept under mosquito bars— mosquito nets hung over the beds.
> I remember my room being shared with 6" spiders and 2" cockroaches. There were

"Abergyle." Spanish Point, Pembroke West, Bermuda
Winter of 1911/12

> fireplaces for cooking, so-called Bermuda fireplaces, a couple of feet off the floor.

Spanish Point was a picturesque area, and FRG did a number of small watercolors in the vicinity, featuring lush flowers, plants and palms. Mrs. VerBeek was an artist, too, who worked in brilliant splotches of almost pure color. FRG's more subtle gradations appeared, by comparison, to be almost monochromatic.

The Grugers bicycled and walked a lot, and FRG, when not working, took many photographs of the breathtaking scenery and the ships at anchor in Hamilton harbor. Every day the artist cycled the two and one-half miles into Hamilton, where he rented a studio on Front Street, down by the docks. The studio was a second floor back room with north light, and was about fourteen feet square.

Gruger followed a steady work schedule each day, reading and illustrating the many stories sent him by the *Post.* He arranged with the customs officials and officers of the Royal Mail Line ships to deliver his drawings to New York on a regular basis. His illustrations entered the United States duty free, as did all original works of art.

FRG encountered a major problem caused by the damp climate in Bermuda. The watercolor washes dried too slowly, delaying completion of his drawings as he worked against a deadline. A cousin in Pennsylvania came to FRG's rescue by sending him a special electric heating device for his drawing board. This remedied the situation, for it kept the paper dry, thereby preventing it from wrinkling.

Owen Johnson and F. R. Gruger at "Abergyle."

"Stover at Yale" was still appearing in *McClure's Magazine* when the Grugers were visited by Owen Johnson. He and his wife were in Bermuda on their honeymoon. The two men posed for a picture in front of "Abergyle" which afforded a beautiful backdrop, situated as it was just a hundred yards from the water.

The Grugers returned to Avon in May, and during the next six months FRG completed two additional Owen Johnson stories for *Century Magazine*, as well as nearly one hundred illustrations for the *Post*.

In December, 1912 they revisited Bermuda, renting another house called "Maycliff." The plumbing at "Abergyle" had been too primitive although the house and grounds were vastly more spacious and beautiful than "Maycliff." From the new location, not as far out on Spanish Point, the children could dive from a cliff. They watched the filming of a portion of *Neptune's Daughter* with Annette Kellerman, some scenes of which were taken virtually in their back yard.

Another bit of excitement occurred when the house caught fire, as Ted remembers:

> Bermuda has no coal, and although the island at that time was pretty well covered with cedar, you weren't allowed to cut it down or burn it. So most everything ran by kerosene; lamps were lit with kerosene and cooking was done with it. We cooked on a kerosene stove—it caught fire one night and burned out the kitchen. Father ran next door (we had no telephone) and called into

Hamilton and reported the fire. They expressed sorrow to hear about it, but where were we? So father explained, and the man on the phone replied:

"Sir, we're very sorry indeed, but that's out of our district, we can't do anything about it."

"What'll I do, just let her burn?"

"'Fraid you'll have to, Sir."

A boyhood friend, who was down for a vacation, and I finally put it out, using small shovels to toss soil on the fire. The floor was pretty well burned, some of the furniture was too, and the ceiling rafters were charred, but they didn't give way.

During the winters of 1912-13 and 1913-14 the Gruger entourage to Bermuda had included a governess, a Miss Fisher, to serve as a qualified teacher for the children. Elizabeth was now fourteen years old, Ted was eleven and Dorothy seven. Ted reminisced:

> The first year our parents looked around for schools for us children, and there weren't any good schools so we were put in a Catholic convent. Our parents found the instruction there concentrated on religion to the detriment of the "three Rs."

According to Elizabeth:

> Our education was less conventional but lots more fun. Father had always believed that to study history and geography and literature separately was to lose much of their real significance...Therefore, not being in school in the usual sense of the word, we benefited from this theory of Dad's, and our regular studies were tied together by the novels which Mother tirelessly read to us.

FRG painted a watercolor at "Maycliff" of a table and a couple of benches in a clearing in the woods which the youngsters referred to as their "little red school house."

In the fall of 1913 the VerBeeks left for England, to take up residence at St. Ives in Cornwall, after which the Grugers sailed for Bermuda. Encouraged by glowing accounts contained in letters from the VerBeeks, FRG planned to take the family to join them in the spring of 1914.

After Florence, Elizabeth, Ted and Dorothy were settled at "Maycliff," Fred returned to New York and wrote lovingly to his wife:

Be careful of them (the children). They are precious jewels of ours, sweetheart. You gave them to me and they are the most valuable possessions we will ever have.

FRG was a prolific correspondent. It was not unusual for him to write letters of thirty or more pages. Since his letters travelled to Bermuda by boat, he kept informed of the scheduled departure of each ship:

The *Caribbean,* I am told, does not sail until Thursday...which will give me time to make it another fine long letter. Did you survive the thirty-six page one? Or was that too long? I don't want to inflict too much of my writing upon you, but as I so love to read all the details of your doings, I supposed that you might like an account of mine...

When F.R. Gruger first arrived in New York in January, 1914, he considered sharing the studio occupied by John R. Neill, but then decided against it. As he wrote his wife:

I couldn't work with Johnny Neill because of the small quarters and interminable visitors. Besides that, half of his rent plus what I'd have to pay at the Y.M.C.A. would be only eight dollars less than I am paying and now I have a private bath, everything all spotlessly clean.

Reunited, the two artists renewed their friendship. Neill, in his illustrations for *The Scarecrow of OZ* on which he was then working, drew the initials "FRG" in the script in the ruff around the neck of the figure Googly-Goo. He also lettered "Dorothy Gray Gruger" in the foliage which was sketched as part of a chapter heading. Neill presented FRG with copies of his most recently illustrated *OZ* books.

On February 16, 1914 Fred wrote to Florence in Bermuda:

Phone rang a few minutes ago and I went down to the basement to answer same. Johnny Neill. Johnny has tickets for the opera tonight and asks me to go with him. I am going. I intended working tonight but I guess as long as I can be a guest I will go to the uproar. M. Caruso, the pinhead, will sing and so will a lot more. I do not think I will care much for the singing. But it will be a fine sight, no doubt, and when I get home tonight I will sit down right here and tell you about it...

At six o'clock I left the studio and went down to meet Neill [for dinner]...At eight we went across the street to the Opera House and took our seats in the balcony. It was my purpose and intent to throw an egg at Caruso. I had it with me in my hat. I have always detested the man. I suppose I do yet; but when he opened his mouth and pours out that marvelous voice, your arm loses its strength and your purpose fades away. I didn't know what the opera was, nor what it was all about. I leaned my head against a post and simply listened. Could you have only been there and Elizabeth! If only you had. My, it was glorious. Honestly, I was ashamed of myself...
[I was] lifted into another world by the music, the light and the color and glamour. The place seemed unreal, strange, a world of fancy, existing only in the spirit. When the curtain finally fell together and the great audience sat silent for a moment and then slowly rose to go home, we followed in the crowd and still under the spell of the music went into the snow-covered street...

When FRG decided against sharing the studio with John R. Neill, he rented the flat of Julian Street in the Shropshire Apartments, at 138 West Sixty-fifth Street. Among the building's residents was Raeburn Van Buren, an illustrator for *Judge* and *Life* who would one day create the "Abbie an' Slats" comic strip.

Julian Street, a novelist and close friend of Booth Tarkington's, had agreed to sublet his quarters to FRG for two months. As the artist informed his wife:

> The parquet floor in this room is so nice and the rug so expensive that I have exercised great care of both...I have a big square sheet of paper...that is placed on the floor under my chair and you would be surprised to see what a lot of truck it accumulates in a day. I haven't an idea whence come all the matches. Just now there are about fifty matches and goodness knows how much tobacco and ashes in it.

FRG sent Florence some magazines which contained the writings of Booth Tarkington. "Read those stories aloud to the kids," he suggested. "In the bookcase here is Paine's *Life of Mark Twain* and when Julian Street left he advised me to read it. I am doing it."

Most of FRG's time was spent producing illustrations. The separation from his family was planned to last only until March 21, when he would depart for Bermuda, then leave a few weeks later with wife and children for England. During the two months in New York he intended working night and day, producing as many drawings as possible so as to earn the money required for the European sojourn.

On July 27, 1914 he communicated to Florence:

> I am doing my second story and in consideration of just having been settled so short a time, I think that is pretty good, don't you?

Twelve days later he provided a further progress report:

> Drawings are going fine and when I finish this next installment which will be next Thursday I will have made $800.00 since I left Bermuda...It is quite dark and only five o'clock, but that is due to clouds. I have a fine standard lamp belonging to Julian Street which enables me to go right on with my work...I have a bushel more to do.

But FRG's work schedule was to be constantly interrupted, for his reputation had preceded him to New York. He had long been inaccessible to fellow illustrators because of his virtual isolation in Avon and Bermuda. Admiring artists now wanted to meet the man who was considered among the outstanding illustrators in the country.[2]

Among his many admirers was Arthur William Brown, also an illustrator for *The Saturday Evening Post.*

Brown, Canadian-born but now a resident of New York, explained:

> Around 1908, two young illustrators, Henry Raleigh and H.J. Mowat, and myself had long talks on what constituted good illustration. We favored Gruger for the richness, beauty of composition and characterization of his work. Nearly every week he would have a set of illustrations in *The Saturday Evening Post.* Looking for a style of our own, we thought his was just right for its simplicity of tones and masses that made it reproduce well. To put it mildly, we were crazy about his work and he became our idol. We clipped every one of his drawings for our files and admitted freely that we copied him...
>
> Gruger was a myth to us. We knew nothing about him or where he lived. All we knew was his work. We could tell that he drew with some sort of a crayon pencil and pulled his drawings together with washes of lamp black. When we tried it, we didn't hit it at all. We worked on different kinds of illustration board but their surfaces were too hard and we got a scratchy effect looking nothing like a Gruger.
>
> Charles Norris, married to novelist Kathleen Norris, was, at the time, assistant art editor of the *American Magazine*...He loaned us a Gruger original to gaze at and allowed us to take it to our studios to pore over. We guarded it with care as if it belonged to Fort Knox. We studied it, looked at it through a magnifying glass, rubbed our pencils on the back, and even there on the back was the beautiful grain like canvas that no illustration board gave us. It was paper like we'd never seen before and Charlie Norris had no idea what it was. We were baffled but had the thrill of even touching one of the Master's originals.
>
> Herbert Johnson, then a great political cartoonist, was art editor of *The Saturday Evening Post.* He said, "Brownie, I know Gruger well, he lives in Avon, New Jersey, and I see him down at the *Post* once a week. I'll be the Christopher Columbus and discover what paper he uses. It's probably a secret formula, but leave it to me." Next time I saw him, he said, "Here's the big surprise. It's going to kill you." Breathlessly I said, "Give it to me fast. I can't wait."
>
> It turned out to be cheap cardboard used by printers for placards. In size, it was 30″ × 40″ and sold for $3.00 a hundred sheets. Then he gave me the name of the Philadelphia cardboard house where you could get it.
>
> I thought, will I keep the secret all to myself or

"Oh eyes!" he whispered softly, "Oh eyes of blue!"

Illustration by Arthur William Brown
For SEVENTEEN by BOOTH TARKINGTON
Metropolitan Magazine, February 1915, page 5
Inscribed: "To F. R. Gruger from Arthur William Brown, 16"

Gruger's influence on these three
younger illustrators is clearly apparent.

Early illustration by Hal Mowat.
Date and place of publication unknown.

Illustration by Henry Raleigh
For THE TRAIL OF THE DOG by WILL PAYNE
The Saturday Evening Post, April 27, 1912

A Fanciful Conception of How F. R. Gruger Could Guard His Famous Technic From the Hundreds of Ambitious Young Artists Who Would Possess It.
(Note: Mr. Gruger Keeps His Technic Locked in the Strong Box on His Work Table)
The Saturday Evening Post, April 28, 1928
Illustration signed by Will Carroll and M.C. (Monte Crews).

will I let Raleigh and Mowat in on it? Better nature won out and I flew to the phone and told them about it. Orders started flying to the Philadelphia concern. It became so popular later that it was named "Gruger Board." Johnson found out that Gruger had come across it one day when he was on the Philadelphia *Ledger*...[3]

Within a month of FRG's arrival in New York, Herbert Johnson offered Brown his assistance again, by inquiring:

"How would you like to meet Gruger? You admire him so much."
"Not me," I (Brown) said, "he wouldn't even speak to me. I've swiped his methods too often."
"Don't be silly," was his reply, "Gruger doesn't know you're alive. He's having lunch with me next Tuesday at the Waldorf and I want you to come along. Don't be so self-conscious."
So, after all these years of admiration, I met my idol...
Gruger turned out just as Johnson said he would— kindly and humorous. When we got

through lunch, Johnson had appointments with artists and here were Gruger and I strolling up Fifth Avenue getting acquainted. We naturally talked about our craft, and, all at once he said, "Where do you get those interesting accessories that you put in your drawings? I've clipped some of them, they seemed so real."
I thought—here it is, so I'll come clean. "Look, Mr. Gruger," I said, "I've admired your work for so long, I've imitated you, I've swiped most of those accessories from your drawings and if you don't recognize them, I've done them badly."
As we strolled along, without even trying, we became friends...[4]

Arthur William Brown invited FRG to attend the annual dinner of the Dutch Treat Club, a social circle of successful artists and writers. The Dutch Treat Club, founded in 1910, met on Tuesdays for lunch. The weekly gatherings had originally been held in the St. Denis Hotel, then shifted to the Brevoort. There the dining room was so chilly that James Montgomery Flagg, the club president, painted a mock fireplace with a roaring fire on the wall boards covering an unused one. This was in keeping with

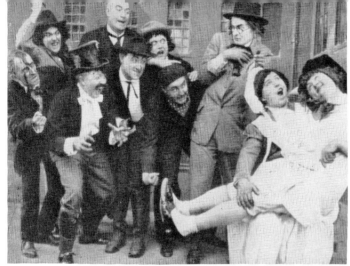

A Picture Made for the Dutch Treat Club. Right to Left: Wallace Irwin, George Barr McCutcheon, James Montgomery Flagg, John Wolcott Adams, Charles Hanson Towne, Will Irwin, Charles Dana Gibson, Rupert Hughes, Julian Street, Bowyer Johnson

Another photo From the Dutch Treat Short. The Gunmen Plot the Downfall of Dicky LeGinny Hen. "We Must Steal the Child and the Papers are Ours!"

Gordon Grant, as proprietor of the "Stone Age Cabaret."

the light-hearted nature of the group.

Featured at the club's annual dinner was a show, usually written by Flagg, which lampooned the illustrators' profession and the magazines for which they worked. Noted individuals from the allied arts were eager to participate. Actor Lionel Barrymore, for instance, served as make-up man at the first Dutch Treat Club play, having transformed Flagg into the Devil, complete with black wig and short pink horns. Barrymore, like his actor-brother John, originally hoped to be an artist and had, in fact, studied at the Art Students League.

The club's weekly luncheons provided a great meeting place for the illustrators and, as Brown once noted, "...it seemed wonderful to me to sit and listen to men like Irvin Cobb, Rupert Hughes, Julian Street and others..." But it was the annual dinner at Delmonico's which served as the high- point of the season. After the meal, tables were replaced by rows of chairs, moved forward toward a stage. The shows were generally musical comedies with talents such as Bill Daly, who would orchestrate George Gershwin's compositions, or the young Deems Taylor writing the music.

FRG reported on the Dutch Treat Club's annual dinner in a letter to Florence on February 15, 1914:

Both [Herbert] Johnson and I were guests of Arthur William Brown, who is a nice chap, I like him and I notice that everyone else seems to...About four o'clock Brown came in tired out. He had been rehearsing since nine in the morning and looked fagged and nervous. He sat around awhile and then he went home to bed—returning here at quarter of seven closely followed by Johnson all out of breath; he had a taxi, which he dismissed and we all went down to Delmonico's in the subway. They have, as you know, a great reputation; Delmonico's, I mean. And their big ballroom was filled with tables, one end occupied by a stage, etc.

The "operetta" was given in place of speeches—although Flagg made several presentation speeches...Flagg is a wonder. He is loved and hated with equal fierceness and altogether a strange and most remarkable personality. He wrote the libretto of the operetta with all its songs. The music was composed by another member of the club and was simply gorgeous—really—everyone was astonished at the per-

Hal Mowat

formance...
Of course as its name implies it was a "roast" of
the magazines. "Biting the Hand that Feeds
Us." The idea being that a rotten sheet, like the
Cosmopolitan, which held itself subservient to
the advertising manager (who in the play was a
very prominent and domineering individual) and
had a tremendous command of money (Cany
Coin in the play) the only woman in it, all
gowned in gold with a $ in her hair—she was sent
out to entice celebrities—clever Fancy—and she
did it. Brown took the part of a distinguished
and high and mighty English author and Cany
Coin was sent out after him—caught him—
brought him in and danced with him, beautiful,
and lovely music. The fellows went mad over it
and roared and applauded till it deafened you...
Everyone in the world of associated professions
was there. All the names we know. I was standing at the top of the stairs and a whole lot of
fellows came up and shook hands, Shinn,
Lowell, Butler, Owen Johnson, Fangel, Dart
and oh, twenty more, I forget whom...
Gibson was there looking handsome and he is
universally loved and respected by the whole lot.
He seems a nice chap, modest and unassuming...
It was all very nice and good humored and I am
glad I went and grateful to Brown...On Monday
next [I will dine] with the Browns who are having
Raleigh and his wife...and a chap named
Mowat. I met Raleigh for the first time last
night—not at all the kind of chap I expected—
great big fellow, he is...

When FRG went to the Browns' for dinner he found
himself, for the first time, with his trio of avid admirers.
Harold James Mowat was, like Brown, a Canadian and a
regular contributor to *The Saturday Evening Post* and the
Ladies' Home Journal. Henry Patrick Raleigh hailed from
Portland, Oregon, and had served on the art staff of the
San Francisco *Bulletin* and the *Examiner* before coming to
New York at the turn of the century. All three men were
eight to ten years Fred Gruger's junior. As FRG wrote to
Florence:

Arthur William Brown by James Montgomery Flagg

It was a lovely dinner and everything was
unassuming, good natured and pleasant. I suppose wherever one is particularly well and kindly
treated one has a good time. You would have
thought I was rich uncle to the group. Heavens
the things they said! I confess to embarrassment.
But they all sound so affectionate and nice that I
just thought maybe they did mean it...
I like Raleigh, so would you, he is a rare sort of
fellow. I didn't think I would care for either him
or Brown, but I have been most agreeably disappointed in my conception of them. Mowat
(whose work is splendid but whose name is not
familiar to you) I thought to be a sort of
backwoodsman—he isn't, he's a most polished
and agreeable person indeed with a splendid
strong face...
After dinner we sat in the studio where there is a
great divan, fully five feet deep on which the
women reclined backs against the wall, while we
four men...got our heads together in a group at
an extreme corner and talked shop. Then we all
sat in front of the divan and held a general sym-
posium.

Grace Brown by James Montgomery Flagg

James Montgomery Flagg

Henry Raleigh

Soon after the Dutch Treat Club's annual show, FRG was invited to attend the Society of Illustrators' dinner. The Society, established by a group of illustrators in 1901, was presided over by Charles Dana Gibson, who had served as president since 1909.

The day after the Dutch Treat Club affair, two artists arrived at Julian Street's apartment to spirit Gruger away. But FRG resisted their efforts:

> This afternoon about half past three...the bell rang and Harry Dart (you remember him, at the time of the Spanish War while we were in New York)—and Charles Wright came in and announced that they had a taxicab and had been appointed a committee of two to come get me and take me out, get me "soused" and see if no perfectly human emotion could be found in the otherwise known "Illustrating Machine." They produced a paper signed by any number of the boys as their credentials and insisted...
>
> After half an hour of the most extraordinary conversation on the part of Dart, during which...I was in hysterics and Wright danced around like a madman, they departed saying that their taxi had rung up four dollars which the Illustrators Society would have to pay.

FRG's failure to accompany the men was caused in part by his desire not to be the center of attention, and partly by a lack of interest in getting "soused." He enjoyed a good time, but was not one to particpate in drinking sessions, where it was his contention that bright, sparkling conversation soon deteriorated into nothing but "booze talk."

Wright and Dart would not depart, however, before eliciting from FRG a promise that he would attend the Society of Illustrators dinner three nights hence. He shared the details with his wife:

> I guess I will go, so you can look forward, upon the next sheet, to see an account of what happens. From what I hear there is to be a play. I was asked to take part, but "Nay! Nay! not I"... Casey (*Collier's* art director) came in and gave me a ticket to the show. I had about made up my mind not to go. But I am glad I went. Saw lots of the boys. Met Moorepark[5] as I was checking my coat, a little later fell into the arms of Owen Johnson...insisted that I come a-visiting...
>
> Sat with Fangel awhile and with Brown. Raleigh wasn't there. During the performance, which was much more respectable than I thought it would be and decidedly clever, the actors, all

men, and of the profession of which I am a humble member, handed out some severe "roasts." Gibson sat in a stage box. They sang a song and shook fingers at him and accused him "of lending his name to be associated with 'Bob' Chambers shame."[6] This was a scorcher I thought. Christy, Fisher and that crowd got it, hard. My, they used a club. Even I got mine. The thing is better understood if I tell you the plot. An artist, real artist, visionary and all that, worked for the love of it and his wife made the living by dancing. She kicked. Magazine art editor fell in love with her, gave the artist a roving commission to go to South Sea Islands—for the same reason that David sent some chap into the forefront of the battle. End of 1st act. Movies—best I ever saw—Take up the tale and show artist on his way to South Sea, shipwreck, desert island. Artist bitten by tsetse fly, contracts sleeping sickness and sleeps a hundred years. 2nd act. Artist gets home in 2014, all artists extinct, everything in his line done by a most remarkable machine. The machine is brought on stage and put to work. The description of three illustrations read, wild tales of jungle and river and all out doors. The machine makes three illustrations all exactly alike and all showing a man in evening clothes leaning over a girl at a piano!

Artist is depressed, looks about for some landmark of the past, asks for art editors—none left—only their progeny—"The fat heads" (applause). The "fat heads" appear. They were funny. Their bodies were bare from the waist up. Their hats came to their shoulders and they had great rope wigs. Their bare bodies from waist to shoulders were painted to represent faces and they had collars around their waists. Great blue, black and brown eyes were fastened on their breasts and, I can tell you, when they bent back and forward the changing expression of the painted faces sent the audience into hysterics. It was the craziest thing I ever saw. Chapin *(Scribner's)* nearly had appoplexy and they had to do something to him. I never heard an audience laugh like that, it was just one great, big, real, contagious laugh.

They had a scene a hundred years hence in an art foundry—owned by a corporation that controlled all art of all kinds in the world. In one corner of the stage was a pneumatic contrivance that conveyed the orders to the "Foundry" at Bethlehem, Pa.

There are openings in the front of the thing in which to insert the carriers and these openings were labelled—Mural, Portraits, Western (cowboy), Society, Gruger and a number of others. The drummer[7] of the concern came in with a roll of paper about a foot in diameter and two feet long that was his list of orders. He unrolled about a yard—orders for portraits, 85 portraits. Three or four yards for this and three or four for that. Then he began and unrolled about two hundred feet, littered the stage with it and announced that it contained orders for 8,564,721 Grugers and a few Raleighs and Brownies and things like that he said—remarking that the publishers of the world generally were amazed at how the two latter maintained their careers of imitating the original. I wasn't struck upon their gentle little touch on my head with their bludgeon but I was sorry for Brown who is a very nice fellow, indeed.

During the next few weeks of his brief stay in New York, FRG attended several of the Dutch Treat Club Tuesday get-togethers:

March 6, 1914

At noon I walked down through the slush and mud and had luncheon at the Dutch Treat Club. It was the most uproarious luncheon imaginable. Funny as a circus. The men sit about a great long table that is capable of seating a hundred and fifty. Each man orders and pays for his own lunch. One is immediately introduced to his neighbors that may be unknown to him and conversation is fast and furious and it keeps one very much on the alert to follow and maintain. I chanced to sit alongside Fuhr[8] whom I knew years ago. We had a good old chat and various fellows came up from time to time and joined in. It was quite a pleasure.

FRG enjoyed the companionship of his fellow artists while he lived in New York. But during January, February and March, 1914, he also developed into a practiced city watcher, observing the pulsating excitement, the daily drama of life in Manhattan. The activities he witnessed here contrasted sharply with the more leisurely scenes he was accustomed to in Avon and Bermuda. Now Gruger painted an unending series of graphic word pictures in the letters he wrote almost daily to his wife:

January 25, 1914

I walk about a good deal at night. And when the pavements are wet and the umbrellas and motors and cars and streets all reflect the thousands of electric lights, it is a wonderful spectacle.

Left to right: Mr. C. Allan Gilbert, Mr. John Barry Ryan, Mrs. Walter Trumbull, and Mr. Charles Hanson Towne

Mr. & Mrs. Owen Johnson. Mr. Johnson is the well known author of "The Salamander" and "Stover at Yale"

COSTUME PARTY OF THE SOCIETY OF ILLUSTATORS AT THE HOTEL BREVOORT, 1915

February 9, 1914

On the street here you really do see skirts slashed up to the knee, and what is more, they *do not attract attention.* Even upon these breezy days when so much of the very thinnest possible silk stockings are visible...The astonishing thing among the women here is the paint used. Girls of eighteen with rouged cheeks and reddened lips, penciled brows and powdered noses. Why, it is amazing. Walking down Fifth Avenue I didn't see but one in a dozen content to remain as the Lord had made her. They look like toys, playthings...

The Museum was full of people. Uncomfortably so. I just looked about and located some new things and had a look at them. They are getting ready for a large exhibition of works of art loaned by the Morgans. A large and rather sumptuous painting by Abbey attracted the largest crowd, by far. And I was surprised to see so many people in The Rodin Gallery and to hear such intelligent admiration expressed. That exhibit alone is worth a long trip to see...

February 13, 1914

It is not so cold, but snowing smartly... The walk up Broadway tonight is very lively. The swirling snow half hides the lights, and all the street is white. The motors carrying people to the theatre and opera are coming down in a procession at the rate of eighty to the block, one

wonders where they all come from... Gaiety is the watchword these days, and to spend money and be seen and envied by the less "fortunate" is the ideal for which many, indeed most, seem to strive... It seems rather more appropriate—in view of the popular scramble for display—to apologize for financial success...

February 16, 1914

The snow has stopped, but although the big 5 and 6 horse snow wagons have been carting it away all day, the snow is still piled three feet high in the gutters and all along the streets are automobiles and big motor vans stalled and making an effort to get away.

It is a very busy night and I have been out drinking in these wonderful pictures of power and effort for an hour. It is a very grand spectacle. Men at work with shovels, the huge black carts...horses under the arc lights, their steaming breath, the labor and hurry, all the white snow trodden gray, the black band of the electric elevated and everywhere hurrying men and women and brilliant lights. Pictures by the score everywhere. Wonderful pictures...

Weaving their shambling way through this crowd of affluence, opportunity and pleasure came the unfortunate wretches whose part in life seems to be to point the contrast and to be the shadows in the picture, I wish I had words to tell you more potently all about it. But not being Mark Twain I can't do it...

February 18, 1914

There were two fires this evening... I had to flatten up against the buildings with the rest of the pedestrians while the "chief" and his charioteer drove at a gallop along the sidewalk on 23d street. Fine sight. It always delights me to see the fine horses and their furious galloping. The streets were too congested with vehicles and great piles of snow to allow the fire chief to move along quickly enough... Just as I came out of Mouquin's along came another engine and then another, hose carts and ladders tearing, screaming down Sixth Avenue and just a few moments ago I heard still a third battery of fire engines go careening out 66th Street...

March 6, 1914

The snow has melted and the eaves have dripped and policemen have waved flags all along the streets to warn people away from the snow that falls from the high buildings...

FRG absorbed the visions of the city streets by night, but each day he toiled long hours over his drawing board. Often, after returning to his studio on Sixty-fifth Street, he would work until 11 p.m., which was his usual time to retire. Gruger strove to complete the accumulation of magazine commissions, so that he could return to Bermuda to rejoin the family. He included regular progress reports in his correspondence:

I have just been putting in the licks endeavoring to get a great big pile of work done so that we could be sure of our trip so far as my industry would insure it... I will be as busy as can be for 10 days more... I made the five compositions for the Mary Roberts Rinehart story for *Colliers* including the cover... Two more stories will be in during the week and I will have to try to grab off a little time in between to go to Avon and to Philadelphia.
Now I am going to put in an hour or two working upon some compositions... I have $1200 worth of work right here and if I can get it done that will be a fine help.

February 18, 1914

I wish I were with you. As soon as I finish what I have on hand I will go to Bermuda to stay until we all come home. I am homesick and I want you all.

March 6, 1914

Tomorrow two weeks, unless something happens which I cannot foresee, I will sail by the *Arcadian* and my, how glad I will be to see you all again...

FRG departed New York, as scheduled, on March 21, and was reunited with Florence and the children. A month later the entire family returned on the same ship. The *Arcadian,* which was on its final Bermuda-New York run of the season, was scheduled to leave for England, and the Grugers had booked passage so they could join the VerBeeks there. But when the entourage stopped briefly in this country, FRG learned that both of his parents were terminally ill. The European plans had to be cancelled.

Just two months earlier, while working in New York, he had notified Florence:

Tonight I only went out to dinner and to send a box of candy to Mamma, whose birthday is tomorrow. I would not have remembered it, I regret to say, had Papa not mentioned the fact in a recent letter.
From the tone of his letter I am thinking that Mother is not very well. He seemed anxious although, as usual, he said little enough...

His parents lingered through the summer months. Travel plans could not be resumed because of the outbreak of the First World War.

notes for chapter 7

[1] Sixteen of these drawings are now a part of Yale memorabilia in The Beinecke Library at Yale.

[2] The August, 1915 issue of *Vanity Fair* named Gruger as one of "a dozen of the most distinguished illustrators in the world and every one of them American." The others were: Charles Dana Gibson, William Glackens, Howard Chandler Christy, Arthur I. Keller, A.B. Wenzell, Reginald Birch, Boardman Robinson, Henry Raleigh, James Montgomery Flagg, May Wilson Preston and Wallace Morgan.

[3] Brown, "Fifty Years with Artists, Models and Authors, p. 51.

[4] *Ibid.*, p. 53

[5] Carton Moorepack, an illustrator

[6] Robert W. Chambers, a fellow classmate of Gibson's at the Art Students League in the 1880s, had turned novelist and written "The Common Law," which was serialized in *Cosmopolitan* from November, 1910 to February, 1911. The story, illustrated by Gibson, concerned a refined artist's model who consented to pose in the nude. It became the sex-thriller of the day. There was consequently much criticism aimed at the creator of the Gibson Girl for allowing his famed female to be cast in such a role.

[7] salesman

[8] Ernest Fuhr, the illustrator

Two of the illustrations by Gibson for "The Common Law". Although the story, which shocked its generation, is about a young woman who poses for a mural painter in the nude, Gibson never depicted her undressed. In fact, in all of the huge volume of Gibson's work, the only nude to be found is the rendition of a distant statue in a European public park.

Charles Dana Gibson

CURTAIN FIRE by Frederic R. Gruger
The First Award in Section I for Black and White Illustration and Design.
Art Directors Club of New York, First Annual Exhibition

FRG in 1916
Drawing by James Montgomery Flagg

Chapter 8

F.R. Gruger celebrated his forty-third birthday the week that Germany declared war on Russia and France.

For the next two years the Grugers lived in Avon, where FRG was busy filling the requests of magazine art editors. During World War I he worked for a dozen publications, with *The Saturday Evening Post* making the major demands upon his time and talent. Between 1914 and 1919, he produced over six hundred illustrations for the *Post* alone, an average of two works per issue per week over the six-year span. Through those years his Wolff pencil drawings accompanied the stories of Pulitzer prizewinning novelists Booth Tarkington and Edith Wharton, as well as Irvin S. Cobb, Fanny Hurst, Ring Lardner, Joseph Hergesheimer, Sinclair Lewis, Theodore Dreiser, I.A.R. Wylie and Don Byrne.

As a result of the war in Europe, New Jersey's coastal resorts gained in popularity, for Americans were obliged to vacation within their continental borders. The community auditorium at Ocean Grove, just north of Avon, featured Enrico Caruso and the John Philip Sousa Band, attracting an audience from Jersey beaches all along the coastline. During the war years young Jascha Heifetz lived in Avon, as did pianist Leopold Godowsky. Avon boasted a tennis club which became the site of weekly dances and occasional productions by the Avon Comedy Club, an amateur company. When there was an infantile paralysis scare coupled with reports that someone along the coast had been attacked by a shark, one comedy routine included the verse:

> Sharks in the water
> Germs in the pool,
> How in the hell
> Are we gonna keep cool? [1]

Sharks provided the major menace off the Jersey shore, although following the sinking of the *Lusitania*, German U-boats were thought to prowl just beyond the horizon and an anti-submarine device, in the form of a huge steel net, was stretched under water across the Narrows in New York harbor.

Most citizens of Avon neglected to arm themselves against attack from the sea, and while FRG purchased a rifle, his primary thought was not self-defense but hunting, *inside* his house. Gruger's studio contained a semi-circular ceiling inscribed within the triangular gable. Squirrels found the space between the shingle roof and the interior plastered lath much to their liking. They scampered about, building nests and interrupting the artist's powers of concentration. Even though FRG had a carpenter plug every hole around the eaves, nothing seemed to help. In despera-

tion, he purchased a twenty-two caliber rifle, and each time sounds were heard he would haul out his gun, get the ceiling section into focus, and fire away. The noise stopped for awhile and FRG claimed to have hit quite a number of squirrels. When the house was reshingled some years later the roofer descended his ladder holding the skeleton of a squirrel with a bullet hole through the head.

By the fall of 1916 the Grugers had decided to close their Avon house and move to New York, where they rented an apartment on Riverside Drive. The idea of maintaining a studio in Manhattan had been in the back of FRG's mind ever since those pleasant weeks two years before. Then, on February 14, 1914, he had written to Florence: "As for having a studio here in New York all the time, I think I would like that..."

Now, with the family comfortably settled at 593 Riverside Drive, Gruger went studio-hunting. Unable to find an appropriate one, he contacted Arthur William Brown and explained his plight. Brown described what ensued:

> Walking along, he (FRG) told me that he felt a few years in New York would give him a new outlook...That was an opportunity I wasn't going to miss, so I told him I had a large studio with plenty of room and why didn't he work there until he found a suitable place. He said it was a good idea and accepted...He moved in, I played it cool and you might say conniving. I made him so comfortable that he stayed two years and what I learned about illustration from him was pure gold.

FRG could not help but feel flattered by the offer, as well as the decoration he found in Brown's studio, for there, upon its walls, were several dozen of his drawings which had been clipped from issues of *The Saturday Evening Post* and mounted for all to see. Brown constantly extolled his guest, and spoke often of his stylistic indebtedness to FRG.

In Arthur William Brown's background Gruger saw similarities to his own. The native of Ontario had begun his artistic career as a newspaper illustrator for the Hamilton *Spectator*:

> The first important drawing I (Brown) did was the sinking of the *Maine* in Havana harbor. The editor handed a blurry clipping of it from the Chicago *Inter-Ocean* to me and said, "Do a good job on this and we'll keep you on..." [2]

Brown stayed with the paper until 1901 when, at the age of twenty, he left Canada for New York. There he

"Mrs. Heman Sutler, up the lake, makes all my clothes," confided Fluff. "She copies the patterns out of the fashion magazines, and they do say she improves them a lot".

THE COUNTRY MOUSE by WALLACE IRWIN
The Saturday Evening Post, March 9, 1918, Page 9.

This was the one and only appearance of "Arthur Frederick," illustrator.
Illustration provided by the General Research and Humanities Division
The New York Public Library Astor, Lenox and Tilden Foundations

studied at the Art Students League under Walter Appleton Clark, whose use of all three names, like Charles Dana Gibson, Howard Chandler Christy and James Montgomery Flagg, influenced the young artist to sign his drawings "Arthur William Brown."

As with FRG, Brown created his first magazine illustrations for *The Saturday Evening Post.* In October, 1903 he produced thirty-two works to accompany a series of articles about a traveling circus, written by a fellow Canadian, Arthur Macfarlane. Brown had received this original magazine commission through sheer perserverance, for as he admitted:

> I did the rounds and got very little encouragement. Some art editors even looked at my great art upside down, they were so disinterested.

Virtually all illustrators had begun in the same manner. James Montgomery Flagg acknowledged:

> I had persisted in showing my wares to dear old Joe Chapin, the art editor (of *Scribner's*), who kept saying, "Let me see some more six months from now." [3]

Everett Shinn once admitted to hauling a portfolio of drawings to *Harper's* for fifty-two weeks before he was even permitted to walk into the office. And John Sloan had occasion to write in his diary:

> I decided to go out in search of work today, so with my packet of proofs under arm, I went...to *McClure's...Associated Sunday Magazine... Century...*and *Everybody's.* Came home rather blue—the usual effect of these trips on me. [4]

Not so with F.R. Gruger. He took considerable pride in the fact that never once had he petitioned an art editor for work. Each of his successive positions with the Philadelphia newspapers and the various magazines had been offered him. His talents were in demand.

Once FRG was established in Brown's studio, his host carefully observed the method of drawing:

> I (Brown) learned many valuable things from him, especially in the flowing line and massing of contrasts in composition...A suggestion he gave me that helped was that if a spot in a drawing gave me trouble, the thing to do was put it in a deep shadow and finish one thing like a toe of a shoe, for instance, and let the rest disappear. He could do it to perfection...
> He never used models except to make an occasional sketch, for he claimed that models could never fit into the pattern of his compositions...He could design any object from memory because he would constantly practice by drawing a telephone or a chair or, for example, a tree which he would draw carefully from different positions and make a study of the construction... [5]

Brown, who was lost without a model or a photograph from which to work, occasionally sought aid from his mentor:

> I remember once when Dean Cornwell was in my studio and I had a drawing on the board of a boy and girl fully drawn down to the waist.He asked, "Aren't you going to finish it?" "Well," I told him, "they're supposed to be in a canoe and I'm waiting for Gruger to come in and sketch it in for me." [6]

Another collaboration between the two artists occurred on an assignment for *The Saturday Evening Post*:

> When George Horace Lorimer, editor of the *Post,* bought a story he liked, he usually insisted on rushing it into the issue then being made up. One day the art editor phoned to say that Lorimer wanted...three illustrations in three days. I said it was impossible. He replied, "Why don't you and Gruger do it together?" And we did...
> The story was sent by messenger, we read it, picked out the situations to be illustrated and went into action. I engaged the models, photographed them, developed the photos and printed them. After that I pantographed[7] them and drew them in carefully. Fred took over from there and finished them. By Friday, just in time to make the issue, they were in Philadelphia. We had a conference as to how to sign them, so decided this new discovery would be named "Arthur Frederick," a combination of both of our first names.
> When the drawings appeared, contemporary illustrators were alarmed. Here was a dangerous rival. They watched for him thereafter until time assuaged their apprehensions. Arthur Frederick, never seen before, was never seen again. [8]

The co-produced artwork accompanied Wallace Irwin's "The Country Mouse," which appeared in *The Saturday Evening Post* on March 9, 1918.

During the same year the artists cooperatively produced drawings for a *Collier's* serial as well, but in this case each subject was signed by one or the other, and the

FRG as a model for one of Arthur William Brown's illustrations

by-line read "Illustrated·by F.R. Gruger and Arthur William Brown."

The studio-sharing arrangement worked well, although it was not fully understood by the neighbors, as Brown recalled:

> On the ground floor were shops, one of them occupied by a shoemaker. The next two floors were my living quarters and a long extension on the second floor was the studio. Gruger had been there over a year and, one day, I was having my shoes shined and while the shoemaker polished away, he said,
> "Business must be pretty good with you, Mr. Brown."
> "Why?" I asked.
> "Well, I see you've got a man working for you now."
> He had seen Gruger going into the studio mornings and going out at night.[9]

Although the two men's methods varied considerably, FRG enjoyed the experience of utilizing the work space and offered to pay rent for his use of the facility, but Brown refused, so Gruger bought him a studio camera and constructed a darkroom instead. He even posed occasionally for Brown's photographs, assuming such characterizations as that of an irate baseball manager, a soldier, and a judge·

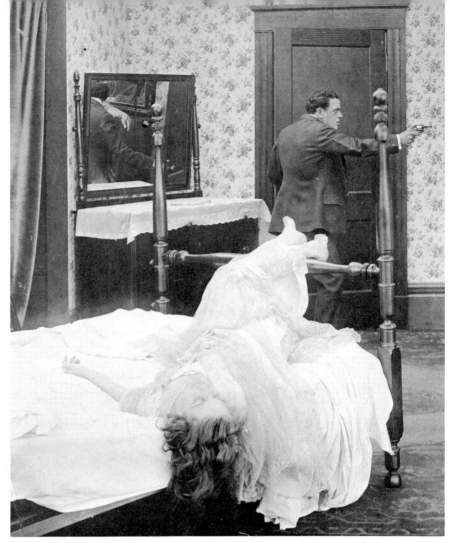

Arthur William Brown, minus his glasses, serves as his own model

Brown used his models as actors to interpret the particular episode he wanted to illustrate in a story, as a photographer recorded the poses and setting.

Arthur William Brown had begun creating magazine drawings from photographs in 1904, when he directed a commercial photographer who lived in the same building to take pictures of a posed model. Although artists such as Eugene Delacroix had painted from photographs as early as the 1850s, Brown was possibly the first magazine illustrator to do so.

During the time that FRG shared his studio, he sometimes made sketches of Brown's models while they were positioned before the camera. In this way Gruger was introduced to a procession of famous personalities, such as Fred Bickel, who posed for one dollar and fifty cents an hour until he began to act in the movies under the name of Fredric March. Neil Hamilton became the original Arrow Collar man, and other models employed by Brown included John Barrymore, Tallulah Bankhead, Norma Shearer and Evelyn Brent.

Arthur William Brown's procedure of posing and photographing people for his illustrations was unique at the time, although in subsequent years it was followed by many other magazine artists, including Norman Rockwell.

Brown would read aloud that portion of a story in which his models were involved. Then they would practice the scene as if they were rehearsing for a stage play.

The illustrator explained his rationale:

Often when they speak a line, they will unconsciously make a gesture or perhaps a slight turn of the body, an accidental thing perhaps, but it will be different and at the same time convincing. When I feel they are giving it pictorial quality and it fits in with my rough sketch, I start to photograph. I make the first exposure even if it is not exactly what I want because it puts the models at their ease...You have to be a good director to get the best out of them so you keep on shooting; sometimes I make a dozen exposures of the scene.

As I'm working with them, before pressing the bulb, I talk to them, telling them to take the expressions, try and feel that they are the people in the story—I may move them closer or farther away from each other, raise or lower an arm, tilt heads away or toward me, watch every tiny detail—and with "Hold it," I snap the picture.

When I develop my negatives, the next step is to make contact prints and see what I've got. These are studied carefully before I make enlargements to work from. Sometimes one will be perfect or I may use parts from each shot, often changing arms or other parts of the pose to fit in with my design...[10]

During World War I, Charles Dana Gibson as President of the Society of Illustrators, formed and became head of the Division of Pictorial Publicity under the Federal Committee of Public Information. Top illustrators were invited to design posters, billboards and other publicity materials for the war effort. Included in the picture are, left to right, Jack Sheridan, Wallace Morgan, Devitt Welsh, Herbert Adams, Gibson, Frank Casey, Frank Sheridan, Adolph Treidler, Harry Townsend, and C. B. Falls.

Arthur William Brown was more gregarious and socially-inclined than FRG and, as a result, artists were continually dropping by the studio. Gruger was caught up in the affable atmosphere. Among his mementos of the two years spent at 233 West One-Hundredth Street were a group of illustrations given him by Henry P. Raleigh, May Wilson Preston, Harvey Dunn, J.C. Leyendecker and James Montgomery Flagg, as well as Brown.

While most of the gifts were either magazine illustrations or cover designs, Flagg produced an eleven-by-fourteen inch profile portrait of FRG, a pencil sketch dated "1916."

After the United States entered World War I on April 6, 1917 Flagg, Gruger and the other magazine artists were mobilized to produce posters and propaganda. Charles Dana Gibson, as president of the Society of Illustrators, was directed to organize the artistic talent of the country into a Division of Pictorial Publicity. Eight artists, including Harvey Dunn and Wallace Morgan, were commissioned captains and sent to France to record the action of the American Expeditionary Force at the front. Flagg and Brown travelled to cities such as Washington and New Haven where they painted billboards for the cause. In all, some 323 artists created 1,438 posters, cartoons, newspaper and magazine advertisements.

One of the crucial needs was for war posters, but the illustrators, many of whom had previously worked only in pen-and-ink and on a small scale, were initially ill-equipped to produce them. Painter-author Albert E. Gallatin claimed that

> …the poorly drawn sketches of Messrs. Howard Chandler Christy and Harrison Fisher and others of our popular illustrators were not posters at all…[11]

F.R. Gruger produced several illustrations and poster designs as his contribution. One of the latter depicted a small Belgian girl in tattered clothing, her hand outstretched appealing for aid. On a wall behind her, a shell hole appeared in the form of a halo above her head.

Among FRG's war drawings was a twenty-by-thirty inch sketch showing a battery of howitzers lobbing shells at the enemy, while gun crews struggled to reload the big cannon. The artist also produced a group of illustrations intended for books which were published as good will gestures toward the Allies. One such volume in which Gruger's art is represented bears the title *For France*.

Many of FRG's friends and acquaintances participated in the war drive: Glackens painted his first mural

This popular poster by James Montgomery Flagg was used for recruiting in both World Wars

Harry Townsend, who designed this strong poster, later served as an Artist-reporter with the American Expeditionary Forces in France and Germany. Among others who served were Harvey Dunn and Wallace Morgan.

in twenty years, a great battle scene symbolizing Russia; J.C. Leyendecker created recruiting posters, as did John R. Neill, Edward Penfield, Charles Dana Gibson and Charles Livingston Bull. Artist Henry Reuterdahl, commissioned a lieutenant-commander, served as artistic adviser to the Navy Recruiting Bureau, but none of his efforts could equal the appeal of the Army Recruiting Service poster by James Montgomery Flagg, ''Uncle Sam Wants You.'' Flagg's patriotic portrait had originally appeared on the cover of *Leslie's Weekly* before it was mass-produced in several million copies.

Less than three weeks after the United States joined the Allied cause, the first Liberty Loan Act was authorized to help finance the war through the sale of Liberty Bonds. New York City's bond drive committee installed a picture frame measuring sixteen by eight feet in front of the Public Library on Fifth Avenue, and on each of twenty-two successive days an artist would create a work typifying the spirit of one of the Allied countries.

The so-called Great War demanded art on a grand scale, so the Division of Pictorial Publicity met the challenge by erecting a huge canvas on the steps of the Library. This time the working surface measured twenty-five by ninety-feet. Franklin Booth, James Montgomery Flagg and others painted before a constant throng of people in order to promote the Liberty Loan drives. Such performances demanded talent *and* showmanship, and Gruger possessed only the former. Dudley Summers, a young illustrator-friend of FRG's recalled:

> Frank Booth and Jim Flagg stood up there; they were accustomed to painting on large canvases. I recall seeing Flagg doing this thing for the war effort in front of the Library. Then Gruger told me:
> ''I couldn't stand up there and do a painting. Why it would be a terrible thing.''
> And so he drew one, but it was for someone to copy. It was so like him, this quality of shyness. He didn't realize how big a person he was in the business.[12]

Howard Chandler Christy at work on a poster for a Liberty Loan campaign

Watercolor painting by Harvey Dunn, who served in the front lines with the troops in 1917 and 1918, depicting the movement of American soldiers in France

Photo courtesy of Everett Raymond Kinstler.

The steps of the New York Public Library provided an ideal public forum for war publicity. Here, James Montgomery Flagg paints another of his famous World War I posters, "Tell it to the Marines."

The Grugers spent the summer of 1918 in Avon, and when they returned to New York that fall, FRG rented a studio at 57 West Fifty-seventh Street. The building was a three-story red brick structure, with a restaurant at street level. The second floor was rented mostly to writers, whereas the top floor, consisting of skylight studios, was occupied by artists.

On the opposite corner at the intersection of Fifty-seventh Street and Sixth Avenue stood the Sherwood Building, the first cooperative artists' studio building in New York. Robert Henri had lived there when he first arrived in Manhattan in 1901, and so had John Sloan when he moved to New York three years later.

The structure in which FRG now worked had previously housed the New York School of Art. Founded in 1896 by Douglas John Connah, it was here that Henri developed his great reputation as a teacher, creating a following that included George Bellows, Edward Hopper, Rockwell Kent, Eugene Speicher, Guy Pene duBois, Walter Pach, Patrick Henry Bruce, Randall Davey, Nathaniel Pousette-Dart, Glenn O. Coleman, Gifford Beal, Vachel Lindsay and Clifton Webb. During the 1903-4 season there were some six hundred students attending the school, whose faculty also included William Merritt Chase, Frank Vincent DuMond and Kenneth Hayes Miller.

Now, in 1918, 57 West Fifty-seventh Street was occupied by individual artists. There were six residents on the third floor in addition to F.R. Gruger: Neysa McMein, a portrait painter, illustrator and cover artist; Sally Farnum, sculptor of the Simon Bolivar statue in Central Park and a monument to ballroom dancer Vernon Castle; Edgar Franklin Wittmack, just beginning to produce artwork for magazines and books after having served in the army; Franklin Booth, a former newspaperman and illustrator for *Munsey's, The Ladies' Home Journal* and *Collier's*; Alfred Cheney Johnson, a fashionable portrait photographer; and Theodore Spicer-Simson, a painter of portraits. In addition, James Montgomery Flagg occupied an apartment on the floor below.

All of the artists were quite friendly, circulating freely among each other's studios. Sally Farnum, for instance, would stop by to provide Gruger with hunks of plasticine, with which he sculptured small heads, complaining the while about the abundance of dog hair stuck in the substance from Sally's two pets. And Franklin Booth, whose studio was a few doors from FRG's, often stopped in for a chat, seek a critique of his work, play a game of dominoes or solicit company for dinner.

For FRG the autumn of 1918 had brought with it a

Franklin Booth in his studio, 1934

new studio and an additional circle of friends. It also marked the beginning of another activity, for simultaneously with the move to 57 West Fifty-seventh Street he began to teach at the Art Students League, located less than two blocks away.

notes for chapter 8

[1] Conversation with Elizabeth Gruger Van Buren, May 18, 1973

[2] Brown, *op. cit.,* p. 6

[3] Flagg, p. 81

[4] Bullard, p. 96

[5] Brown, *op. cit.,* p. 53

[6] Brown, *Ibid.,* p. 54

[7] A pantograph is a jointed instrument which Arthur William Brown employed to copy mechanically a photograph while enlarging it to any
[8] desired size.

[9] Brown, *op. cit.,* p. 54

[10] Brown, *op. cit.,* p. 55

[11] Brown, *op. cit.,* p. 38

[12] Gallatin, *Art and The Great War,* p. 36

[13] Conversation with the author, January 7, 1973

Neysa McMein shown with one of the pastel portraits for which she was famous.

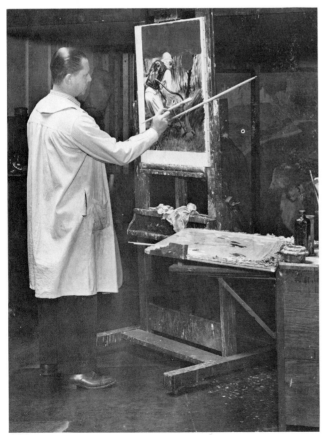

Edgar Franklin Wittmack, for many years cover artist for *Popular Science Monthly*

Sally James Farnham, sculptor

The statue of Simon Bolivar at the Avenue of The Americas entrance to Central Park, New York.

Wallace Morgan. "Women's Sewing Circle", brush and ink drawing. 16¾″ x 9⅝″. Date and place of publication not shown.

Howard Pyle "Dragging the Duke Out of the Coach," from A SOLDIER OF FORTUNE written and illustrated by the artist. *Harper's Monthly Magazine,* December, 1893. Black and white oil on canvas. 16 x 24 inches.

Henry Reuterdahl. "A Variety of Craft, including a Passenger Whaleback" from *The Century Magazine,* "Chicago's Great River-Harbor." Date not known.

Thomas Fogarty. "We pick on, forgetting heat and fallen logs in the thought of delicious pies." Date and place of publication not known.

Chapter 9

When F.R. Gruger joined the League faculty to instruct a class in Illustration, such courses were little more than two decades old.

One of the pioneer teachers of the subject was Howard Pyle, the Wilmington-born artist. Having gained a reputation as an illustrator for *Harper's* and *Scribner's* during the 1880s and early 1890s he determined to become an Illustration instructor. Since no recognized art school existed in his native city, Pyle came to Philadelphia where, in 1894, he offered his services to the Pennsylvania Academy, but was turned down. The rejection was followed by an overture from nearby Drexel Institute and by 1896 Howard Pyle was appointed director of the newly established School of Illustration there.

For the next dozen years, almost until his death in 1911, Pyle became the foremost teacher of Illustration in the region. His students at Drexel included Frank Schoonover, Violet Oakley, Jessie Wilcox Smith, Maxfield Parrish and Elizabeth Shippen Green, the latter two having been previously enrolled at the Academy. When he opened his own school in Wilmington, with summer classes at Chadds Ford, they were attended by N.C. Wyeth, C.W. Ashley, Sarah S. Stilwell-Weber, Harvey Dunn and others.

Howard Pyle taught at the Art Students League during 1904-5, by which time the faculty there included illustrators Howard Chandler Christy, Henry Reuterdahl, Henry McCarter, Thomas Fogarty and Wallace Morgan. Fogarty was in his thirteenth year at the League when F.R. Gruger joined the staff, and the veteran teacher was an admirer of the newcomer's work. According to Thomas Fogarty, Jr., subsequently a League Illustration instructor himself:

> My father used to hold Gruger up as one of the deans of beautiful illustration and storytelling any time there was any reference to a periodical Gruger illustrated, for at that particular time father had nothing but praise for him. He admired his work. [1]

FRG taught at the Art Students League by invitation, and according to Ted Gruger:

> They wanted to know what he would expect in the way of compensation, so he named a figure, and it nearly knocked them over. They said no, they couldn't possibly afford him in their budget, so he said well, then, I'll work for nothing. No, no that wouldn't do either, because many of the other instructors there were making their living by teaching, and it wouldn't be proper at all for somebody to come in and contribute his time. It would sort of put them in a bad light. So then he said all right, I'll work for whatever figure you want to pay me.

Dudley Gloyne Summers, a twenty-six year old student from Birmingham, England, was appointed monitor of the class. He explained:

> I became monitor just because Gruger said he wanted me. He saw that I was interested in the whole idea and he became interested in me. The monitor's job was to take attendance, write it in a book and then pose the model and get the chairs out. It was regular lackey work. We used the underside of the chairs—the legs—for our easels, so the ones standing in back could see. You could put out just so many chairs, and then there were easels, and the next thing you know you had a full class. [2]

For his work, the monitor received a scholarship. Summers arrived at the League the year before by way of Boston, and had studied anatomy with George Bridgman while working as a catalog illustrator. When FRG joined the League faculty, according to Summers,

> ...it was a wonderful thing, because he very patly put down in simple language what my trouble was. And then I was all right and I carried on quite awhile on that basis, and my work began to improve and show a little more cohesion. Eventually I got a story to do for *MacLean's Magazine* in Canada, which Gruger was influential in getting for me.

FRG's League class met on Friday nights, and it quickly became one of the school's most popular offerings, having an enrollment of one hundred and twenty-five students. Summers explained:

> Gruger was there only one night a week. He never gave any problems. We had drawings from the models and work on the drawing we intended to show him when he came in. There wasn't any formality about it. The students could take any story to illustrate they wanted. There was no limit to what you could do.
>
> He had to show that drawing was so important to him. He had sketchbooks which he filled with drawings from the model, and yet I've never known him to use a model in his pictures. He knew what to do without the model. He was amazing in that regard. When you look at those drawings you'd say he certainly had an extraor-

dinary group of models to call in. But he didn't
do that...

As students he had us using Gruger Board...but
in the class you could use any media. I used to
draw with his media, the Wolff pencil...but that
pencil was FR and I knew of no man who could
use it as well. I turned to charcoal, wash,
gouache and oil paint. In the class he didn't care
what you worked with.[3]

Although sketching and painting went on during the
week, the big attraction on Fridays was FRG's critiques,
which involved work produced between classes, according
to Summers:

We all put our drawings on the walls. Some
nights we had fifty people, and the next week
we'd have the full quota. He would start off at
the left-hand side slowly and go down, through,
across the line, and every drawing would be
commented upon. He compared them with other
drawings on the same wall, and one student's
work helped another man's work, and the next
thing you know, you got the whole picture...The
drawings were arranged four or five high. We
pinned them up that way. They weren't very big.
The compositions might be eight-by-ten or
fifteen-by-twenty. He very rarely worked large
either...

Gruger had a quality of shyness. He said he just
couldn't keep his mind on what he was doing if
he had to look at who he was talking to, the
students, so he would look at the drawings and
not turn his head around to the class at all. He
would talk to the wall. It was all right with us.

FR would go from one work to the other and he
would point out: ''Now in this picture I would
say there's a bit of misunderstanding about what
you're trying to do with balance here. It doesn't
check that way...Now this one does that, you
see?'' and he'd go down the whole line.

We didn't do any drawing on the night he was
there; that was the criticism night. He mentioned
Henri...[4]

Robert Henri was conducting an afternoon Painting
Class at the League at this time, and Margery Ryerson, one
of his pupils, recounted how his method contrasted with
FRG's:

Henri didn't criticize the whole class every time
he came; he just criticized a few. And if he didn't
like your work, he might not say anything...He
might give the whole criticism to one or two people, or he might go around and give almost
everybody one. He was unpredictable...About a
third of the class left every month. It was a very
changing class; they were leaving because they
didn't like it, it wasn't what they wanted. It was
during the war and there were maybe one or two
to ten men. The rest were women and the trouble
was they were elderly women, people with gray
hair, who had retired from school teaching...
The class ten years earlier was a much better
class. That was his class and he had it all his own
way.[5]

One of the handful of younger students in Henri's
class was twenty-year-old Elizabeth Gruger. FRG's older
daughter had previously studied art with John Weygandt
at the Darlington Seminary in Pennsylvania, and she
recalled:

I was always thinking of illustrating but Father
said, ''You're not going to be an illustrator so
why don't you go ahead with your painting?'' At
the League I studied with Henri, DuMond and
Bridgman.

She also sometimes sat in on FRG's class, and on the
occasion of her first appearance, one of the students who
knew her made the introduction by stating: ''This is a
Gruger original.'' But Elizabeth never enrolled. She was
able to elicit personal criticism of her work in his studio:

With Dad you did a great deal of work yourself.
He was always very graphic when he would explain something to you. He never touched a student's work. Sometimes he would make little
sketches on scraps of paper. He brought
something of you out and made you do it.

F.R. Gruger's comments to his students in the League
class were lucid, honest and to the point:

I will criticize your work but you'll get the
truth—you may not like it but it will be the way I
see it.

If the composition is right, the detail will fall into place.

Illustration may become a great art, but to
become a great art it must be creative. It cannot
hope to compete with the camera in the reporting
of facts. It has no business with the outer shell of
things at all. It deals with the spirit...

I shall never forget my father's[6] caution when I
said I intended having a try at being an artist...to
make illustrations. Doré was in my mind and

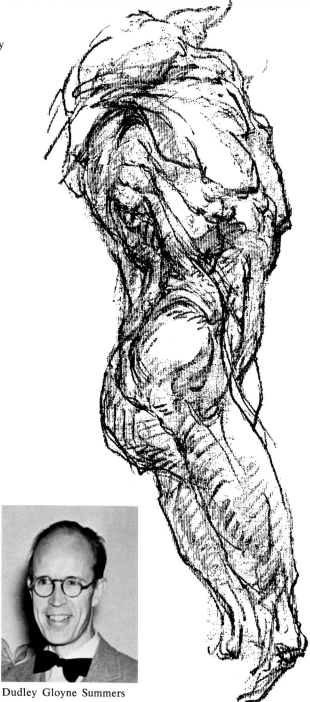

A typical example of Bridgman's anatomy class demonstration drawings

Abbey and Howard Pyle…"All right," he said, "make your illustrations, but learn to draw—not just to put on paper what you're looking at but as though the people in your pictures are real people. Like this: 'If this man has this sort of hands he'll have this sort of feet…this kind of brow and eyes and body—he will sit just so in this kind of chair and on his table and on the mantle shelf will be—but if he is married you'll have to find out what sort is his wife before you know about the shelf and chairs and carpet and all that says two live in this room.' " I really have worked very hard to do just that.[7]

When one of his students asked how to draw a ghost, FRG said just go out and look at one. That evoked a roar of laughter, but then he went on to explain that if anyone sat in a subway train and observed the reflections of people in the windows opposite, the images would appear to be ghost-like.

In the classroom FRG extolled the praises of Rembrandt and Rubens, and on occasion he brought in black-and-white reproductions of their work. "He was really enthusiastic about Rubens," Summers remembered.

As a teacher, Gruger was all business. There was nothing flashy, no showmanship in his style. By contrast, George Bridgman was a rollicking individual who awed his pupils with his demonstrations, as John J. Floherty, Jr. recollects:

Bridgman would come out into the classroom, on the walls of which had been tacked enormous sheets of newsprint, huge, bigger than doors. He had an old fashioned teacher's pointer with a piece of charcoal taped to the end of it. He would walk up and down and begin to expound, say, on the human thigh, and while he'd talk, he would draw a tremendous human thigh on one of those pieces of newsprint. Or he might draw a leg six feet high. He was so remarkable about it, apparently drawing with no effort whatsoever. And, of course, we in the class would scribble our sketchbooks full. He wouldn't look at our work particularly, at least he didn't look at mine. He expected you to get what he had to say by his illustrated talking.[8]

Gruger and Bridgman were widely respected in their fields. When the *Encyclopedia Britannica* planned to publish a new edition a decade later, it was Gruger who was commissioned to write the article about "Illustration" and Bridgman the one on "Anatomy."

FRG displayed a continuing interest in his students, even to the point of recommending them to the magazines.

Dudley Gloyne Summers

As Dudley Summers recalled:

If there was anyone in there who was ready for a story, it somehow got to an editor's ears. FR heard of the stories and would give a name.

Some of the pupils did work on the outside, and brought drawings to his studio for criticism, Summers remembered:

I thought that FR was very wonderful to take some of his valuable time for his students. He would just invite them over when they had some things. I moseyed up to his studio once a week and about four o'clock he'd lay aside his picture and let me have a criticism of my drawing. Now that was a very unusual thing. He was the most extraordinary character you'd ever run across. I had many, many teachers but I never had one who took as much interest in me.[9]

Other League students made their way to his door. Donald Teague, for instance, was enrolled with Bridgman and DuMond at the time:

My contact with Gruger consisted of only one visit to this studio which, as I recall, was only a block or two from the Art Students League. This came at a time when I was just starting as an illustrator and I felt great diffidence in calling on him. He received me very cordially, however, and gave me not only an hour of his time but also a couple of *Saturday Evening Post* illustrations...[10]

Orison MacPherson had been a student of John Sloan's at the League. However, his Wolff pencil drawings for the *Post* and *Country Gentleman* were influenced mostly by Gruger, whom he often visited.

FRG taught at the League for two years, but by the spring term of 1920 the strain of his dual careers as teacher and illustrator was beginning to tell. Florence, Elizabeth and Dorothy were vacationing in Florida when he wrote, revealing his plight:

March 1, 1920

...have been working hard and tomorrow will have words with the League to see if I can get out of the rest of my course there. In that case I'll gather up a bunch of work and beat it to see you and the children...

March 3, 1920

I didn't get home until half past eleven last night...there was a very large class and they kept me hanging around for a long time...

March 13, 1920

My days are pretty full, believe me. This being Friday is a League night and I am amazed to see the kind and quality of the "congregation." One man for whom I do drawings is now in it! The head of a big advertising firm also with his entire staff. It makes it somewhat a difficult task and I'll be glad when May 29th comes and I can give Dorothy seventeen kisses and one goodbye to the teaching game.

March 21, 1920

Summers informed me today that there are now 140 students in our class!...

As Elizabeth explained:

He stopped teaching because he was busy and it took an awful lot of his time. Even after he gave up teaching at the school he would have students stop in and bring their work. It was exhaustisng and he always became very involved...

Among FRG's pupils at the League were many who one day would become professionals: Herbert Morton Stoops, associated with *Collier's, Cosmopolitan* and *Blue Book,* and elected president of the Artists' Guild in New York; R. John Holmgren, a magazine ilustrator and one-time president of the Society of Illustrators; Edward Ryan, an artist for *The Saturday Evening Post* and other publications; H.L. Barbour, whose artwork appeared in *Good Housekeeping;* as well as illustrators A.J. Trembath, M.P. Thayer, Norman T. Mingo, E.J. Dinsmoor, Barbara Bonner; and, of course, Dudley Gloyne Summers, a long-time artist for *The Saturday Evening Post* and other magazines.

As Gruger's final semester at the Art Students League drew to a close, his class presented him with two books: *The Minor Ecclesiastical, Domestic and Garden Architecture of Southern Spain* and *Farm Houses, Manor Houses, Minor Chateaux and Small Churches from the Eleventh to the Sixteenth Centuries in Normandy, Brittany and Other Parts of France.* The two volumes were inscribed with the names of sixty-four of his students.

William Reusswig, who attended the League after FRG's departure, reminisced:

I missed studying with him and I was always sorry I did. There was a fellow named Wilmot Emerton Heitland who took over the Illustration Class after Gruger. He was the guy I studied with.[11]

Although FRG had abandoned the classroom, his influence on the teaching of Illustration was now widespread.

Harold N. Anderson, a well-known illustrator whose work has appeared in many leading publications, explained:

I attended the Fenway School of Illustration in Boston which had a very short life—1912 to 1918— and a relatively small enrollment. Harold Brett, one of Pyle's pupils was one of my in-

Herbert Morton Stoops
YOUTH RIDES WEST by WILL IRWIN
Collier's Weekly, April 12, 1924

John Holmgren
Judge Cover, June 16, 1928

Orison MacPherson
JOSEPH'S BRETHREN by LEONARD H. NASON
The Saturday Evening Post, January 30, 1932

Dudley Gloyne Summers
THE MUMMY by JOHN GALSWORTHY
Redbook Magazine, November, 1924

Edward Ryan
College Humor,
publication date not known

structors. N.C. Wyeth and Harvey Dunn visited us at intervals. Chase Emerson was another instructor—one of the best of teachers. He frequently called Gruger to our attention, praising him as the finest of them all.

Of course, we all studied Illustration so we were all familiar with Gruger's work. Particularly in Composition Class, Emerson would expound and elaborate on why he thought Gruger was such a great illustrator. Mr. Emerson was so enthusiastic about Gruger's work and so often lauded him to us.

Gruger's drawings didn't have the pictorial splash of the painters but they were the epitome of story-telling, which is what illustration should be. Each picture bore scrutiny and study. The wealth of important factual detail was amazing.[12]

Garrett Price, best known for his *New Yorker* covers, stated:

We all thought a great deal of Gruger. In art school most of us imitated him or tried to. At the Art Institute of Chicago we paid a great deal of attention to Gruger; in fact, there was one of his originals hanging on the wall in the hall of the school.

I worked on Gruger Board. A friend of mine who was on the Chicago *Tribune* went down to New York just for a trip and he came back with some of it, and he gave me a sheet. We all thought that if we'd get the same kind of board Gruger used and the same kind of Wolff pencil we'd be able to do that. At the time there was a teacher of mine at the Art Institute named R.F. James, and he was a great imitator and worshipper of Gruger's. He got a whole carload of that board shipped into Chicago...

And John Falter, a long-time cover artist for *The Saturday Evening Post*, recalled:

When I was in the Kansas City Art Institute, my Illustration instructor, Monte Crews, held up F.R. Gruger along with Wyeth and Pyle as a giant to be aware of and study. We did, even going so far as to buy 3B carbon pencils and ordering Gruger Board from the Philadelphia Art Supply Company.

Crews brought in many of Gruger's reproductions from the *Post*. We were greatly influenced by him because we tried to work in his style. Monte worked in that media consistently, and worked as a cartoonist for the *Post* under the name of Will Carroll...

During March of 1920, while FRG's wife and daughters were wintering in Florida, son Ted was midway through his second semester at Yale University:

I [Ted] think my attention was first focused on Yale when Father was doing the "Stover at Yale" illustrations. Up to that time I really didn't know what a college or university was, and this brought it to my attention. As is very often the case with youngsters, you get to know something or get familiar with the name and you build up a certain allegiance to it...

Then there were two families with whom we were really very close and friendly who were Princeton people. They were so doggone aggressively Princeton that I guess I just, out of contrariness, took the part of Yale.

Whenever there was a Yale-Princeton game, they would hold forth at such great length about how wonderful Princeton was and what Princeton was going to do to Yale. Of course, Yale usually beat Princeton. So I just naturally developed an affection for it.

I took Business Administration at Yale, and I think it was the first time it was offered in an American university and it was a very good course.

Ted wrote to his Father:

March 13, 1920

Yale is entered in ten athletic meets today, five of which are against Harvard. We are pretty sure of winning everything except fencing with Columbia.

FRG was an enthusiastic football fan but during his son's four years at Yale his work continually interfered with plans to attend the games in New Haven:

Hurrah!... I see by the papers that we won. I suppose you feel good. I'm sorry I wasn't there to see it happen. Circumstance was too strong for me though. It happens that I have a most ghastly lot of work to do...

I greatly regret that I can't be up to the game. I'd like to very much and am disappointed that I cannot make it. Particularly so because I don't want your friends to imagine your family is not interested in your interests. We are. All of us are, as you know.

...Now then go up and trim Harvard. I had a bet on Yale vs. Princeton and came out sorry it wasn't bigger. I suppose you are too hoarse to read this letter!

Photograph of James Montgomery Flagg as Lincoln

Flagg and his father Elisha in 1926.
From *James Montgomery Flagg,* by Susan Meyer

FRG's schedule was upset by the arrival of a former Academy colleague and *Ledger* artist, John Weygandt:

March 17, 1920

I didn't get a chance to write you yesterday, being very busy and having Weygandt arrive unexpectedly and one thing and another turn up all day. I took him down to dinner at the Alps with Booth and Kidder and when we came up I had to stick around and be genial host until time for the League. Weygie slept at the studio last night and I'm planning to send him to several exhibitions at a long distance—he doesn't realize at all that a day has but a few hours in it at best and that every one of those hours counts like the deuce...

March 20, 1920

Yesterday we had another snow, rather slushy, rainy, cold and dismal snow. So then when it came time to go to the Dutch Treat Dinner at six o'clock... I took me a taxi and went in style— "Delmonico's," said I, sinking back luxuriantly among the cushions!
It was a good dinner and a good show. At my table were Grant[land] Rice, Rex Beach, Charlie Williams, a Mr. Roberts, Jim Flagg, Jim Flagg's Papa, Arthur William Brown and me. And there you are. Plenty to eat and talk about. Very nice things, both. Mr. Flagg, senior I had never met before—he is a most pleasant man and looks a few years younger than Jim, who introduced him as his son. They really do look like brothers. There were three little plays and some excellent songs and, by the way, the Dutch Treat Club has the best and most expensive male choir in the world—two Metropolitan singers on it—among others—and they can make the silly songs they have to sing sound perfectly wonderful...
The Dutch Treat show was pretty good, all told, some really remarkable parts to it. Jim Flagg as Lincoln was most convincing and his address in character very good. Orson Lowell as George Washington was wonderful—just G.W. in the flesh, and Bill Walker as Henry VIII divided honors with the very best. All three have taken great pains and the result was surprising. And it is amazing that folks who know how, can take a silly little fool song intended to be more silly just because it is set to superb music, and make it sound splendid. It was a great treat, Dutch or not and it was Dutch to the tune of five dollars.
I got home at about 12 o'clock and hopped right into bed, me having to work today (Saturday)...

FRG's intention of joining his family in Florida—to "gather up a bunch of work and beat it to see you and the children," as he had written his wife—was never realized. Before he could handle the flow of stories being sent him by the art editor of the *Post* and a half-dozen other magazines, the resort hotel had closed for the summer and

Advertising layout, with rough sketch by Gruger

The published advertisement, as illustrated by FRG

Florence, Elizabeth and Dorothy returned to New York.

The following winter Florence's younger sister, Emily, and her husband Howard Megary, together with the Grugers rented a house in Dobbs Ferry, a small community north of Yonkers, New York. The three-story Victorian structure was situated picturesquely on a bluff overlooking the Hudson, with ten acres of beautiful grounds surrounding it. FRG commuted daily to New York City, travelling the twenty miles from 99 Broadway, Dobbs Ferry to his studio on Fifty-seventh Street.

F.R. Gruger was beginning to do more and more advertising art, producing magazine ads for General Electric, Yuban Coffee, O'Sullivan's Heels, Palmolive Shaving Cream, the Squibb Drug Company, Johns-Manville, the Alexander Hamilton Institute and the Curtis Publishing Company. Such advertising agencies as J. Walter Thompson, Barton, Durstine & Osborn,[13] the Ralph H. Jones Company and N.W. Ayer & Son used his services.

Thirty years earlier the potential of advertising art was first demonstrated when Frank Doubleday, of *Scribner's*, drew the reader's attention to the back of the magazine by sandwiching Arthur B. Frost drawings between the ads. Now virtually every well-known illustrator was being employed to promote commercial products, and being paid handsomely for the work.

Early in 1920 a group of these artists sought to promote their profession by organizing the Art Directors Club of New York, and in March of the following year, the club sponsored its "First Annual of Advertising Art in the United States." This exhibition held at the National Arts Club, attracted entries from such notable illustrators as N.C. Wyeth, F.R. Gruger, Maxfield Parrish, J.C. Leyendecker, Henry Reuterdahl, Harvey Dunn, James Preston, Arthur William Brown, Franklin Booth, Norman Rockwell, Edward Penfield and Dean Cornwall. A total of 302 works was displayed.

FRG was represented by six drawings, one of which was awarded the First Prize for Black and White Illustration and Design. The artwork, utilized in a newspaper advertisement for the Curtis Publishing Company, depicted a battle from World War I.

An FRG illustration was also awarded First Prize in the Second Art Directors Club annual, and his work continued to win honors until 1927, after which he stopped submitting. He was usually given a great deal of freedom in creating his advertising art, and his judgment was seldom questioned. A rare exception is recalled by his son:

> I remember his telling us about one set-to he had with an advertising customer. The object was to present a thermos bottle, the customer's product. His drawing showed a thermos standing on a table. They weren't pleased because they wanted it to stand out like a sore thumb. So they insisted that he polish it up and make it a lot

Advertising illustration for the Gruen Watch Company, 1926

more apparent. Father refused to do it and explained why. They insisted and announced they would get another artist to do it. Father said O.K. do that and take my name off the drawing. When the picture was published it looked silly, because the thermos was not in the atmosphere of the illustration, but seemed rather to hang in the air. They had the good grace to admit the mistake.

In the spring of 1921 FRG's brother-in-law, Howard Megary, learned that he was being transferred to London by his company, so the two families who had been sharing the residence at Dobbs Ferry decided to make the trip together. FRG took satisfaction in the fact that he could schedule his holidays when it suited him, and not according to the calendar: "Our vacations are easily movable along the twelve month scale of the year," he once observed. And now there was an opportunity to realize the plans of 1914, when another trip to England had been so abruptly cancelled.

Before their departure, FRG offered the use of the Riverside Drive apartment to his old friend, John R. Neill. Neill had just completed illustrating *The Royal Book of OZ* and would soon begin *Kabumpo in OZ*, the fifteenth and sixteenth in the OZ volumes. He was living on East Thirtieth Street with his wife Margaret and their infant daughter, using the premises as both studio and living quarters. "You must find the studio too small now to live in," Gruger told him. "Why don't you take our apartment?"

So with the Neills comfortably settled at 593 Riverside Drive, the Grugers and Megarys set sail for Liverpool on June 7, 1921 on the R.M.S. *Albania*.

notes for chapter 9

1 Conversation with the author, January 3, 1973

2 Conversation with the author, January 7, 1973

3 Ibid.

4 Ibid.

5 Conversation with the author, January 14, 1973

6 Refers to FRG's father, John Gruger.

7 FRG teaching notes

8 Conversation with the author, December 28, 1972

9 Conversation with the author, January 7, 1973

10 Letter to the author, January 28, 1973

11 Conversation with the author, December 28, 1972

12 Letter to the author, November 29, 1972

13 Now known as BBD & O

She felt sure this careless speech masked a sentimentalism intensely congenial to her own.

CHILDREN OF HOPE by STEPHEN WHITMAN
The Century Magazine, November 1915, page 16

Chapter 10

The ocean crossing was a joy to FRG, who never tired of observing the changing patterns of waves, the formation of white caps and the churning wake. He particularly enjoyed the company of several passengers, among them Charles Hanson Towne, managing editor of *McClure's* and Harold Everett Porter who wrote under the pseudonym of Halworthy Hall.

The Grugers and Megarys spent a couple of weeks in London, then rented a country house in Shoreham, near Sevenoaks, Kent. The estate, known as Darent Hulme, had belonged to Sir Joseph Prestwich, a distinguished geologist and Oxford professor. It came complete with six servants, two gardeners and a chauffeur.

One of the Grugers' neighbors was Lord Dunsany, the Irish writer, whose estate of several thousand acres was just outside of Sevenoaks. And, as Elizabeth noted: "Just below us in the valley was the stone cottage where William Blake had lived and worked, to earn the title of grandfather of the moderns."

It soon became apparent that FRG's reputation as an artist had preceded him. According to Elizabeth:

> I went to art school in London and they said "Are you F.R. Gruger's daughter?" When I answered "Yes" they said "Will you have him come into the class?" and the same thing happened in Paris. Every time I went into a school, students would ask, "Is your father coming in?" or "Will you get him to come and see our work?" He was always very good about doing it.

FRG worked much of the time, producing illustrations for *The Saturday Evening Post* and other magazines. But he also delighted in touring the countryside and in going to the galleries and monuments in and about London.

Occasional visits to and from Lord Dunsany were pleasant and interesting. "England was still pretty class conscious at the time," Ted remarked, "and because father was an artist he was welcome in many places to which his brother-in-law, who was just a businessman, would not have been invited."

Ted had been spending the summer in France, working in the war-devastated region of Verdun as part of the Mission of American Students, a reconstruction unit assembled by the Ivy League schools. When Ted informed his father he would be arriving for a brief visit, FRG wrote back:

August 8, 1921

> It is good news indeed that you...are coming over to England and I trust that you will make

the plane trip without getting seasick, but if you do, don't forget there is a cuspidore for the purpose and that it isn't good form to stick your head out the window as much on account of the pedestrians as for yourself...
> When you are about forty-five minutes north of the channel keep a lookout on your right for a white cross on a hillside...The top of the cross is only a few hundred yards from our house, in fact we walked up there this evening after dinner to get its bearings from your course. There may be someone on board who has flown over several times and who can point out Sevenoaks to you. Shoreham is the village about five miles north of Sevenoaks and is distinguishable by reason of its triangular shape with the Darent River forming one side...

Ted remembers that flight, which represented the first commercial air service between Paris (LeBourget) and London (Croydon):

> To the best of my recollection we were in the air somewhat over an hour. The plane was a converted World War I French Spad, a fabric covered bi-plane with a radial Nome engine. A single pilot occupied the port seat in a two-place open cockpit. The enclosed cabin, accommodating three passengers, was between the cockpit and the engine. Engine lubricant was castor oil, the aroma of which encouraged the vulnerable to the use of heavy paper bags. Neither my classmate nor I was sick, but the third passenger was. Planes flew in pairs so that if a mishap overtook one the other could report it, there being no radio communication. At mid-Channel we reached 10,000 feet so that, hopefully, we could glide to land if the engine gave out. On the return trip the pilot, an affable Frenchman who no doubt felt an urge to show off this remarkable machine, invited us individually to share the cockpit with him. After strapping ourselves in, he put the plane through non-acrobatic paces to show us how it was "driven." Each of us stuck his head out of the cockpit and had it nearly blown off. The idea of danger didn't enter our minds, for we were only 19 years old.
> I still retain a mental picture of our progress through stupendous canyons of cumulus clouds splashed with crimson and gold by a setting sun. We had excellent weather and uneventful crossings both ways, but were not able to see Sevenoaks or the cross.

Ted returned to New Haven with the student group,

A Sicilian elevator
GOLDEN CITIES OF ITALY by HENRY JAMES FORMAN
Harper's Magazine, August 1923, page 307

and the following month FRG returned to New York, leaving the rest of the family behind.

He resumed work as an illustrator full-time. By the fall of 1921 he was also drawing for *Good Housekeeping, Woman's Home Companion, Cosmopolitan* and, shortly thereafter, *Harper's Bazaar.* The softly-shaded Wolff pencil compositions signed "F.R. Gruger" soon appeared with the stories of such authors as Fanny Hurst, Stephen Vincent Benet, Arthur Train, W. Somerset Maugham, F. Scott Fitzgerald and I.A.R. Wylie.

FRG had determined to return to England in time to celebrate Christmas with his family. When he arrived at Darent Hulme he brought some exciting news: *Harper's* was sending him on a sketching trip through Sicily, Calabria and Malta to produce a group of illustrations for a forth-coming book by Henry James Forman.

The Grugers left England on January 26, 1922, their twenty-fifth wedding anniversary, stopping off in Paris and Rome on the way. "We went to the National Museum, St. Peter's and the Vatican," Florence recalled. The Sistine Chapel was closed, they learned, because a new Pope was being elected. On to Naples, Messina and across the straits by ferry. "Sudden, violent storms all day," FRG observed. "Bay superb—waves breaking over ramparts…"

The Formans met them in Taormina, Sicily, where FRG immediately warmed to his literary colleague. Henry Forman had recently served as editor of *Collier's,* but relinquished that post to devote himself full-time to writing. The Grugers were now joined by other notables, as Elizabeth remembers:

> We were spending the winter in Taormina. John Marquand and Harold Porter were there too, which made a most entertaining group.
> To gather their material for Mr. Forman's book, *Grecian Italy,* he and Dad set off for Calabria, Malta and several Sicilian towns where the Greek ruins are particularly fine.
> They were gone about two weeks and had a most hilarious trip, during which Mr. Forman threatened to describe Dad in his book as a companion who sat in every chair he came to, and drank coffee endlessly. Dad assured Mr. Forman that that would be fine, as he would depict Mr. Forman in his drawings as an aged, studious soul, while he would make himself dashing and debonnaire.

FRG returned with only a handful of sketches. As was his habit, he had soaked up with his coffee the specific characteristics of each town, enabling him to produce illustrations at a later date which made every Grecian ruin

Henry James Forman

specific and unique. When the Forman volume appeared, it contained three watercolors and fifteen black-and-white drawings.[1]

FRG had written his son from Siracusa:

February 14, 1922

...At one point in this historic land of fable and romance and mythology we pass the place where Polyphemus chased Ulysses and hurled rocks after his fleeing boats. Some rocks—they are still to be seen sticking up in the sea, and this morning huge waves were breaking over them, so, as they seemed to be solidly stuck in the bottom, I take it old one-eye had a husky right arm.

Sometime I hope you will get to see this place and it will be clear and lovely weather, and Etna unclouded and shining in the sun. With his great mantle of snow and plume of sulfurous steam he's an impressive giant. They used to think Vulcan labored there and all around are myth upon myth.

Even the Sicilian cart horses are decorative
GRECIAN ITALY — GOLDEN CITIES OF ITALY
by HENRY JAMES FORMAN
Harper's Magazine, August 1923, page 311

After travelling through Sicily and southern Italy, the Grugers returned to England. Darent Hulme was for sale, and Sir Joseph Prestwich's heirs offered it to them. Although Elizabeth and Dorothy were excited at the prospect, FRG pointed out that he already owned one home in Avon, rented a house in Dobbs Ferry, and an apartment and studio in New York City.

When Darent Hulme was bought by others, the family took up residence at Speldhurst Close, a sprawling, ivy-covered stone house located four miles away, rented from Francis Alexander MacKinnon, the 74-year-old head of the MacKinnon clan.

Having decided that the family would remain in Europe during the summer months, FRG returned to New York and offered John R. Neill the use of the Avon house. The Neills moved from Riverside Drive to the summer home just in time for the birth of their second daughter.

When FRG returned to England, Arthur William Brown came with him. Florence met them at Waterloo Station and they had lunch at Harrod's. Brownie remarked that FRG was travelling back and forth across the Atlantic with such frequency that his friends had begun referring to him as "the long-distance commuter."

The Grugers had a summer of travel, visiting Paris, Strasbourg, Stuttgard, Munich, Berlin and Pottsdam, before taking a boat trip down the Rhine and returning to England by way of Brussels and Bruges. When FRG sailed for New York in September, his wife and daughters remained on the Continent. Their arrival in the French capital was noted in the *New York Herald.* After a short

The ruined cathedral of Messina
TAORMINA THE BEAUTIFUL by HENRY JAMES FORMAN
Harper's Magazine, August 1923, page 312

stay they wintered in Madrid, Algeciras and Gibraltar. Ted joined them for Christmas, and when they journeyed to Algiers and other North African points of interest, they were accompanied by one of Elizabeth's suitors, Peter Penn-Gaskall, the last descendant of the William Penn family in England.

During the period from October, 1922 to March, 1923, FRG wrote his wife daily, detailed letters from New York. He kept careful note of the movements of the fast mail-carrying vessels.

The following excerpts from this correspondence provide a unique insight into the life and times of the illustrator: his working habits, problems, productivity, pleasures and everyday activities and interests. They amount to an intimate chronicle, an historical picture by one who was able to illustrate with words as well as with pencil and brush:

October 12th, 1922

So far to-day I'm well along with two drawings for *Good Housekeeping*. Tomorrow I must do two for the *Post*. If I finish them by tomorrow night, which I must, then I will have made two thousand two hundred the first month—for tomorrow will be the tenth and I arrived in New York on September 11th...

Next month will yield $4000.00 at least, and November another $4000. So I'll be able to pay up everything, I think, and have enough to send you and to pay Ted's and my little trip.

I have on hand yet to be done:

Harper's	$2000.00
1 serial for *Redbook*, 7 parts	3500.00
1 story for *Redbook*	500.00
1 story for *Cosmopolitan*	650.00
1 story for *McCall's* (1 drawing)	250.00
1 serial for *Woman's Home Companion* (3 parts)	2500.00
2 drawings for J. Walter Thompson at	1000.00& 2,000.00
1 series for *Post*—5 parts	1875.00
	13275.00

I'll proceed to announce that the *Post* drawings are done, but I didn't finish them until four o'clock! The weather was so very damp that I had to keep one drawing before the fire while I worked on the other.

Booth and Wittmack came in and suggested dinner. After dinner they suggested movies—we went to see Richard Barthelmess in a melodrama...the acting and presentation were superb.

October 16, 1922

So far things have gone well—I have four drawings underway. Three for the *Post* and one for *McCall's*. They all look good. I must say the last eight drawings have been good ones! These look as though they would be better. All I have to do is finish them by Thursday and then I'll be ahead of my schedule. Which will help me do better stuff for *Harper's*.

October 20, 1922

I went up to Brownie's last night to dinner, as I said, a very good dinner as usual. After dinner we went to the theatre a short way from their house and saw "Blood and Sand," an excellent movie of the Spanish story. It was well directed, well acted and well photographed...

Some days ago "Doug" Fairbanks was at the Dutch Treat. Brownie wanted me to go. But not I...I was too busy. Brownie went and called me later to say how interesting it was and to invite me to dinner. When I got there I found a drawing on his board, all done except the background. I put that in for him in fifteen minutes! That's how he got the time—it would have taken him all afternoon to do that background.

I haven't anyone to make up my lost time for me. Don't blame Brownie, as the drawing of a tree and a few flowers is just relaxation for me (when it's on someone else's drawing). I didn't mind at all.

Last evening McKeogh's[2] secretary phoned me...and asked if I could do one in a hurry! Of course, I said "yes." The manuscript came in this morning's mail and I made the drawings all today, except an hour's work, and tomorrow they will be in Philadelphia...they show no trace of haste!...I most earnestly pray that I shall be able to keep up this pace...

Brownie and I went down to see the "Prisoner of Zenda"—which is a wonderfully acted, directed and photographed picture. We enjoyed it greatly.

Forman came in yesterday to luncheon...We had a long chat and a very pleasant one, you see he said many lovely things about my unusual and lovely family...

October 23, 1922

From Ted's letter you will see that it is our purpose to leave here on December 10th or thereabouts. I have already notified all editors and other dependents!...It is most probable that

Inspiration Pictures, Inc., Charles H. Duell, President
announces

RICHARD BARTHELMESS

Supported by DOROTHY GISH *in*
Joseph Hergesheimer's colorful romance

"THE BRIGHT SHAWL"

A John S. Robertson production   Screen adaptation by Edmund Goulding

Of the many characters created by Barthelmess we believe his panto-
mimic artistry is most appealing in this story of a young American's encounter
with the impulsive Cuban lady of the Bright Shawl.   A drama of hearts,
flowers, swords—and a great soul.

To make "The Bright Shawl," the entire company spent several months
in Cuba. It represents sincere artistic effort while striving for the maximum
of popular entertainment.

Advertising illustration by Franklin Booth for a Richard Barthelmess movie, 1923

we will go direct, although I'd like very much to get a chance to see the Prado and the New Gallery in Madrid...

Tomorrow Booth lends me his car. I have to go downtown and hunt paper. The big stock I have is at last exhausted and no new supply in sight—I phoned Brownie to go with me...We went downtown and visited a dozen paper and cardboard houses! We came away laden with sample sheets of paper. Out of this caravan I hope we will find something that is good and that will allow us to make drawings without going mad with the misbehavior of so paltry a servant...

October 27, 1922

We dined at Keen's Chop House and had steak and kidney pie, excellent. After that we went to the first night of Griffith's new picture "One Exciting Night." It was all the title claimed for it—some excitement! Griffith made his usual speech afterward...The audience enjoyed it immensely; and squealed and squealed with excitement and laughed convulsively...

Brownie came in during the day and brought me a loaf of Italian bread...Booth came over and we went down to the Alps to dine...to the Rivoli...They had a wonderful picture taken under the sea. Exquisite landscape peopled by fishes...the audience spellbound...We are a great people, even if we only develop this beautiful new art.

During the light I am making color drawings and late in the afternoon and at night I work on the black and white. In that way a lot of work gets done...

October 31, 1922

This is Sunday night (October 29th) and I am happy to say, I have finished one of Forman's things. Malta. If it does not sound too much like a boast I should like to admit the color picture to be a "pippin." Everyone agrees with me...It seems to have made quite an impression upon the gang...

Last night I went to the theatre. Eddie came in just before dinner waving a pair of tickets and suggested that I put away the shovel and the hoe for a few hours and hie me to the playhouse, which I did much to my satisfaction and amusement. The play was "Captain Applejack," and very good. I liked it. It was funny (which cheered me greatly) and pleasing to look at...

November 3, 1922

Yesterday Forman phoned me asking if I would be on hand at the Harvard Club to dine with him. I was. After that we went to see a play with a queer and very bad title, "Six Characters In Search of An Author." That's pretty bad, but the play was very good and I was glad I went. I met more authors and actors and writers than I knew there were...

November 6, 1922

Yesterday morning I went down and had my hair cut. It was a gloomy day, but warm and without rain. Having a new drawing to start and long hair I seemed too much of an artist to work, so I went downtown and had, what I believe the surgeons refer to as a cosmetic operation, performed, and I was annointed with oil and shampooed all complete.

November 13, 1922

Eddie, since his painting of the sea was accepted by the (National) Academy for exhibition, has been so far up in the clouds that I haven't seen him since yesterday. His painting is a remarkable performance and well deserves to be accepted and well hung...

Late this afternoon in came friend Forman, all enthusiasm, all joy! Wells, of *Harper's*, called him up and told him that the drawings I had made for Malta were not only beautiful drawings but the best I had ever done and a new note in pictures of that kind...

November 17, 1922

Last night I went to see the opening of "Merton of the Movies." Everybody was there. Forman sat at the other extremity of the same row in the balcony. Neysa had a seat in the front row of the balcony with one of her steadies. Brownie and Grant Rice were downstairs and there were lots more whom I knew around and about. The papers this morning give the play a good write-up, but I wasn't pleased at all with it. It seemed indecent to parade this poor young fool around the open stage in all his spiritual nakedness and make sport of him and laugh at his poor poverty. I was rather ashamed to be there...

After dinner I took a short walk and then, returning to the studio, I got into my rags and sat

"The Race of the Natchez and the Robert E. Lee" by Dean Cornwell.

down to read a new story. It's from the *Cosmopolitan* and written by Arthur Train...

November 21, 1922

McKeogh had been here on Friday bringing with him a story to be done by Tuesday (tomorrow) which had come in so late that they did not have time to set it up. He brought the original and Miss Herr read it to me while I was doing another drawing for the *Cosmopolitan*. I got to bed early and lay in comfort reading Forman's book, "The Man Who Lived in a Shoe"...
Eddie says he will have tickets for "Hamlet" tomorrow night. John Barrymore is the Hamlet and so I imagine Booth and I will go with him.

November 27, 1922

It was quite cold last night when Booth, Eddie and I came bounding up the Avenue full tilt from the theatre, tearing along at top speed so that we could get some hot chocolate before the bar closed...I must say that John and his gang did a good job. The whole production was magnificent and Barrymore as Hamlet surprised us at his excellence. This is the eighth production of "Hamlet" I have seen and the others are already forgotten, except the younger Salvini, who did a

most impressive Hamlet. But this outclassed them all...
Yesterday, after finishing my drawing, I went out to luncheon with Booth—we met Dean Cornwell at the restaurant and another artist. We all ate buckwheat cakes and sausage and then Booth and I went over to the Academy show.
John R. [Neill] came in Friday evening and we all had dinner at the Alps—Booth came over too—we sat in my studio afterward and talked and had a good time—John R. told all about the joys of paternity and about how he put the kids on the pot at 11:30 and 2:00 o'clock at night. He made quite a joke of it and had us all gaily laughing at his misadventure in fatherhood—he couldn't get room at the club so I offered him a couch in Eddie's room...Saturday morning I slammed my door preparatory to my descent to breakfast and Eddie's opened and we all went to George's together where we met Booth and had a foursome for breakfast—Booth asked John how he had fared and John said fine, fine. Eddie piped up and said it was just like home and that Johnnie had got up twice and tried to "put me on the pot"—He said John had held him by the shoulders and kept saying "do it—Daddy can't *hear* you *do* it." John R. denied it vigorously and paid the breakfast check!

December 3, 1922

As you have probably gathered...this is Sunday. It is evening now and the lights are burning and a rather hard day's work is done. A large drawing full of detail which was rather stubborn is now defeated and all that remains to do to it is a few minor matters that give no trouble.

December 4, 1922

Things have come about in such fashion that I find it impossible to go over to France at the time I had planned...I cannot arrange matters satisfactorily before the end of January. There are some papers in relation to the sale of the house at Avon[3]...one of us must be there...Then there are a set of six profitable advertising drawings just offered me which I would lose if I took the 13th sailing. I have counted up carefully and find that to go with Ted at this time would cost fully five thousand dollars. I haven't done many advertising drawings this time and they are what makes the real profit, so that I have only averaged twenty-five hundred dollars a month since I have been home, and as you know expenses are a whole lot...

December 8, 1922

...the newspapers have tried to make us aware that we are about to become stiff with cold because of coal shortage, but most do not fear that as much as we should. The various states are taking steps to prevent profiteering and recently the coal administrators have confiscated large supplies which had been delivered to the large estates of some rich men so that the less fortunate might have wherewith to keep the fire burning. And then one turns in thought to regard the huge *Berengaria* in which Ted is happy and lucky to be crossing to spend two happy weeks with you, and is appalled at the huge amount of fuel she withdraws from the common store to carry a few hundred people on just a few days' journey.

December 11, 1922

Saturday afternoon Brownie called me on the phone and asked me to come up for dinner. I went. Max Foster and his wife arrived shortly after dinner...

You have no idea how shockingly disappointed I was when I found I had to give up my trip over to you, but, well, it just couldn't be done. There is too much to pay and there was too much right in my hands to do so that I simply couldn't make it. As for the bright idea, that is modified by an occurrence today. The *Harper's Bazaar* man came in and asked me to go over to Seville, meet Baron de Meyer and do the Easter festivities there—all expenses paid! All kinds of things happen, when least expected—don't they.
Have a look around and see if you can find for me a suitable place I can use as a studio...North light preferred. After that an eastern light. Not south or west. If the weather is cold then some heating device because I can't work when I am cold...

December 13, 1922

We are to go see Douglas Fairbanks in "Robin Hood" or, as I rather suspect, Robin Hood as Douglas Fairbanks which is the way it usually is...

December 24, 1922

The Fifth Avenue shops were all open and lighted with young folk going in and out, gaily buying the last almost forgotten token. All along were people gazing into glittering windows where costly temptations were almost enthroned in royal fashion. Everyone seemed all dressed up. Everyone seemed happy, and I felt very much alone.

December 28, 1922

Last night I went with John R., who came in about dinner time, to the movies where we saw a new rendering of Tarkington's "Flirt". It wasn't at all like the story but as the "pitchers"...go, it was pretty good. Eddie went with us.

December 31, 1922

They are getting all ready for a New Year party. Silent as were the halls on Christmas Eve, so noisy will they be tonight. I prefer the silence. And I am all the more determined the Prohibition is a boon to mankind, especially if he wants to do any work and has the mischance to dwell in this building.[4] For the flowing bowl is about to flow, and indeed, has already begun, though it is only five o'clock, and dark already.

January 1, 1923

(At Eddie's party) my wine glasses remained turned bottom up as did some others, happily…I suppose this sort of thing must be a great joy, otherwise wherein lies its temptation and its great hold upon people. But this morning everyone is sick and heavy and wretched in just proportion to the exhilaration of last night, and they have headaches and regret and, I think, some digust—yet they'll do it again at the next opportunity. Happily I am of the temperament that is able to look on and see and, to some extent, understand, while I am not tempted to pass judgment…

Neysa (McMein)[5] did not grace Eddie's party, having got up as far as the Vanderbilts now. I told that to Forman but I fear he thought me harsh as I am inclined to believe he thinks Neysa entitled to the full 100% sex appeal which she was accorded at a recent contest, but Alex Woollcott being one of the judges, and Brownie and I not concurring, we have our suspicions of the findings—I think I rated .03% myself, so maybe I'm not a fair judge.

January 5, 1923

I have only been to two movies in a long while. I went to see the Tele-(something-or-other) which is a stereoscopic device…They did a very ingenious thing as a special number. A large translucent screen was put over the proscenium arch. Then at the back of the stage they set two lights about six inches apart. In between they had four dancing girls. In each seat was a small device which contained a revolving shutter before the lights, so that you first saw the screen with one eye and then with the other, and at the same time the lights were obscured alternately. The result of this was that the screen seemed to disappear and the shadows of the dancers became solid and drifted to and fro over the heads of the audience. I sat well back, and these fresh women came and precious near kicked my dignified nose. It was quite astonishing and amused the audience hugely. That will probably suggest a new use for this device…

I really want to spend the whole time I am in Spain with water colors or oil, seeing what I can do in the way of gathering up some more experience in color than I have. I think it would be the most profitable way to spend the time…Last week I had to refuse almost $1200.00 worth of work. I still have a lot and when it is finished I'll have enough money for all we need this time.

New Year baby cover by J. C. Leyendecker
The Saturday Evening Post, December 30, 1922

January 8, 1923

Work has been going along fairly well but I am doing one of Forman's color drawings and it has given me a tussel…I have been working four days on this drawing and in that time could, ordinarily, have done a full story. If, however, I can make a reputation with my color drawings, it will ultimately pay me…I am working on four drawings at once, come to think of it, so what had Caesar on me! *He* never did.

January 16, 1923

You will be proud of me when you see the picture of the market place in Palermo which I made for the Forman article—everyone else is and Forman is thrilled with it. *Harper's* seem to think it a good one too and, which is more to the point, so do I!

It's lonely here today…There's no one about except Sally, who came in a few moments ago to get a plaster tool. All the rest are on some lark or other (Neysa's at the Vanderbilts—I guess—so's not to let it get cold!). Eddie's at his uncle's house—and everywhere is silence except for Sally scratching plaster and my pen scratching paper, for I'm making pen drawings today.

Nine-fifty P.M. and the drawing's done! After having been engaged upon water color and

A TOUCH OF ETERNITY by WALLACE IRWIN
Redbook Magazine, April, 1923

crayon drawings, pen drawings go hard. But by dint of sticking at it one does get through. But y' gotta work.

I have a lot of colored inks here and when I begin to get myself in form to do this advertising drawing I got my colored inks and had a go with them and it may be said that they present all sorts of possibilities. Some day it will be fun to try a colored illustration with them.

January 23, 1923

I have been working on the lovely story for the *Post* of which I wrote you and I think I have made one drawing, at least, which you will rightly claim. I have been asked for it by several people already, but I have told everyone that all drawings belong to you until you have decided that they are not good enough for you to accept...

Today I have to forgo a serial for *Good Housekeeping* that would have been a six thousand dollar commission. That's all right though because something will arrive to take its place as soon as I return from abroad, and anyway I can't keep up this pace indefinitely. Today I made two drawings for the *Post*. Tonight I have another ad. Tomorrow two more drawings for the *Post*. Tomorrow night another ad and so it goes.

January 26, 1923

...dinner at Brownie's and an evening at the Follies.

January 29, 1923

The Formans have just left and I feel like a birthday cake all nicely iced with sugar ... They are a funny pair and fully convinced that no one ever sees them at it.

Last night I went down to the Algonquin again and met a chap named Huchinson, who is a most delightful writer. He was many years in China and I wanted particularly to ask him questions about a Chinese story I have on hand. Apparently the story is not very exact itself so I do not need to worry about accuracy so much as just finishing them up as soon as possible...had a very nice little dinner, although it was necessary to wait for a table, but that was pleasant in its own way. Many people whom I know pass through the lobby. Evey Shinn, for example...

The pavements are all white with snow again and the elevated looks very black against the sky, and I had breakfast all alone this morning because I got up at half-past eight and no one else did! They don't, often.

Since I have been here this trip I have had offered to me twenty-five thousand dollars worth of work which I have had to refuse. In a very short time now I'll know what I can do and when I can sail and you may depend upon a cable as soon as I can be sure.

February 6, 1923

Today I finished another drawing for the *Post*. Three since yesterday morning. By tomorrow night I'll have that serial all done and will begin

"So Nicoletta is false to me! Ha!" I fill the goblets with red wine and, turning aside, empty the contents of this ring into the one destined for you. "Let us drink to the fair Nicoletta," I cry.

THE POISONER by ARTHUR TRAIN *Cosmopolitan Magazine,* March, 1923, pages 78 and 79

on the *Redbook* serial. I have to complete two or perhaps three for them.

...I have yet to do the following things:

Cosmopolitan	3 pic	$ 650.00
Harper's Baz.	1½	350.00
McCall's	4	800.00
Hearst's	5	1000.00
Harper's Mag.	6	1000.00
Redbook	9	1500.00
		5300.00

These have to be finished before I leave and I am doing them at the rate of one or more a day. I did all I could to hurry them but could not afford to let the standard go down. As it is I am in great demand...

February 14, 1923

Yesterday Eddie came to my door and asked me to step into his room and see something interesting. I did so. There were several men in there who had with them a box about half the size of a suit case. On opening the front one saw two black knobs and a pair of telephone receivers with a spring band to keep them over the ears, that's all. It was near to twelve o'clock and the box being pointed in the general direction of Washington the receivers were given to me and I could plainly hear the great clock at Arlington beating out the time signals for noon. It was then turned toward Newark and the voice of the man who announced the weather forecast and stock quotations was much clearer than is usual by phone, ensuing music being exceedingly

well rendered. Having that set with one anywhere ensures communication in one direction, with all sorts of sending stations whether you are in the subway or in an automobile upon the road, or in a closed room, as we were. Quite wonderful, isn't it?

I'm making a set of drawings for *Hearst's International,* today, and they are going very well even tho' they are in two colors. Black and red, black and green, black and blue and so on. I was afraid I'd have a lot of trouble with them, but apparently not. One is drying over the radiator as I write this. Tonight I am planning to start a pair of black and whites for *McCall's.* Speed is the watchword! I have six drawing boards at work this minute! And only one pair of hands!

Another good day's work done and a night's to do... Tomorrow I hope to finish this story, the next drawings are of the kind that one does quickly. I wouldn't boast, for that is fatal, but in this case I am fairly safe. I still have a lot to do, but there are only a few drawings among them that give me pause at all. The rest are just regular drawings. The rest of *Harper's* stuff can be finished in three days. The only thing that is a bother is the first installment of the *Woman's Home Companion* story, which has been shoved ahead, but I'll leave out a *Redbook* and that will give me time and the *Redbook* one won't be needed until October...The drawing I finished today is of the interior of a newspaper office of the late Nineties—about the time I went on the *Ledger.* So it should be authentic, and it is.

...I have wrapped up a lot of old drawings securely and have set them upon the new shelf in

Illustration by James H. Crank for *The Saturday Evening Post*

the hall designed, executed and erected for that purpose. There are a lot of them. I may say, also, that I have destroyed a lot of them too. Prefunctory drawings...not worth saving. I didn't destroy any that had a sign of anything worthwhile in them...

I didn't do much tonight except start a drawing. Crank[6] (who isn't one at all) came in about quarter to eleven and we have been sitting here talking about everything in the world for near an hour. He has the studio that Spicer-Simpson had...

After dinner, at the Algonquin I met Evvie Shinn and Richard Barthelmess, also Gibson of *Cosmopolitan*. After a bit of talk Evvie and I started off northward. He was in a hurry and stuck me into a taxi—although I'd have preferred to walk. He was all dressed up for a party and said he was in a semi hurry. He's nearly divorced for the second time! He said I had the only wife he ever heard of who was good for life and didn't quit half. Said I was always a good picker and how is John Neill. I said I thought John R. about usual...

The next job I have on my hands is a stinger. It is a portrait of Lincoln's mother—Nancy Hanks. There isn't any portrait of her, except one that Robert Lincoln has and won't lend—So I'm said to be the only artist capable of doing it without giving offense to the family: And as it is for the Western Electric Company, it is important not to offend Bob, because he is the President of some other big company and us fellows got to stick together! How'd you like to tackle that?

February 22, 1923

Now that the editors are all muzzled by George Washington's splendid services (for which I thank him) I will get to work before any more of the day disappears in idleness—and I kinda think there is a sort of holiday tomorrow too...

All the art editors weren't muzzled, one of them came in to see me and laughed when I read from this letter what I had said about them.

McKeogh comes in tomorrow to take up the matter of a raise in price for *Post* stories. I told him that I lose seventy-five dollars on every drawing I make for him. He's been after Lorimer and I don't know what the result will be, but he phoned to make a date for tomorrow and I hope some profit shall come out of the interview. I suggested quite a raise in price and will stick to it if I can.

February 27, 1923

Some weeks ago I went with a number of others, Booth & Bee, Jack Troube and a lady and Eddie and me, to see Will Shakespeare. Did I mention this before? It was a wonderful play and at the end of it Queen Elizabeth made a speech to Shakespeare that was, or is, or should be, a classic. If Elizabeth wasn't like her characterization—then, she should have been. Everybody that saw that play was greatly impressed with it. I wish you all could have seen it. You would have appreciated it, each of you, and yet—it failed. It was too good for Broadway. Brownie says it was because the young people wouldn't be bothered to go to it, and they are the ones who spend the money! Poor Broadway!

It [a drawing] is done, and with it is finished the two weeks of high pressure work such as I haven't experienced in a long while. I am glad it is done. It was for a story for *Hearst's* that I got stuck with and couldn't get out of doing. I didn't like it—had no sympathy with the way they wanted it done, although it started well enough, and the way they wanted it done did not develop until later. I made them pay a thousand dollars for it though, which eases the smart a bit. Now I shall go ahead with more agreeable work which should yield me, barring ill health, just about a thousand a week until you return...

This afternoon I worked on a little sketch for Sally. I did it largely for my own pleasure though. It is for some kind of a memorial and she didn't seem to be getting the right sort of thing and had several turned down—so I had an idea and took a hand. It is a youth's figure with wings—it's just to suggest youth—in relation to the war. So I have made him offering the Roman salute, which I think a splendid gesture. It was a pleasant relief from the crayon pencil...

Another little commission amounting to two thousand dollars came in this morning in the mail. I can well remember when that would have cheered me mightily. Now, it's only a job to be done. But it all helps. Especially as there are but five drawings in it...Since I have been home I have made $13,600.00. That takes work. I have the bills almost all paid and I have a balance in the bank...

March 2, 1923

In a letter just mailed I told you...why I thought it necessary to "can" my trip [to Spain]. Since it became known that I am to remain home manuscripts have poured into the studio. Seven thousand dollars worth this week! I think it best to make this money. I also think it best to stop work during the summer and have planned to return to Europe all together, as I said, Venice, Florence, Milan, The Alps, Prague, Budapest, Switzerland and England, perhaps Spain. All of us together. Counting the *Post* stories that will come in I have enough work to pay me a thousand dollars a week until we leave! And more to come when we return...

The reason I am sure these things will pay that much is that I have added all of 75% to my prices and have got away with it. The *Cosmopolitan* is responsible for that...

March 9, 1923

I thought the family as a whole would be better served by my remaining here at work until the summer season, when work and the desire to do it is naturally slack. We can then blow the money saved in one grand bust!...

It's a frightful night out... There is about three inches of snow and frozen rain on the sidewalks. Taxis and motors are in endless and apparently hopeless jams. Rubber coated and booted traffic police, greatly increased in numbers, are nearly frantic with their task and every driver is demanding right of way with horn and klaxton. Mad as Paris gone mad!

But the beauty of the spectacle of the theatre district made us glad we were held up long enough to look into the amazement of lights and thronged with motors and scurrying people. It was wonderful.

There is no city to compare to New York, nor anywhere in the world a street like Fifth Avenue or Broadway. And, lighted by the huge electric signs, the white street, thronging crowds of hurrying people in the pelting sleet, the glitter and color of the jammed mass of cars, the noise of horns and shouting of numbers of directions made a carnival of excitement that would be hard to match anywhere else.

Florence, Elizabeth and Dorothy returned to New York in mid-April. They all attended Ted's graduation from Yale and then spent the summer at Bar Harbor, but once again FRG's vacation plans were thwarted. He accompanied the family on the drive to Maine, stopping off at the Boston Public Library to see the murals of Abbey, Sargent and Puvis de Chavannes, but then hurried back to Manhattan and his work. "I'll come up as soon as I get two *Post* installments ahead," he wrote Florence optimistically, yet as the summer slipped away Fred remained in New York City, laboring amid heat and humidity to fill a never-ending flood of requests for his art.

FRG's refusal to compromise his high standards of illustration in order to accelerate production was rewarded by a continual outpouring of praise from the various magazine staffs and authors. From art editor Arthur McKeogh of the *Post:*

Having seen your two sets this morning I am waving the old headpiece on high and leading a vigorous cheer on the part of the Art Department ending with three long GRUGERS...Every one of these pictures is a knock-out, and we are very much indebted to you.

When Karl Edwin Harriman, editor of *Redbook,* sent FRG a three-part story to illustrate, he wrote:

> ...I think you are going to say you have never read a more fascinating, unsolvable mystery story; and there isn't a man in America whom I want to illustrate it so much as I do you.

And after author Phyllis Duganne saw FRG's drawings for her contribution to the June, 1923 number of *Harper's Bazaar,* she informed the editor:

> ...I do want to write before another day goes by to tell you how much I like Mr. Gruger's illustrations for "It Can't Be Done".
> They have lots of nice things about them, but the nicest—and the one that no writer ever has the right to expect—is that he has made the people look exactly as I thought they did! The sketch of Owen Musgrave is what is known as Perfectly Priceless, and it has fired me with ambition all over again to do a story about him that has been percolating inside my skull ever since he first walked into Eleanor's story.
> Thank you for them. And won't you tell Mr. Gruger how pleased I am, too?

During the summer FRG learned that the building at 57 West Fifty-seventh Street had been sold and would soon be demolished. Forced to relocate, he scoured the area for new quarters. Drawing table, books and other belongings were gathered up by F.R. Gruger and the circle of friends who had shared the floor for five years: Eddie Wittmack, Franklin Booth, Neysa McMein and Sally Farnum. As steam shovels began gnawing away at the brick walls of the Fifty-seventh Street structure, FRG made the move to another address—80 West Fortieth Street.

notes for chapter 10

[1] Prior to the book's publication in 1924, *Harper's* Magazine ran four articles by Forman about Southern Italy, Sicily and Malta, between July and October, 1923. These were illustrated by twenty-four of Gruger's drawings, the three watercolors being used as frontispieces to the magazine. *Good Housekeeping* also ran one article with three illustrations in March, 1925.

[2] Arthur McKeogh, art editor of *The Saturday Evening Post*

[3] The house was put on the market because there seemed to be little prospect of the family continuing to use it to any extent.

[4] 57 West Fifty-seventh Street

[5] The popular magazine cover artist who became best known for her portraits of such beautiful women as Mary Pickford, Ethel Barrymore, Irene Castle and Norma Talmadge.

[6] James H. Crank, a magazine illustrator

"Owen, gloomy and with his usual hang-over, grunted wanly from his arm chair."

IT CAN'T BE DONE by PHYLLIS DUGANNE
Harper's Bazaar, June, 1923, page 79
Reproduced at the same size as the original.

Howard Chandler Christy painting a portrait of Marion Davies

Chapter 11

When F.R. Gruger moved into his new studio in October, 1923 the premises were already a hive of artistic activity. Illustrators J.C. Leyendecker and Norman Rockwell were there, as was Leon Gordon, a well-known portrait painter and advertising artist. The building, which was called the Beaux Art Studios, had acquired an aura of notoriety because its penthouse was occupied by Marion Davies, a former chorus girl who had posed for magazine covers by Harrison Fisher and Howard Chandler Christy. Now the twenty-six year old beauty was being groomed for the movies by William Randolph Hearst, who visited her regularly.

For two months prior to occupying his new quarters, FRG shared Arthur William Brown's studio again. But by October he was comfortably settled in Room 63 of the building at Fortieth Street and Sixth Avenue, facing Bryant Park. His brother-in-law wrote:

> Your new studio, I gather, is quite an elaborate affair, for which *The Saturday Evening Post* and others will suffer, owing to the excessive rental you must pay. Fortieth Street, overlooking the Park, seems an ideal situation for a studio in that nothing can be erected in front to interfere with the light.

In the meantime the Grugers' living quarters were anything but settled. Having completed plans for another trip to Europe that winter, they were temporary tenants of the Robert Fulton Hotel, preferring that to uprooting John R. Neill's family from the Riverside Drive apartment. Fred and Florence now dined out almost nightly, often choosing the Algonquin Hotel because it was only four blocks from the Beaux Arts.

The Algonquin restaurant was a meeting place for people in literature and the arts. Alexander Woollcott (who lived next door to the studio building on Fifty-seventh Street), Charles Hanson Towne, Dorothy Parker, Franklin P. Adams and Henry Forman were among the habitues. The Grugers dined there or at Keen's Chop House or other neighborhood places, often in the company of Booth, Wittmack, Brownie or the Neills. The Beaux Arts Studios had its own restaurant, the Gold Room, located on the floor below Marion Davies' penthouse, but it soon closed due to Prohibition.

FRG and Florence went regularly to the movies or the theatre to see such silent films as "Rosita" starring Mary Pickford, "Three Ages" with Buster Keaton, "The Hunchback of Notre Dame," "Cyrano de Bergerac" or the latest comedies of Charlie Chaplin and Harold Lloyd.

Florence and her daughters sailed for Europe aboard the *President Polk* in mid-November, and FRG joined them the following month. Ted was there, having been sent by his new employer. After the family travelled together through Belgium and France, Dorothy, just nineteen, was enrolled at the College Montmorency in Paris, a finishing school which offered "French Instruction for Foreign Young Ladies." Her courses of study included Ancient Literature, the History of Art, Domestic Economy and classes in millinery and lingerie.

FRG rented a studio at 2 Rue des Italiens, working there for about four weeks. At the end of that time he acknowledged:

> My drawings are nearly finished I'm glad to say. My stay in Paris has produced four thousand dollars and that's more than enough to pay our expenses until I reach New York I should imagine.

Elizabeth entered the Academie Julian, studying art at the school which had proven so popular with several generations of Americans. Now the parents left their children and Paris, and set out for Milan, Venice, Trieste and finally Alexandria.

Egypt was a favorite destination for travellers who had completed the tour of Europe, especially since the discovery of King Tutankhamen's tomb in 1922. FRG was stimulated by the prospect of viewing this burial chamber of an Egyptian king, the only such chamber ever to be discovered intact, containing all its treasures.

Florence made copious notes of their travels which were typed in narrative form when they returned home:

> We had come by boat from Trieste—a five day trip down the Adriatic and across the Mediterranean, where fur coats and steamer rugs were necessary to one's comfort—but the next morning when we awoke to brilliant sunshine, and from the four tall French windows of our bedroom—a corner room on the ground floor—we could walk out into the tropical garden of the hotel,[1] and we realized that we had left winter behind us...

One evening they drove to the Pyramids and the Sphinx, observing that:

> ...as we sped through the city out toward the Nile the brilliant moonlight softened and beautified everything—palm-shaded gardens, Bougainvillea-hung houses, Moorish-designed buildings, with shadows within the arches black as velvet.

Across the Nile they rode, joining a long line of sightseers:

> Leaving the car we walked halfway around the base of the great Pyramid, meeting a continuous line of Bedouin-guided tourists, some on camels, some on donkeys, many walking, returning from their moonlit view of the desert, the three vast Pyramids and the Sphinx...The sightless eyes and mutilated features have a majesty, a calm, and a sense of infinite knowledge that is awe-inspiring...(while) the great Pyramids, like silent guardians, were outlined against the midnight sky.

The next morning they boarded a river steamer for the six hundred mile trip up the Nile, viewing the colossal statues of Rameses at Memphis, and the pylon temples at Abydos and Luxor along the way. Finally, on the eighth day, their destination was at hand:

> ...entering small boats that were drawn up beside our steamer, we were rowed across the river... Thereafter a delightful donkey ride... Into the valley we rode and the sun, almost overhead by now, beat down with pitiless force while the glare from the bare rocks and the heat from the burning sands made a furnace of this narrow, winding valley... The ride seemed endless!...
> Finally we were rejoiced to see the rude wooden gate protecting the entrance to the Valley of the Tombs of the Kings. Here, outside the gate was a crude shelter under which the donkey boys and their little beasts could rest; and inside the gate gleamed the white canvas tent of soldiers guarding the treasures in the tomb of Tut-Ankh-Amon.
> Showing our tickets, and entering through the narrow gate, we climbed a fairly steep path, slowly (for the temperature here was 130°)... till we reached a rough stone wall and, leaning over it, we gazed into the pit from which the entrance to Tut-Ankh-Amon's tomb can be seen. A few laborers were working here removing stones and debris, but the tomb was closed. It was just the time when Carter[2] and the Egyptian government were having their controversy and, in consequence, no one was allowed to enter the tomb—even Carter himself being barred. It was a great disappointment...
> We had applied for tickets of admission into the tomb but there was no help for it, so, taking some pictures of the deep excavation, we passed on up the hillside...

The fact that FRG recorded the site on film was, for him, a normal procedure, because the artist was an avid photographer. Back in New York his still and motion pictures of the Egyptian journey would become the source of many an evening's entertainment for family and friends.

This interest in photography dated back to the 1890s, to days on the Philadelphia *Public Ledger*, when he had taken pictures of street cars, trees and barns. During his first trip to Europe in 1905 FRG had written to Florence:

> I have had my ship negatives developed and I wish I hadn't as many were ruined which I could have saved I'm sure... I'll send you prints when I return to Paris.

The illustrator enjoyed the camera as a diversion, a hobby which allowed him to record all sorts of natural and man-made objects. With each clicking of the shutter the image was captured, not only on film but also in the artist's own mind.

Soon after the construction of the Avon house, he had a darkroom built under the first floor stairway and eventually another, in a third floor space adjacent to his studio. As early as 1907, Gruger had begun experimenting with color photography, then a complicated procedure which resulted in pictures on glass plates. In one such early effort, Florence, her copper hair shining, is shown holding a large yellow bowl of red and green peppers on a blue apron-covered lap.

For black-and-white shots FRG used a graflex camera with a focal-plane shutter. He photographed a wide variety of subjects—a close-up of locomotive wheels, automobiles, machinery, bridges, a waterfall, men in straw hats, women with parasols, sailboats, the surf and bathers along the beach at Avon.

FRG's fascination with photography led him to produce pin hole cameras for his children, as well as to construct cardboard models of cameras and special lens fittings for the enlarging equipment. He also built a stereopticon, a stereo-slide viewer which produced a merged, three-dimensional picture.

When FRG returned to his Fortieth Street studio, he and Arthur William Brown began making experimental home movies. On one occasion he wrote to his son:

> Recently we have had several movie shows here in the studio. They seem ever popular.
> Some evenings ago we dined at Brownie's. Rube Goldberg, the cartoonist, dropped in. He has the same sort of camera and recently took it abroad with him. Brownie says his pictures are no good,

Typical Arrow Collar advertising illustration by J. C. Leyendecker

Cover painting by J. C. Leyendecker
Collier's Weekly, September 29, 1917

and he is maliciously anxious to have Rube come down here and see mine which Brownie considers particularly good. My vanity being tickled, I shall make Rube very welcome.

When FRG bought a Bell & Howell movie camera for Ted, his instructions for its use resembled a credo for his own compositions:

> Get life and motion and occasional shots at the historic buildings which give the locale and whenever possible use the signs and railroad station labels for your titles...
> When making pictures in a town of major historical interest one is inclined to over-emphasize the historical aspect. Go out after the picturesque side always and especially go out after the life and movement in the town... Take five or six second shots of the most important historical spots and eight or ten second shots of life and movement. Take a larger number of those at various points. Then when they are all spliced together the picture will convey the idea of the time with emphasis upon its life and picturesque qualities.

During the summer of 1924, FRG alternated between his studio at 80 West Fortieth Street and Avon, retiring to the seaside resort on weekends. It was during this time that he became well acquainted with J.C. Leyendecker, whose studio was a floor below his. A Chicago-born illustrator just two and one-half years Gruger's junior, Joseph Christian Leyendecker had begun illustrating for *The Saturday Evening Post* in 1899, only shortly after FRG. Over the past decade he had become one of the *Post*'s leading cover artists, at the same time gaining a reputation for his depictions of the idealized American male in a series of advertisements for Arrow Collars, the House of Kuppenheimer Clothes and Interwoven Socks.

Leyendecker, a bachelor, commuted to New York from his home in New Rochelle, where he lived in partial seclusion. Yet while in Manhattan he enjoyed the company of the Grugers. Evidence of their friendship exists in the form of a painting presented to them, one which had been reproduced on a 1917 *Collier's* cover. It had been made by Leyendecker during the period when FRG's own drawings for *Collier's* were accompanying stories by Mary Roberts Rinehart and Edna Ferber.

J.C. Leyendecker had shared the Beaux Arts studio with his brother Frank, also an illustrator, but when Frank died in April, 1924, J.C. decided to move to a smaller space down the hall. In October he sublet his duplex apartment to FRG.

The new quarters were spacious—an entrance foyer, living room, kitchen and two-story studio on one level, with two bedrooms and a bath on the mezzanine. Several of the rooms had paneling and decorated ceilings, while the floors were connected by a handsome stairway with a wrought-iron balustrade.

J.C. Leyendecker was soft-spoken, retiring and not very social. Nevertheless, he and FRG often dined together or relaxed in each other's studios. Leyendecker, after observing his fellow artist at work, once commented: "You paint in black-and-white." And in his role of friend and neighbor, he stopped by before Christmas to trim the Grugers' tree.

Here were old friends, Troillus, Cressida, many others; the same noble company who swept through those other pages, leaving her dazzled.

BARBRY by HENRY MILLER RIDEOUT
The Saturday Evening Post, May 12-June 9, 1923

FRG enjoyed Leyendecker's former apartment because it provided increased work space, but he noticed one drawback concerning its location, at the corner of the building facing Sixth Avenue and Fortieth Street:

> The Sixth Avenue Elevated seems to try to annoy. They send every train along with one flat wheel which makes an ungodly noise and makes it hard to hear over the phone...

On the other hand the Beaux Arts was but a block away from the New York Public Library, a convenience for occasional research.

Although an avid reader, FRG was more likely to buy a book he wanted than to depend upon the Library. His acquisition of books in the field of art as well as that of general literature was continuous. FRG's interest ranged from classical literature to modern, which had been true even when he was a youngster. He once remarked:

> I have been tucked into the corner of the davenport renewing a slight acquaintance with the stalwart shades of Aristophanes and Phidias, Socrates, Sophocles and diverse others, surrounded by democratic politics which seem strangely familiar!

The space at 80 West Fortieth Street, as well as later on at his home near Gladstone, N.J., provided amply for the expansion of his collection of books, which was extraordinarily diversified.

The roomy apartment, No. 52, was suitable for more entertaining than had been the case previously. Once settled, and after Florence had seen to some redecorating, the Grugers entertained as many as twenty people at one time. During the winter of 1925-26, Leyendecker, Neill, Booth, Wittmack, Brownie and Forman were frequent visitors. Norman Rockwell also dropped in occasionally. Twenty-two years FRG's junior, he later recalled: "Because he was older than I was, I just didn't pal around with him."

Rockwell had begun his long association with the *Post* eight years earlier, and often since then an issue of the magazine would include a cover by him and several illustrations by FRG. About the latter, Rockwell said simply: "I admired him very much." [3]

In February, 1925 Gruger was visited by a student committee from the Brooklyn Institute and asked to speak there. On March 18th he did, with Florence noting:

> Mr. Rockwell was here to dinner—afterwards he and Fred went over to Brooklyn where Fred gave a talk at the Art School.

The invitation extended to FRG was probably a result of his having been featured in an exhibition at the Anderson Galleries a few months before. This show, held during November 1924, presented, in addition to FRG's, works by Henry Raleigh, Wallace Morgan, James Preston and George Wright. Gruger was represented by ten drawings, among which were illustrations for stories by Owen Johnson, Booth Tarkington, Joseph Hergesheimer and Irvin S. Cobb.

FRG was self-conscious about exhibiting, considering it a form of self-promotion, so he never sought such opportunities and seldom accepted invitations to participate. As early as 1901, when the Newspaper Artists' Association held its first exhibit in Philadelphia, his work was absent. Nor was he represented in any of their subsequent shows, or in the Pennsylvania Academy annuals. His work appeared in the annuals of the Art Directors' Club in New York, but was submitted by others. But the invitation from the Anderson Galleries was different, since the chief concern of that establishment was the sale of fine books. [4]

All five of the exhibiting artists were illustrators. Although showing together for the first time, they were not strangers to one another: George Wright had been a student at the Academy when FRG and Preston were there; Wallace Morgan, once an artist-reporter for the New York *Herald,* had known Gruger during his brief stint on that paper; and Raleigh had likewise been on the art staff of the *Herald.* But the common bond between them now was that each illustrated for *The Saturday Evening Post.* It was no coincidence that, on the opening day of their Anderson Galleries' exhibit, the *Post* had a full-page ad in *The New York Times.* The magazine boasted a circulation of "More than two million and a quarter weekly," and while a copy regularly consisted of over two hundred pages of stories and ads, it still cost only a nickel.

During the 1920s a surprising number of illustrations showed the influence of Gruger's style, for there were half a dozen men who unabashedly followed his lead. One of the characteristics which set his work apart from many of the others was his failure to incorporate pictures of pretty, well-groomed types of people whose near-classical appearance had become the vogue. Beautifully attired, svelte females who populated the illustrations of Gibson, Flagg, Raleigh, Leyendecker, Pruett Carter and Charles D. Mitchell were not a part of Gruger's artistic vocabulary.

"I can't do it, I can't do it at all—it's not me," he would tell Arthur William Brown.

Brownie suggested that FRG study the fashion magazines, and agreed to help him absorb the formula for portraying the nattily-dressed fashion plates. But the

Shortly after the above illustration appeared in print, FRG received the following letter,

August 31, 1923

Dear Mr. Gruger,

I am refinishing my studio and would like very much to buy one of your originals for my wall. I was particularly struck by a picture you made for a *POST* serial entitled "Barbry". It showed a young girl dreaming in an attic beside an old trunk. Above was a vision of classic heroes. This is one of my favorites, but if there will be any difficulty in securing this particular picture I would be pleased to have one of your own choosing.

Cordially yours,
Norman Rockwell

It is very likely that this illustration may have inspired Rockwell to use a similar device in his mural, "The Land of Enchantment" in the New Rochelle Public Library. The mural was also reproduced in *The Saturday Evening Post,* December 22, 1934.

"Aren't you even going to lift your hat to other women if you remarry, or whatever it is you are going to do?
Illustration by John LaGatta, *Delineator,* October 1929

John Lagatta, a younger illustrator, was just appearing on the scene with his ultra glamorous
females, the kind of "'chromium-plated women" that Gruger never attempted to depict.

glamour girl was not Gruger's forte, and he did not attempt to draw what he referred to as "those chromium-plated women."

Speaking once on the subject, he stated:

> One may perceive the charm of smart clothes and exquisite equipment, of beautiful women and well-dressed men, of trimmed hedges and smooth lawns and weedless paths...I could never do anything with it so I left it to others and contented myself with admiration of what they did.
> For me the weathered street, the lived-in houses, the old trees...Used belongings, comfortably worn and pushed about into homely order long before the incident of the story occurred. To remain, bearing the scars of use, long after it has passed.
> Perhaps that is the poetry of character.

FRG had refused an invitation to be a judge in the Miss America Beauty Contest in Atlantic City for essentially the same reason. One year a group of well-known artists were invited to serve in that capacity. Flagg, Christy, Rockwell and Brownie were among them, as was Gruger. But while the others accepted, enjoying their perquisites, which included chauffeur-driven limousines, suites of rooms and lavish banquets, FRG declined. "I'm not a pretty girl type of artist," he said, implying an inability to pass judgment on what he didn't draw.

For several years the Grugers' personal schedule followed the familiar pattern: summer months in which FRG worked in New York, joining his family on weekends at Avon; winters in which Florence travelled to Europe, to be joined by FRG at a later date. For four years Ted and his father maintained an apartment in Paris, one which Ted selected in 1925. It was on the Left Bank not far from the intersection of the Boulevards du Montparnasse and Raspail. FRG wrote to his son, whose job had caused him to be transferred to Paris from Brussels:

> You can use it of course for the major part of the time and we will camp there occasionally...

One year FRG and his wife had planned to embark for Europe in November, but on the 28th of that month Florence noted in her diary:

> We were to have sailed this morning on the *Rotterdam*—hope to make the *Mauretania* on December 15.

As the date approached it was apparent that there was still too much artwork to be completed, so FRG persuaded her to leave without him. Before long they were reunited in Paris and by spring were touring Naples, Capri, Amalfi and Sorrento.

During the summers FRG looked forward to the weekend trips to Avon, where he could escape the oppressive heat of New York City and the view from his studio window of Bryant Park, full of men sleeping on the grass. Sometimes Eddie Wittmack or Franklin Booth accompanied him and they would all relax on the beach, take motion pictures of their activities or play Michigan Rummy. On occasion they also went for a Sunday drive to Rumsen, N.J., or to view the huge dirigibles at Lakehurst. One year, just prior to Florence's birthday, she and FRG drove to Lancaster, where they revisited the old homes and schools of their childhood.

Because of the ready availability of the Paris apartment, the Grugers sold their Avon home in 1926. Unable to get to Europe that year, FRG wrote to Ted about the events in New York:

September 23, 1926

> Wednesday night Mother and I went to the Strand to see if we'd agree with you about Mary Pickford's "Sparrows"...
> Tonight at the Algonquin all the tables were empty— where there should have been two hundred diners there weren't a dozen—a waiter who stood in front of my table eyeing the array of empty chairs and neatly folded napkins turned and remarked, "Well, I hope it won't rain—I guess maybe Dempsey will knock that Tunney out early!"
> There were six sections to the noon train and dozens of extra trains of maximum capacity were run through the day to accommodate the mad crowds that are rushing to the arena in the Sesquicentennial grounds...[5].

The following summer FRG was in the Beaux Arts Studio without the possibility of a weekend retreat. In May of that year a drawing of his, produced for the Gruen Watchmakers Guild, had won the Gold Medal for Black-and-White Illustration at the Art Directors' Club annual. [6]

Perhaps as a result of the award, an increasing number of art editors offered commissions to Gruger, for at that time he produced his first work for *McCall's* and an increasing amount for *Harper's Bazaar, Cosmopolitan,* the *Post* and *Woman's Home Companion.* For the last mentioned he did the drawings, two in full color, for Edna Ferber's "Show Boat," while for the *Post* he was regularly illustrating stories by I.A.R. Wylie, Joseph Hergesheimer and Donn Byrne.

"I'm going to tell you something that you ought to
know," Marion said; "I think you ought to hear the
whole story."

ONE OF MY OLDEST FRIENDS
by F. SCOTT FITZGERALD
Woman's Home Companion, September, 1925

The 1920s was FRG's busiest period, the time when he produced the greatest number of illustrations for the largest number of magazines. His production was astonishing, amounting to over one thousand drawings for sixteen publications.

FRG had gradually acquired a reputation for doing period drawings, having mastered the concept of the total picture, including its architecture, costumes, types of furniture and characters. There was authenticity in his compositions. As he wrote in a letter to Ted:

Things continue to amble along about the same. I sit down at the same hour and push my pencil around on the same kind of paper for about the same number of hours each day; but not with the same results. Sometimes better, sometimes not so good.

This may sound a bit monotonous but, strange as it may seem, it is not. Each story is a sort of adventure into somewhere else. Since I seem to have graduated out of the field of commonplace everyday life for which I have rather less aptitude I am having a good time. I have just made a short visit to Boston in the late (18)40s, conducted by the fertile imagination of friend Hergesheimer and tomorrow I shall return to the stricken field hard by Bethlehem some seven hundred years ago, in company with Mr. Donn Byrne. I am having a good time. Last week, in the same good company, I drifted about in a small town in Ireland shortly after the Norman invasion there and enjoyed that...In the interim...I took a back somersault into the dim past at the request of a genial Mason from "The Masonic Outlook" and I had reason to be thankful that I had read the "Golden Bough"...

During the summer of 1926 FRG had seen a good deal of Arthur William Brown, until he and Flagg decided to take a trip to Hollywood. FRG showed no desire to join them, having spoken to Henry Forman after his trip there the year before, and concluding: "Hollywood it seems contains not a single human intellect..." Brownie and Flagg vacationed in California for six weeks, staying at the Ambassador Hotel, where F. Scott Fitzgerald and John Barrymore had adjacent bungalows. Brownie enjoyed relating how he and Flagg hobnobbed with the celebrities:

John Barrymore lived...with his pet monkey in a cage. "The only virgin west of the Rockies," John said of her.
Both Scott and his wife, Zelda, loved practical jokes and Zelda had Barrymore crazy because every morning she would put under his door a love letter signed "Rex, the wild horse." [7]

This sort of caper didn't appeal to FRG, who was content to settle for a trip to Bermuda with Florence the next year. As he wrote to Ted:

October 29, 1927

Suddenly I grew very much fed up with work and suddenly I arose and, tossing my implements of labor upon my table, I proposed to Mother that we hie us to Bermuda. So, after a perfectly smooth and partly sunny voyage, which was very enjoyable, we find ourselves here...
Of course, the first thing we did was to visit Spanish Point. Spanish Point is completely shut. Many trees are gone, several of the graceful places are no more and old Abergyle is but a ruin. A field of onions struggles along where the two rows of cedars pleased us so much—a recent tornado ripped off the roof and left a most ghastly ruin—two black chimneys and a dreary gable survive and out of all the little grove of palmettos that used to live in the angle of the wall only one poor dwarf remains. At Maycliff we saw Mrs. Gorman standing at the door and Mother went in to talk to her.
...over on this side of the bay everything looks lovely as ever and Mother and I have picked out several agreeable locations and several charming houses and find the idea of a winter home as inviting as ever. But Grugie (Elizabeth) is to be married on the last day of the year and we can't be leaving Da (Dorothy) alone...

That winter FRG began dreaming of a four-month tour around the world:

November 11, 1927

... We started to see how far it would be to Hawaii... Bali... Benares and Delhi... and felt that we would enjoy the long train rides the more if we had pleasant memories of Rangoon and Mandalay and Singapore to chat about... Calcutta and Bombay... it was only natural that we return by way of the Red Sea, Suez, the Mediterranean and make a detour to Paris...
All this should convince you that we are still youthfully aware of what joys the future may hold!...

FRG had just celebrated his fifty-sixth birthday. Like other successful magazine illustrators, his earnings were considerable. Following the advice of Arthur William Brown, he ventured into the stock market, as he informed his son:

September 16, 1927

I myself have started in to gather up all the American Water Work stock I can buy. I didn't start soon enough but bought a hundred shares at 88 in time to benefit by a hundred percent split and the new shares stand at sixty-odd now. I shall buy more as I can...
I believe the A.W.W. will split again in about a year, it also yields some eight percent on my investment...

October 12, 1927

I have just blown myself to some three hundred shares in three separate Public Utilities. I am assured by those authorities in whom I have confidence that each share I purchased at from $20 to $27 per in ten to fifteen years will be worth about a thousand what with stock dividends, splits, and the like. They are managed by a very careful sort of gang of financial and business geniuses and while I am a skeptic in all such matters, yet I believe my advisers are well informed and sincere.
Brownie originally paid around twenty-five dollars per for his Water Work stock some three years ago—that has increased in value now to the equivalent of five hundred dollars per share. The companies of which I speak are the same structure and managed by the same type and recommended by the head and front of one of our first-class brokerages who is a great friend of Brownie's and who made Brownie's fortune for him...

But Brownie's "fortune," as it turned out, was made and lost on paper. Just prior to that fateful day in October, 1929, when the stock market began its plunge, Brown and his wife Grace were vacationing on the French Riviera. Unfortunately they returned to New York just a few hours too late to save the million dollars they had amassed in stock assets.

The stock market crash apparently had little effect on FRG's style of living. In April, 1930 he and his friend Dudley Summers were vacationing in Bermuda, from where he wrote Florence:

April 21, 1930

...Lord it's silly to live in the ghastly climate of N.J., N.Y. and such places when one could enjoy existence so much more in such a place as this or the Riviera...

The men stayed in Hamilton but roamed over the island taking 16 m/m movies.

April 24, 1930

...I am afraid my pictures are not good because I couldn't keep the lens free from salt spray long enough to make a picture. I fear there will be few good pictures to show you...

April 27, 1930

...Color photography is a difficult problem. I've never been so at sea... My speed, I take it, is a five dollar Brownie bound in pink leather.

The following September Florence went to Bermuda, and FRG wrote from New York:

...have a grand time and do any old thing your little heart desires and the hell with what it may cost...

Although the Depression was taking its toll among illustrators, his work was just as sought-after then as before:

March 7, 1929

Dear Mr. Gruger:
I wonder if you can imagine with what thrill I picked up the *Cosmopolitan* just now and saw with what superb discernment and brilliancy you have done my Rarirks.[8] You *have said* in your drawings what I tried to say in 100,000 words. I am your debtor!

Fannie Hurst

December 14, 1930

Dear Mr. Gruger:
I was delighted when I learned that you were to illustrate my story,"The House of Darkness;" I had written the *Post* that I hoped you would. On a recent trip East I saw some of the originals in the offices of the *Post*...
Costain[9] has written me that the other originals that have come in since I was in Philadelphia are even better than the ones I saw. They must be good, then! I am very glad that you had time to do them...

Sincerely yours,
C.E. Scoggins

February 7, 1931

Dear Mr. Gruger:
...Your pictures not only inteprreted almost what I saw in my own mind; they must have added tremendously to the atmosphere for the reader. That's why I wrote Costain I hope you'd do them. In the story I had tried for a certain mystic touch, and unimaginative pictures could have spoiled it in no small degree...

Sincerely yours,
C.E. Scoggins

June 10, 1934

My dear Mr. Gruger:
I have been getting up my nerve for some time to thank you for the perfectly delightful illustrations

"The pain that lies under the heart," Avery had written in his strange inchoate torment. "Avery," cries Rarick, "was that your only heritage from me?"

FIVE AND TEN by FANNY HURST
Cosmopolitan Magazine, July 1929, page 55

His deep voice rolled on into prayer; its quiet volume covered their uncertain murmurs.

THE HOUSE OF DARKNESS by C. E. SCOGGINS
The Saturday Evening Post, January 10, 1931, page 29, 30

"Where did she go? What became of her? Was she murdered? What happened to Eve Durand?"

BEHIND THAT CURTAIN by EARL DERR BIGGERS
The Saturday Evening Post, March 31, 1928, page 5

"John Stafford, what have you been up to? After what I told you. And Mr. Lincoln! I am surprised."

THE FATHER by KATHERINE HOLLAND BROWN
Woman's Home Companion, October 1928, page 25

you have been doing for my Boyd stories. I have always been an admirer of your work in the *Post* —especially of the drawings for "Behind the Curtain." But naturally I have liked none as well as your pictures of the Boyds. They are all so exactly as I tried to describe them, even the house, that I now begin to find myself looking at the drawings and taking my own descriptions from them. I am still whooping over the one of the two old woodsmen in "Caviar to Candida," and I am more grateful to you than I can say.

Sincerely,
Walter D. Edmonds

From the editorial staffs of the magazines there was also continued praise:

May 2, 1928

Dear Gruger:
The drawings for the second part of "The Father"[10] are especially beautiful. I am ever so grateful to you...

Sincerely yours,
Henry B. Quinan
Art Editor
Woman's Home Companion

April 15, 1929

Dear Mr. Gruger:
I want to say again that these pictures that you are doing for Fannie Hurst's story are to my mind just about the finest thing of the sort that ever have been published anywhere. I thank you most sincerely.

Sincerely,
Ray Long
Editor, *Cosmopolitan*

June 30, 1930

Dear Fred:
I am so enthusiastic about the latest set of pictures[11] that you have sent us that I can't wait a minute to tell you that I think they are just about the best you ever did in your life.

Sincerely,
Ray Long
Editor
Hearst's International Cosmopolitan

Bessie Y. Riddell, art editor of *The Saturday Evening Post,* had likewise been a long-time Gruger admirer:

Rodney was led up to his post beside the commanding officer, the band struck up "When the Caissons Go Rolling Along" and the entire garrison — horses, foot guns and tanks — went by in review.

May 31, 1927

They are lovely pictures which you sent us this morning for Charleston.[12] Mr. Lorimer thought the hoodoo scene a wonder...

February 15, 1928

The illustrations for the first two installments of the Biggers story[13] have just arrived and they have so far exceeded our expectations that I don't know what words to use in thanking you...

December 1, 1930

Thanks for the illustrations which you left for us this morning.[14] They were wonderful. Mr. Lorimer is delighted with them. When Mr. Costain saw them he said, "It is too bad Mr. Scoggins can't see these originals because he would have been more thrilled than ever."

Soon after this last letter, Mrs. Riddell was replaced at the *Post* by a new art editor. FRG was naturally a bit apprehensive. Bessie Riddell had been a devoted friend.

In 1925 she had hired Dorothy as assistant art editor. Although the starting salary was only $20 per week, FRG's younger daughter had performed an important function for the artist, as Elizabeth recalled:

Dorothy used to try to protect father while she was assistant art editor of the *Post*... When the editors would want to phone and rush him she'd say, "I won't call him and if you do he'll be sore, because he will not hurry." And she used to keep them from pestering him, which was a help.

But her job lasted for only two years, and on November 28, 1927 FRG wrote to Ted:

Mr. Lorimer has been elected Vice President of the Curtis (Publishing) Company and as a result of necessary reorganization of the *Post*, Da is out. They are going to put men in place of as many women. I had a long letter of explanation from Lorimer...

As it developed, Fred's foreboding about the new art editor of the *Post* was unwarranted. W.T. (Pete) Martin was carefully primed to follow in his predecessor's footsteps:

When I became art editor, Bessie Riddell had one word for me. She said, "I want you to take care of Mr. Gruger, Mr. Mowat, Rockwell and Raleigh. Those are the four you have got to be careful of and take care of them and give them work. And they're sacred, practically," is what she said...

We never changed 'em (Gruger's drawings), not even an eyelash or an eyebrow. We just used them the way they were. Rockwell would submit five or six sketches and we'd O.K three or four of them and then he'd work from them. Gruger, we'd send him manuscripts and we'd take the drawings when they came in and we just published them, that's all.

RODNEY by LEONARD H. NASON
The Saturday Evening Post, January 21, 1933, pages 6 and 7

FRG's first communication from Pete Martin was in the form of a telegram:

June 15, 1932

WE SENT OUT SIX THOUSAND LETTERS TO OUR MAILING LIST TELLING THEM WATCH FOR YOUR ILLUSTRATIONS AS BEST TWO COLOR JOB ANY MAGAZINE EVER DID[15]...

July 11, 1932

Here is the next Marquand story.[16]
Mr. Marquand was in the office the other day and said some very nice things about your pictures.

Very truly yours,
Pete Martin

December 16, 1932

As I tried to convey in my telegram the enthusiasm about your pictures for "Rodney,"[17] is pretty tremendous around these parts.
Everyone seems to feel that what you have done in this set proves pretty definitely the infinite superiority of honest craftsmanship to the freaky sort of thing people seem to be doing elsewhere.
We are deeply grateful to you also for doing four fine pictures for us in so short a time.

Very truly yours,
Pete

All *Post* illustrators did not fare as well as FRG during the year these letters were written. Arthur William Brown once recalled:

All through my working life, I've kept an accurate account of all my commissions, with one exception, and that was the year 1932. I notice only two entries in January for the whole year and they were the *Post* and *College Humor.* The way things were going, I must have quit cold and said "to hell with it."

Even during the decade of the twenties, some periodicals reduced the number of illustrations used; others were forced to discontinue publication altogether. *Munsey's, McClure's* and *Everybody's* printed their final issues in 1929, and the *Century Magazine* ended the next year. The Depression took a similar toll in the thirties.

In 1932 FRG drew only a few illustrations for the *Woman's Home Companion* and *The Delineator,* and in May of that year he did his last work for *Cosmopolitan,* the final of ten Irvin S. Cobb "Judge Priest" stories, which series had begun in November 1930. But he continued to produce for the *Post,* the *American, Good Housekeeping, Woman's Home Companion* and occasionally others.

He was composing two illustrations for a J.P. Marquand tale, "Jack Still," when he consented to a rare interview in the spring of 1932. The occasion was an article for the *Post* about magazine illustrators, to be entitled, "Yes, We read the Story." The author, Wesley Stout,

127

In response to a request for a sketch or photo of himself for POST readers, FRG made the above drawings, with the written caption, "Of them that look at my drawings many think I look like this — but I don't — not a bit!

P.S. Nor like this either.

would be named editor of the publication six years later, upon the retirement of George Horace Lorimer.

The long article recounted interviews with four of the *Post*'s most prominent artists: Gruger, Arthur William Brown, May Wilson Preston and W.H.D. Koerner, with each relating his philosophy and experiences. FRG explained candidly:

> The man who says "I know nothing about art," and then proceeds to criticize a picture usually is well within his rights. He does know about the things the artist is drawing. Illustration is the craft of portraying to the reader things he does know. For example, he knows people. He is as much entitled as the artist to say whether the man the artist has drawn is the man the author has described. A picture of masons laying a brick wall must satisfy a bricklayer...
>
> Then an artist either must meet all these realistic exactions or must avoid the issue. If the former he is in danger of being no artist, but a draftsman and copyist. I knew in my case, at least, that I must draw romantic pictures and stay away from what I could neither attain nor interest myself in. I try to illustrate moods more than things, and pick my spots accordingly...

Ironically, just four days after the article appeared, FRG received the following letter from Pete Martin, the *Post*'s art editor:

> All through the good times we consistently advanced prices to our contributors, and we have held off cutting them in the hope that prosperity, if not just around the corner as many of our leaders have predicted, was within reasonable reaching distance. However, though there is a better feeling in the air, we are afraid that recovery will be slow and that it will be a long time before we get back to the old level. Under the circumstances, we feel justified in asking you to share the Depresseion with us and to accept a cut in your price from $400 to $350 a drawing beginning with the next story we send you.

There is no indication that this arrangement gave FRG much concern. On the contrary, he was, at that very time, planning the construction of a new country home in New Jersey.

notes for chapter 11

1 Shepard's, in Cairo

2 Howard Carter, the English archaeologist who discovered the tomb

3 Conversation with the author, December 31, 1972

4 The Anderson Galleries had also been the scene, in 1916, of the Forum Exhibition of Modern American Painters, a landmark show which included such artists as Arthur G. Dove, John Marin, Marsden Hartley and Alfred Maurer. A decade later the Société Anonyme exhibited there as well.

5 Gene Tunney became heavyweight champion of the world that night by defeating Jack Dempsey.

6 The jury of awards consisted of Charles Dana Gibson, Robert Henri, Joseph H. Chapin of *Scribner's*, author Matlack Price and George Wright.

7 Brown, *op. cit.*, p. 60

8 The family in her story, "Five and Ten," which appeared in six installments accompanied by fourteen FRG illustrations

9 Thomas B. Costain, a member of the editorial staff of the magazine

10 by Katherine Holland Brown

11 "The Bracelet," by Robert Hichens

12 One of an eight-part series on American cities by Joseph Hergesheimer

13 "Behind That Curtain," by Earl Derr Biggers

14 For "The House of Darkness," by C.E. Scoggins

15 For "Black Wolf," by Walter D. Edmonds

16 "Far Away"

17 "Rodney," by Leonard H. Nason

Photo by Joseph Janney Steinmetz

F. R. Gruger, working on illustrations of "Dakotahs Coming!" *The Saturday Evening Post,* January 15, 1938

W. T. Benda

Work of some of the illustrators resident in the studio buildings on West 67th Street

Harry Beckhoff

Gilbert Bundy

Walter Biggs

Chapter 12

When F.R. Gruger first considered building a home near Gladstone, New Jersey, he and Florence were already living in the Netherwood section of Plainfield, just twenty miles away. They had moved from New York in the winter of 1929-30 wanting to be near their married daughter, Elizabeth, and had rented the house at 755 Berkeley Avenue. By 1931 FRG had studio space in a downtown office building.

He was not very demanding about requirements for his studio, except when it was of a permanent nature, as in the homes he built. During the summer of 1928, for instance, the studio apartment in Paris was used in order to produce illustrations for *Redbook* and *Harper's Bazaar*.

The following summer he made some for the *Post, Good Housekeeping* and *Harper's Bazaar* in a cottage in Birdcliff, Woodstock, New York, which he had rented after being introduced to the area by Dudley Summers, who usually vacationed there. In addition to Summers, neighbors included John LaGatta and Charles McCarthy and painters Eugene Speicher, John F. Carlson and Henry Lee McFee.

While still living in the Beaux Arts Building, FRG rented a studio at 138 West Fifty-eight Street, seeking to escape from the increased amount of activity in the apartment, for Dorothy had returned from Philadelphia and Ted from Europe. The following year, 1930, saw yet another move, to the Rubens Studios at Fifty-seventh Street and Seventh Avenue, but FRG found the place depressing, precipitating his relocation in Plainfield.

When FRG purchased a tract of land in Chester Township near Gladstone, he offered an existing farm house on the property to Elizabeth and her husband, Morris VanBuren.[1] A new home was to be built for FRG. John A. Frank, an architect and a cousin, was asked to design it, but before the plans for a new house were completed, the VanBurens decided to remain in Plainfield, so the farm house was modified to Fred's and Florence's needs. As John A. Frank explained:

> The Gladstone house was an alteration and an addition to an existing farm house, the original building becoming the central part of the house. On the east toward the highway we added a studio, and on the west side a garage and kitchen. The original farm building was a two-story affair; the new house which I designed was to have been built further east on the property...[2]

The remodelled home was occupied in the summer of 1933. The fact that the Grugers now lived in Morris County, New Jersey, named for one of their son-in-law's ancestors, would not have been lost on FRG who once remarked proudly: "Great on early Americana, we are."

Although FRG valued his privacy, he missed the camaraderie and convenience of working in New York. A year after completing his country home he once again rented quarters in Manhattan, this time at 33 West Sixty-seventh Street, where he was soon joined by his old friend, Arthur William Brown. Harry Beckhoff, another illustrator who also shared the premises, recalls:

> In our building at 33 West Sixty-seventh Street there was Gruger, Brownie, Dean Cornwell, Gilbert Bundy and Johnny Gannam.
> Practically the front of the whole street was full of studio apartments. None of them had skylights; there were big side windows and north light. The building had duplex apartments, but Gruger's was just a regular big room, with a kitchenette and a bedroom. That's the way mine was, and Brownie's.

Most of the residents were artists. Dean Cornwell was creating book illustrations and working for *Cosmopolitan*; Gilbert Bundy's art appeared in *Judge, Life* and *Esquire*; Harry Beckhoff's in *Country Gentleman* and *Collier's* and John Gannam's on the pages of *Collier's* and the *Woman's Home Companion*.

Walter Biggs, illustrating for *Good Housekeeping, Woman's Home Companion* and *McCall's*, was there too, and Beckhoff remembers:

> Gruger, Arthur William Brown, Walter Biggs and I every once in a while used to go out and have breakfast together over at Child's Restaurant at Broadway and Sixty-seventh Street.

In the buildings along Sixty-seventh Street there were a good many other illustrators, including W.T. Benda, who lived next door; Eddie Wittmack, at the Hotel des Artistes a block away; and FRG's old friends, Everett Shinn and Wallace Morgan.

Gruger and Morgan had first struck up an acquaintance in the art department of the New York *Herald* in 1898, and renewed it the following year when they shared the press boat covering the America's Cup Race.

As a writer observed long after these events:

> The humanness of Gruger, the humor of Morgan, were mutually attractive, and a bond of liking and respect started then which still continues today—when they are co-deans of American Illustration.[3]

As for Everett Shinn, Ted recalls:

They were not singing yet; they were just hurrying. It was just a sound at first, like wind, like it might be in the dust itself, and cousin Drusilla hollering, "Look out!"

Father and Shinn must have come into contact fairly frequently because they both had apartments on the same block on Sixty-seventh Street. I remember one time crossing the street with father on our way to breakfast. We met Shinn coming back, stopped and had a brief chat. It is the only time I remember having met him...

FRG's illustrations from this period continued to draw praises from his colleagues:

February 14, 1934

I can see no reason why I shouldn't tell you personally that Mr. Scoggins should be very much indebted to you. So also should Mr. Hergesheimer and Mr. Lorimer. This week the *Post* really looks like something. It has been very drab—pictorially— lately...
This sounds like a blooming valentine. I just couldn't help getting off this bit of "gush." Your drawings are so damn worthwhile.

Dud[4]

November, 1934

...I enjoyed your pictures for Faulkner's story "Raid"[5]—Have been reading it on the boat to N. London on my way home to Scotland (Connecticut).
Hope to see you when we are back in the city—
Saw Billy Glackens and E. Shinn last week, also Franklin Booth...
Good luck and best wishes to you all in Gladstone.

J.R. Neill

April 16, 1935

Dear Fred:

This is a fan letter from three great admirers of yours, John Gannam, Harry Beckhoff, and your ob'd't servant, myself.
We want to tell you that your wash drawings in the *Post*[6] were, as they say in Hollywood, colossal.

RAID by WILLIAM FAULKNER
The Saturday Evening Post
November 3, 1934, pages 18 and 19.

Keep doing them that way and you'll soon have the New Trenders known as Victorians.
The drawings were delightful in their character and freshness. Do more vignettes...
Sorry I missed you Friday as I was away an hour...

Sincerely,
Brownie

Letters of appreciation also continued in an undiminished stream from the *Post*'s art editor, Pete Martin:

May 11, 1934

Thanks a lot for the illustrations and for the very effective layout which accompanied them.
I have used up my small store of superlatives in the past in regard to your work...

May 15, 1936

It seems that every day I am under the compulsion of writing you a letter telling you how much we like the work you are doing for us now, and today is no exception to the rule. Mr. Lorimer said some very nice things about the pictures Brownie brought over for you[7], some very, very nice things indeed...

Many of Gruger's admirers had become the proud possessors of his original illustrations. Hundreds of them were given away, free for the asking. Fellow artists, magazine editors, writers, art students—none who made a request was turned away. Novelist Clarence Budington Kelland, for instance, once reminded the artist: "I have hanging in my bedroom a small drawing of yours...It is the only picture in my house...", while from *Post* author Horatio Winslow:

Costain writes me that, thanks to you, I am going to have one of the originals which you made to illustrate "The Sun of Mithra."[8] I'm delighted about this as I've admired your stuff for a long time...

C.E. Scoggins wrote:

...Of course I'm going to ask if I may have some of the originals.[9] One of our prize possessions is an original of yours from one of my yarns some years ago.[10] My wife studied under Duveneck in Cincinnati, and your technique enchants her...

From writer Hugh McNair Kahler:

If I'd been given a chance to choose a Christmas gift from the *Post*, I'd hardly have dared to ask for the one I got from you and from them. It's a long, long time since I felt as I've been feeling ever since I found those two illustrations.[11]

From Pete Martin:

The author of "Contrabando," Mr. Karl Detzer, has written to the Editors saying how much he liked your pictures,[12] and also, wished to know what the possibilities are of getting one of the originals.

From author Glenn Allan:

Your swell illustrations for my "Pipe Major" story[13] arrived today and I can scarcely tell you how grateful I am to you. I am a new *Post* writer and never dreamed that I should have the honor of an FRG to hang over the desk...

133

And from Edward W. O'Brien:

> We were all extremely pleased with the illustrations you did for the last story...[14] I will now have one framed to go along with my vast collection of three so far. We are still waiting for you and Mrs. Gruger to come and see the blacksmith shop picture which hangs in our living room, and which I never tire of examining.[15] While Rockwell's scene in the first story is a wonderful picture, I believe that the dark background of your shop scene more nearly catches the atmosphere...[16]

Although FRG continued to be a generous donor, he retained more of his work after the mid-thirties, when Franklin Booth pointed out that perhaps his family might need to sell some of his pictures one day.

Gruger's rise to prominence on *The Saturday Evening Post* paralleled the career of George Horace Lorimer, and for four decades the two men were among the major contributing factors to the magazine's remarkable success. The December 26, 1936 issue of the *Post* was the last to carry Lorimer's name in the masthead, and he died the following year. When he relinquished the reins the great era of this illustrated magazine came to an end. At the same time the event signalled, in a sense, the demise of the Golden Age of American Illustration.

FRG continued to produce occasional drawings for *Post* stories for a few years, but his approach to illustration was no longer in favor. *Post* artwork was taking a new direction, imitating the movie's favorite device, the big close-up. Like other weeklies and monthlies it had succumbed to the so-called "He and She" art, with oversized faces four and five inches high, and little else. Instead of pictorial illustration with a feeling for the characters and their environment, the public was now served decoration in double-page spread, full color and irregular shapes.

As Brownie lamented:

> Somewhere in the 1930s a decided change was apparent in American Illustration...The editors of magazines decided the readers wanted entertainment and were going to drag you into stories with pictures that had a wallop. So many of the details we used to put into drawings were eliminated.[17]

Photography had also begun to make inroads into the Illustration field, crowding drawings and paintings off the pages. The Eastman Kodak Company's earliest promotions of photographs, rather than artwork, in advertising, was beginning to pay off.

Frontispiece and book jacket

"I don't live anywhere," she said at last.
FROM THE LIFE by HARVEY O'HIGGENS
Harper & Brothers, Publishers, 1919

134

They laughed some more at Sharkey. But walking matches were a fad all over the country.

UNCLE SHARKEY AND THE WALKING MATCH
by EDWARD W. O'BRIEN
The Saturday Evening Post, June 21, 1941

Readily enough the vintner rehearsed for him the town talk on the subject.

THE KING'S MINION by RAFAEL SABATINI
The American Magazine, April 1930

Photographs had also replaced drawings for most book illustrations. An artist like Gruger created eighteen illustrations to accompany the text for Lorimer's "Letters From A Self-Made Merchant To His Son" when it was published in 1903, and he continued to provide illustrative material over the years for books by William Allen White, Booth Tarkington, Anne Warner, Owen Johnson, Richard Harding Davis, Arthur Cheney Train, Henry James Foreman, Harvey O'Higgins and others. But during the Depression the number of drawings in each volume was reduced, and in most cases either limited to a frontispiece or eliminated altogether.

By the end of the 1930s the economic situation had improved but the magazine industry never recovered completely. More publications ceased, including *The Delineator* (1937), *Pictorial Review* (1939) and *Scribner's* (1939).

In the May 1, 1939 issue of *Time* there appeared an article entitled "U.S. Illustrators" which reviewed the accomplishments of this vanishing profession:

> As worthy as Gibson to be called the dean of
> U.S. illustrators, in the opinion of many artists,
> is a stolid, 68-year-old Philadelphian who lives
> in a white frame house and raises chickens in
> Gladstone, N.J. Frederic Rodrigo Gruger...
> After 1899 when George Horace Lorimer
> became editor of *The Saturday Evening Post,*
> Gruger became the mainstay of that magazine.
> The *Post*'s romantic and period fiction by such
> experts as Joseph Hergesheimer and Donn Byrne
> got half its atmostphere from Gruger's old-
> fashioned, deep-browed men and frail but credi-
> ble ladies.
> Though limited in range, Gruger's draftsman-
> ship and handling of dark and light masses could
> be compared with the French masters Daumier
> and Forain. He never used a model. The kind of
> cheap cardboard on which he drew with carbon
> pencil and lamp black is now known as Gruger
> board...

In that same year a New York photoengraving firm celebrated its fiftieth anniversary by issuing a series of twelve monthly folders featuring a dozen of the country's top illustrators.[18] The first, appearing in March, 1939, honored F.R. Gruger and his work. The May number included this note:

> In the last couple of weeks *Time* gave a brief
> resume of what these men have meant to this
> country, and to art throughout the world. It's in-
> teresting that they, as we did, picked Mr. Gruger
> as the dean of today's masters.

Continuity illustrations, interpreting the "Book-of-the-Month", released for reproduction in newspapers by King Features.

TAPS FOR PRIVATE TUSSIE by JESSE STUART

The next year FRG received a request from author Jerome Mellquist:

> I am preparing a book on Modern American Art which is to contain a chapter on Cartooning and Illustration. I like your work and am thinking of using an example of it in my book. May I see you at your convenience to discuss this further?...

In Mellquist's book, *The Emergence of an American Art* (1942), Gruger is described as:

> ...the perfect accompanist. His pictures always balance. Light and shade agree; draughtsmanship tells. He is as sound as old silver, and frequently his drawings have a similar beauty. He stands as the fulfillment of all that these men started out to do...
> Illustration is now a reminiscence of its own better days. Gruger alone retains his sound crisp excellence and expands with the years that pass...

The following year, as World War II raged on in Europe and the Pacific, FRG's last illustrations appeared on the pages of the *Post*[19], bringing to an end this forty-five year association.

During the war he did several series of illustrations of current best-sellers for King Features Syndicate, for reproduction in newspapers. The first illustrated Jesse Stuart's *Taps for Private Tussie*, and this was followed by *The Lost Weekend, Duel in the Sun* and the *Immortal Wife*. Each of the parts included three pen-and-ink drawings, arranged in a horizontal row, comic strip fashion. There were 120 installments over a three-year period.

In 1946, having concluded his career as an illustrator, FRG returned to the classroom once more, lecturing at Pratt Institute and, at the urging of Arthur William Brown, teaching a course in Composition to war veterans at the Society of Illustrators. FRG noted that none of his students had ever heard of him.

The following year Brownie, having been elected president of the Society, saw to it that FRG was chosen an honorary member.

In October, 1951 the Society of Illustrators celebrated its fiftieth anniversary with an exhibition of the "Big Four": Harvey Dunn, F.R. Gruger, Wallace Morgan and Norman Price. It was FRG's last public honor.

Visitors to the Society's headquarters on East Sixty-third Street saw a choice sampling of Gruger masterpieces: the principal illustration for "True Thomas" by Stephen Vincent Benet, the New England ladies from Joseph Hergesheimer's "Java Head," drawings for the "Mr. Moto" series by J.P. Marquand, "The House of Dawn" and "The House of Darkness" by C.E. Scoggins, George Agnew Chamberlain's "Man Alone," Donn Byrne's "Crusade" and Alice Duer Miller's "Sunrise." A dozen illustrations selected from thousands; the presentation of a career spanning half a century.

In August of that year FRG turned eighty. As he wrote to a friend:

> One of the troubles of long life is the departure of one's contemporaries. Many of mine have gone...[20]

Indeed, the preceding years had seen the passing of John Weygandt, William Glackens, John Sloan, May Wilson Preston, Wallace Morgan, John R. Neill, Franklin Booth, Neysa McMein, Henry Raleigh, Harold Mowat and Norman Price.

In November, 1952 Fred, Florence and Dorothy left for Mexico by car. They had travelled as far as Texas when FRG was taken ill. He was hospitalized in Corpus Christi for two months before being flown back to New York City where he died of cancer in Doctors Hospital on March 21, 1953. The funeral was held without services, after which F.R. Gruger, in accordance with his wishes, was cremated. His ashes are buried at the base of an American beech tree on the property near Gladstone.

IMMORTAL WIFE by IRVING STONE

notes for chapter 12

[1] Edward Morris Van Buren, Jr. had an illustrious family tree: His grandfather, Joseph W. Reinhart, had been president of the Santa Fe Railroad and his great-uncle was Charles Reinhart, the illustrator. President Martin Van Buren was a collateral ancestor. He was also a descendant of Lewis Morris, a signer of the Declaration of Independence and of Gouverneur Morris, who headed the commission which wrote the final draft of the United States Constitution.

[2] Conversation with the author, May 19, 1973

[3] "Wallace Morgan," *American Artists*, Phila., Gatchel & Manning, Inc., June, 1939

[4] Dudley Summers

[5] *The Saturday Evening Post*, November 3, 1934

[6] Illustrations for "No Hero," by J.P. Marquand

[7] Illustrations for "Put Those Things Away," by J.P. Marquand

[8] In the January 9, 1932 issue of the *Post*

[9] The illustrations for his *Post* story, "The House of Darkness," which appeared in six consecutive numbers beginning December 13, 1930.

[10] "Cat's Paw," *The Saturday Evening Post,* August 18 and 25, 1923.

[11] For "The Great Day," which appeared in the *Post* on January 4, 1936

[12] Appeared in five consecutive issues of the *Post*, beginning June 27, 1936

[13] The *Post*, February 25, 1939

[14] "The Far Away Look," the *Post*, December 13, 1941

[15] "Uncle Sharkey and the Walking Match," the *Post*, June 21, 1941

[16] Letter to FRG, June 23, 1941

[17] Brown, *op. cit.,* p. 75

[18] The twelve artists featured in the Gatchel & Manning Company publications were: F.R. Gruger, Robert Riggs, Norman Rockwell, Wallace Morgan, Walter Biggs, Charles Buckles Falls, John LaGatta, Floyd M. Davis, Al Parker, J.C. Leyendecker, Dean Cornwell and Harvey Dunn.

[19] A single drawing accompanying "The People's Choice," by Edward W. O'Brien, in the November 3, 1943 issue

[20] Letter to Edward Ryan of the Bell Syndicate, *Art Students League News,* March 15, 1952, p. 6

Norrie swore the Republicans were bewitched and bewildered, and it sure looked like a Democratic year.

THE PEOPLE'S CHOICE by EDWARD W. O'BRIEN
The Saturday Evening Post, November 3, 1943

On following pages, generally in chronological order, is a sampling of illustrations by F. R. Gruger. Because the use of color in the magazines was extremely limited during most of Gruger's career and because his work was so ideally suited to depict all the nuances of black and white in reproduction, FRG was not often assigned color illustrations. However, the few he did, as included in this book, indicate that Gruger had a good color sense which could have only added further lustre to his career.

Yet paradoxically we do not miss this color, for Gruger's pictures always convey a *feeling* of color in the figures and settings so that the viewer's own imagination can readily supply it.

Perhaps it is this involvement of both the artist's and the viewer's imaginations that most characterizes and elevates the work of this distinguished artist.

Walt Reed
Westport, Connecticut

SEEING FRANCE WITH UNCLE JOHN by ANNE WARNER
The Century Magazine, 1906
Collection of the Philadelphia Free Library

"My father would sit for hours, thinking, thinking"

TRAGEDIES by ESTELLE STURGIS
McClure's Magazine
October 1911, Page 610

THE BIG IDEA by WILL PAYNE
The Saturday Evening Post
September 9, 1911, Page 5

With This Material Lute Morrow Completely Lined the Soap Box

The Next Thing Meredith Remembered He Was in Icy Cold Water, Swimming.

MY LADY'S GARTER by JACQUES FUTRELLE*
The Saturday Evening Post, July 27, 1912, Page 17

There was a crash and a Shrill Scream

Second Use. THE MINE LAYER by C. J. CUTCLIFFE HYNE
The Saturday Evening Post, November 21, 1914, Page 17

*Jacques Futrelle was lost in the "Titanic" a few months before
this story was published.

He chalked squares upon the barn floor and practiced and practiced until he could hit a ball as many times as he pleased just over the chalk line.

THE CHAMPIONSHIP by GOUVERNEUR MORRIS
Everybody's Magazine, July, 1913, Page 21

He sat down in a battered chair before his ancient typewriter and, lighting his cigar, pondered the strange words that had been spoken to his chief in his hearing.

SAVED BY PROXY
by
EARL DERR BIGGERS

The American Magazine
June, 1914
Page 45

That's Fur Me to Know and for You to Find Out

"The Lining of My Stomach Is Not What I Could Wish the
Lining of My Stomach to Be"

SOMETHING NEW by P. G. WODEHOUSE
The Saturday Evening Post, July 10, 1915, Page 17

At His Own Table Belknap-Jackson Writhed Acutely

RUGGLES OF RED GAP by HARRY LEON WILSON
The Saturday Evening Post, February 20, 1915, Page 20

THE JOURNEY by LAURA SPENCER PORTER
Frontispiece, *Harper's Magazine*, January, 1924

Sunshine and shadows, a stirring past and a vivid present.

GRECIAN ITALY by HENRY JAMES FORMAN
Boni and Liveright publishers, 1924.

Frontispiece illustration in transparent watercolor, 12″ x 8″. The book is inscribed by the author, "To Frederic R. Gruger whose work is the best part of this book — and this on the word of the author, at that."

Palermo's market place is almost Oriental in color.

The streets of Cosenza are a fit setting for mediaeval drama.

The above illustrations have been reproduced from plates in the book, since the location of the originals is unknown.

A compositional study in oil. 6½″ x 8½″.

"Won't you say hello to me?" the woman persisted and smiled again. "I'm not allowed," Magnolia explained. "My mamma won't let me talk to show-boat folks."

SHOW BOAT by EDNA FERBER

Woman's Home Companion
April, 1926, Pages 9 and 10

Note: The location of the original art is not know. These two subjects have been copied from the reproductions in the magazine.

"What with the carousing by night and the waste by day a Christian soul can hardly look on it without feeling that some dreadful punishment will overtake us all."

He Felt Foolish, Drinking from a Girl's Hand. The Tea Was
Scalding and Very Sweet.

BLACK WOLF by WALTER D. EDMONDS
The Saturday Evening Post, June 18, 1932, Page 17

This and the illustration on page 151 were made four color as per
original instructions. However, for reasons of economy they were
reproduced in two color as explained in the telegram on the next page.

Compositional sketch.

Two preliminary compositional sketches.

"You're a Brave Boy," She Whispered. He Flushed and Wriggled Away

These two illustrations were copied from magazine reproductions because the location of the originals is unknown, but the compositional sketches were reproduced from the originals.

N24 76 DL=H PHILADELPHIA PENN 15 956A
F R GRUGER, UNION BLDG=
    9 WACHUNG AVE PLAINFIELD NJ=
NOTHING WRONG WITH ILLUSTRATIONS EXCEPT
THEY WERE TWO COLOR INSTEAD OF FOUR WE
SENT OUT SIX THOUSAND LETTERS TO OUR MAIL-
ING LIST TELLING THEM WATCH FOR YOUR ILLUS-
TRATIONS AS BEST TWO COLOR JOB ANY MAGAZINE
EVER DID REASON FOUR COLORS GOT SO EXPENSIVE
WE HAD TO CALL IT OFF FOR WHILE WAS AFRAID
TO TELL YOU BECAUSE DIDNT WANT TO UPSET YOU
MIDDLE OF RUSH WORK MAKING YOUR LAST COLOR
SET THREE COLOR AND TWO COLOR=
    W T MARTIN. S24N

Squirming slightly under Aunt Celestia's eye she planted a small panicky kiss on his ear.

THE FATHER
by
Katherine Holland Brown

Woman's Home Companion
August, 1928
Page 15

THE MAGIC OF MOHAMMED DIN by F. BRITTEN AUSTIN
Redbook, August, 1918, Page 37

From time to time Gervase smiled a little, quietly, when he thought no one was looking.

"SOMEWHERE IN —" by PORTER EMERSON BROWN
McClure's Magazine, July, 1916, Page 29

They walked the length of that block, the three together,
and there the episode ended.

ANGELA'S BUSINESS by H. S. HARRISON
Metropolitan Magazine, November, 1914, Page 25

"Zat Ees Funny too. Now Zat I Die You Talk of Money and Prison."

JERMYN THE MUNIFICENT by JULIAN HINKLEY
The Saturday Evening Post, December 5, 1914, Page 5

It flattered her to be seen so constantly in the company of the great Kimball, and admired of all women — Page 690

HER OWN SORT by CHARLES BELMONT DAVIS
Scribner's Magazine, December, 1915, Page 695

155

THE FLYING FISH by ARTHUR SOMERS ROCHE
Collier's Magazine, August 3, 1918, Page 12

Sanford Low Collection
The New Britain Museum of American Art

JAVA HEAD by JOSEPH HERGESHEIMER
The Saturday Evening Post, October 19, 1918, Page 17

"Most of the Captains Like China," Tauo Yuan said, "They Are
so Far Away from Their Families —"

JAVA HEAD by JOSEPH HERGESHEIMER
The Saturday Evening Post, October 19, 1918, Page 19

It Was a Good Demonstration of the Real Thing, All Right. I
Ain't Never Needed Anyone Since Then to Tell Me What War Is.

THE TAKER-UP by HARRY LEON WILSON
The Saturday Evening Post, January 4, 1919, Page 9

Property of Mrs. D. G. Summers

D. G. Summers said that he had asked to have this
illustration because it contained a lot of what FRG
had talked about in his class at The Art Students
League.

"It's all very well to talk of patience," Triona fumed, "but when one
is hag-ridden as I am—" Boronowski smiled again. "Histoire de
femme —", Triona passed his hand through his brown hair. "Yes,"
he said; "If you want to know it's a woman. She is the day-spring
from on high. And the best thing that could happen would be if she
knew I were dead."

TALE OF TRIONA by WILLIAM J. LOCKE
Good Housekeeping Magazine, July, 1922, Page 81

"Fred don't!" Jean's frightened breath caught. "Don't make a scene. He doesn't mean anything. Let's go, I'm tired and it's almost daylight. Dear - won't you?"

A LAW UNTO OURSELVES by RITA WEYMAN
Cosmopolitan, July, 1922, Pages 88/9

Janet Spence might have been a suppliant crying for mercy as she crouched there on the floor. Mr. Hutton had suddenly begun to devise a means of escape, but it was to late. "Marriage is a sacred tie", she sobbed. "And your respect for it even when the marriage was an unhappy one made me admire you and — shall I dare say the word — yes, love you. But we are free now, Henry."

GIACONDA SMILE by ALDOUS HUXLEY
Hearst's International Magazine, September, 1922, Page 24

The Next Moment a Cavalcade of Gentlemen Shot Past on Prancing Horses. Father Led All the Rest, as Was His Nature to Do.

MY BOOK AND HEART by CORA HARRIS
The Saturday Evening Post
September 1, 1923, Page 5

And Now at Last He Was Ready to Turn Back, Spent and Empty
Handed, to the Familiar Misery Whence He Had Come.

THE ENGLISH TUTOR by PERCIVAL GIBBON
The Saturday Evening Post
April, 14, 1923
Pages 5 and 7

"Really Sargent", Said the Commissar, "You Do Collect the Most
Extraordinary Specimens. What on Earth Is That Old Creature
There?"

THE LUNCHEON by W. SOMERSET MAUGHM
Cosmopolitan Magazine, March, 1924, Page 71

THE PYRAMID OF LEAD by BERTRAM ATKEY
The Saturday Evening Post, July 12, 1924, Page 22

"Am I Supposed to Adventure into the Bowels of the Earth" He Said Plaintively

As Long as I'm Active It's Well Enough, but Let Anything Stop
for a Minute, If I Get Alone on Diggery in the Woods . . .
Shadows and Dreams.

BALISAND by JOSEPH HERGESHEIMER
The Saturday Evening Post, August 9, 1924, Page 22

"I'd have run away if it hadn't been for a little crippled girl
I'd got fond of. She wasn't more than nine and I was a whale
of a feller about eighteen."

HEAVEN by BASIL KING
Cosmopolitan Magazine, December, 1924, Pages 86, 87

Bog Worked on the Kelly With a Drill Crew for Five and Six
Dollars a Day, Often in Water and Mud.

HOME FOLKS by GEORGE PATTULLO
The Saturday Evening Post, March 7, 1925, Page 4

"I Wish You'd Forbid Me to See Him."

IN PRAISE OF JAMES CARABINE by DONN BYRNE
The Saturday Evening Post, May 8, 1925, Page 3

"So You've Come Back With a Double Load of Baggage," He
Said Sneeringly, "The Trunk and Her."

MAN ALONE by GEORGE AGNEW CHAMBERLAIN
The Saturday Evening Post, January 9, 1926, Page 37

It Was Just as Culbertson Had Said, Only There Was Something
Else Culbertson Had Not Touched Upon — A Majesty, a Power

SUNRISE by ALICE DUER MILLER
The Saturday Evening Post,
April 10, 1926, Page 33

"Go out and feed the chickens and stop shivering there like a wet cat," said the innkeeper's wife disdainfully. "Leave your criminals to me" and she proceeded up the stairs with the laden tray. She sniffed disdainfully as she looked at the eleven men gathered about the table. Criminals indeed! They looked like common fishermen, laborers, small tradesmen.

TRUE THOMAS by STEPHEN VINCENT BENET
Good Housekeeping Magazine, March 1926, Pages 24/5.
J. C. Leyendecker, who occupied an adjacent studio at 80 West 40th Street, came in for a
chat while this illustration was in progress. He studied it a bit, then remarked: "I see you
have symbolized Judas." He wanted FRG to do it over in full color in oils, but the publication schedule did not allow the necessary time.

"I pretend not to notice that Pepita and Urdanta were in love, but with a man like Urdanta, things could not remain peaceful for long."

THE VIRGIN WARRIOR by BLASCO IBANEZ
Cosmopolitan Magazine, October, 1926, Pages 64, 5

Sanford Low Collection New Britain Museum of American Art

He Loosed His Clasp from the Nose of the Boat, Lifting His Hand in Salutation, and Suddenly Doubled Over, Disappearing into the Depth with a Boiling up of a Myriad Starry Bubbles.

VILLA BEATA by BEATRIX DEMAREST LLOYD
The Saturday Evening Post, April 30, 1927, Page 14

The Chant Was Like the Broken Breathing of an Inconceivable
Animal. Fearnes Was a Part of It "Efe Bruton, Efo que Name Rulon!"

CHARLESTON by JOSEPH HERGESHEIMER
The Saturday Evening Post, July 9, 1927, Page 11

GRANDMOTHER BERNLE LEARNS HER LETTERS
by I. A. R. WYLIE
The Saturday Evening Post
September 11, 1926, Page 8

He Had to Explain Twice, for at First It Was as Though She Were
too Frightened even to Listen.

While he worked at the memorial he had dreamed — so vividly that once or twice he had looked up and called a name.

THE OLD PEOPLE by I.A.R. WYLIE
The Saturday Evening Post, April 17, 1926, Page 5

Christ's teaching revises our estimates of men. An outcast may go into the Kingdom of Heaven before a canny man.

THE WISDOM OF FOLLY
by WILLIAM LYONS PHELPS
Good Housekeeping Magazine, May 1930, Page 85

"Don't cry! It's not your fault you're ugly."
Susie wailed the louder.

JANE'S FIRST LAME DUCK by JOHN GALSWORTHY
The Delineator, April, 1929, Page 11

In passionate tones she cried out in Gaelic to the piper, pointing to the door.

THE PORTCULLIS ROOM by VALENTINE WILLIAMS
The Saturday Evening Post, June 17, 1933, Page 18

The Emperor held her hand, looking at her with a strange smile.
While her two suitors — the suave Vicomte and the shy English
boy — watched her covertly.

THE EMPEROR'S AIDE DE CAMP by SIR PHILIP GIBBS
The Delineator, December, 1930, Page 8

Bayard Beatty
Wayne, Pennsylvania

June 20, 1933

The Art Director, The Saturday Evening Post

Dear Sir:
Our family hails from Scotland, so when Mr. Valentine Williams' story "The Portcullis Room" appeared in the "Post" last week, I was delighted. And you've chosen Mr. Gruger, one of the best of modern illustrators, to do the illustrations.

But from early childhood I've known what claymores and dirks and targets were; I wear the kilt, and play the bagpipes.

Now will you please pass this along to Mr. Gruger, because the rest is for him? — I wish to comment on the illustration on page 18 of the June issue.

The ribbons on the pipes should *not* be connected to the *top* section of all drone pipes — the ribbons are attached to the tops of the two smaller drones, then continue across to the middle section of the base drone, and then to the top of the base pipe. Am making a sketch of the pipes in playing position.

If I can be of any assistance to you in this connection, I should be glad to be called upon; for the past few years my hobby has been the Highland dress and the various weapons and ornaments that accompany it. I am "well stocked" with pictures and information about things Scottish.

In defense of writing to you on what you might consider a minor detail, I wish to add that every Scot in America will scan your drawings with keen eyes!

Hoping the above will be of interest, I am,

Yours faithfully,
T. B. Beatty, Jr.

173

Sir Robert, in boyish oblivion of all but his old friend, was asking a dozen questions.

THE KING'S MINION by RAFAEL SABATINI
The American Magazine April, 1930, Pages 14 and 15

RETREAT by WILLIAM FAULKNER
The Saturday Evening Post,
October 13, 1934, Page 17

Then It all Kind of Ran Together, Men Hollering and Horses Crashing all Around Us, and Then Hands Dragging Us.

174

"You Can Lick Him, Shag McCloskey; You Can Lick Him if You Try," She Urged.

THROW HIM DOWN McCLOSKEY by RICHARD MATTHEWS HALLET
The Saturday Evening Post, January 21, 1933, Page 11

"Well, Somebody Here Fired on United States Troops. I Guess This is Authority Enough".

AMBUSCADE by
WILLIAM FAULKNER

The Saturday Evening Post
September 29, 1934, Page 13

She Said: "Do You Think There's Enough Yankees in the Whole World to Whip the White Folks?"
AMBUSCADE by WILLIAM FAULKNER
The Saturday Evening Post, September 29, 1934, Page 12

W.T. (Pete) Martin

MING YELLOW by J. P. MARQUAND
The Saturday Evening Post, December 22, 1934, Page 20

EDITORIAL ROOMS
THE SATURDAY EVENING POST
The Curtis Publishing Company
George Horace Lorimer Editor
PHILADELPHIA

September 14th, 1934

Dear Mr. Gruger:

I think it would be a good idea if you would write a letter to Mr. Lorimer explaining the scheme of illustration you are going to use with "Ming Yellow". I am afraid I have been unable to explain it satisfactorily, and I would hate to have you do a lot of work if Mr. Lorimer does not prove sympathetic to the plan.

Mr. Frank Bensing is in the office now, and we were just talking about you, and he said he has been following your work for twenty years or more, and that he does not remember you ever having done an indifferent picture in that time.

Sincerely yours,

Pete Martin

ART ROOMS

Mr. Frederick R. Gruger
WTM-McK

176

INDIANS AT McKLENNARS
by
WALTER D. EDMONDS
The Saturday Evening Post, May 9, 1936, Pages 12, 13

"Go away!" Cried Mrs. McKlennar. "Quick! I don't Like You
Two! You Are Very Bad!"

These two illustrations and the one at the top of page 175 have been
reproduced from the magazine, the original art not being available.

The only kind of security . . . an opportunity to earn a living.

SECURITY by WALTER LIPPMAN
The American Magazine, May, 1935, Page 71

NO HERO by J. P. MARQUAND
The Saturday Evening Post
November 13, 1935, Page 20

I Found Myself Being Lifted Bodily out of the Water, Choking.
There Was an Excited Chattering of Voices Around Me.

He asked a Few Questions of the Servants. These Dealt Mainly
with the Appearance of the Stranger Mrs. Leidner and I had
Seen Looking Through the Window.

MURDER IN MESOPOTAMIA by AGATHA CHRISTIE
The Saturday Evening Post, November 23, 1935, Page 21

CONTRABANDO by CARL DETZER
The Saturday Evening Post
June 20, 1936, Page 21

He Tossed an Armload of Thorny Faggots on the Fire and the
Signal Leaped Upward

Every Day at Family Prayers Uncle Jason's Deep Voice Had
Engraved That Awful Picture a Little More Deeply on Her Mind.

THE GREAT DAY by HUGH McNAIR KAHLER
The Saturday Evening Post, January 4, 1936, Page 11

Delray, Florida
January 3, 1936

Dear Mr. Gruger:

If I'd been given a chance to
choose a Christmas gift from the Post, I'd
hardly have dared to ask for the one I got
from you and from them. It's a long, long
time since I felt as I've been feeling ever
since I found those two illustrations. I wish
the story had deserved them.

Thanks very, very sincerely,

Truly yours,

Hugh MacNair Kahler

Mr. F. R. Gruger

For his voice could search the heart, and that was his gift
and his strength.

THE DEVIL AND DANIEL WEBSTER
by STEPHEN VINCENT BENET
The Saturday Evening Post
October 24, 1936, Page 9

EDITORIAL ROOMS

THE SATURDAY EVENING POST
The Curtis Publishing Company
George Horace Lorimer Editor
PHILADELPHIA

September 1st, 1936

Dear Mr. Gruger:

Here is a story Mr. Lorimer
selected personally for you, because he thought
you would like it. We hope, very much, that
you will be able to get at it as soon as you
have finished the Mote serial.

Sincerely yours,

ART ROOMS

Mr. F. R. Gruger
WTM-McK

The Old Woman Parted Her Thin Seamed Lips; "You Are Young and Warm. You Should Not Grieve."

DELIA BORST by WALTER D. EDMONDS
The Saturday Evening Post
April 3, 1937, Pages 14, 15

The Other Women of the Household Joined Them Inside,
Chattering as They Examined Her Tattered Clothes.

SQUAW by
WALTER D. EDMONDS
The Saturday Evening Post
April 17, 1937, Page 17

"Can't I Go With You? Please," She Said. "I Can Do Hard Work,
I Can Cook. I Could Get Wood and Cook for a Lot of You." Her
Eyes Looked Pitiful to Him.

THE SPANISH GUN
by WALTER D. EDMONDS
The Saturday Evening Post
July 17, 1937, Page 13

She Straightened Up to Take the Candle off the Chest. "No, Pa's
Waiting. He Will Not Let the French Come By, if They Come
Even So Far As the Bridge."

Collection of Mr. and Mrs. Albert Gold

THE CAPTIVES
by
WALTER D. EDMONDS

The Saturday Evening Post
February, 13, 1937
Pages 10 and 11

Three Silent Men, Soberly Abreast, They Jogged Away Sou'eastward.

THE BROTHERHOOD by ALLAN SWINTON
The Saturday Evening Post, June 26, 1937, Page 14

THE PIPE MAJOR OF LITTLE SORROWFUL
by GLEN ALLEN
The Saturday Evening Post
February 25, 1939, Page 18

"I Drug Him Th'ough the Wiah and Found a Place Where He Could Bide in Peace."

Granny Blackchears taught Thin Jimmy how to read and how
to write his name, and more than that.

THE WITCH DOCTOR OF ROSY RIDGE by McKINLEY KANTOR
The Saturday Evening Post
April 15, 1939, Page 8

"She Can't Go Back on Account of Pat Is A-waitin' to Shoot
Any Man or Beast That Sets Foot in His Clearing."

THE BOBBYCOCK TROUT by McKINLEY KANTOR
The Saturday Evening Post,
May 20, 1939, Page 19

Chicago, Ill.
June 19, 1939

Co. Thornton Martin
The Curtis Publishing Co.,
Philadelphia, Pa.

My dear Mr. Martin:

May I say a word
of appreciation of the illustrations
for the Bobby Cock Trout Story of
May 20th were really something.
A good story is spoiled for me if
its illustrations are vapid and
silly, but Mr. Grugers have strength
and character, a really fine piece
of work. They are decidedly the kind
of drawings you don't find in
ordinary magazines. Long live the
Post.
Very truly,
Lucille Evely Hansen

188

FREEDOM'S A HARD BOUGHT THING
by
STEPHEN VINCENT BENET

The Saturday Evening Post
May 18, 1940
Page 12

He Didn't Know the Roads or the Ways, and Mr. Wade Caught
Him before Sundown.

"Your Grandaddy Shengo was a powerful man. It took three men
to put the irons on him, and I saw the irons break his heart."

189

Inscription reads: "With apologies to Aime Marot from whose painting ('89) I swiped these two horses. French painter circa '60-1900

BLIND McNAIR by THOMAS H. RADDALL
The Saturday Evening Post, August 10, 1940, Page 22/3

Publication of illustrations generated a lot of mail, both pro and con. *Post* readers especially seemed to take a personal interest in everything printed and delighted in finding real or imagined errors. It was the responsibility of the illustrator to make sure that any elements in a picture were accurately portrayed. A serious blunder was very embarrassing to the editors and might well end an offending illustrator's career at the *Post.*

On the right is a letter of enthusiastic approval. At the same time, however, an alert reader named Barbee recognized the poses of the horses as being from the original painting by Marot and wrote about it to the *Post.* This resulted in the exchange of correspondence between Pete Martin and FRG reproduced below.

Dear Pete:

Mr. Barbee is absolutely right. Let's put Canada Dry wise to him.

Yes, Sir. This is a proud day. There are folks above the nickel level. I always said so.

In your customary reply to him I hope you done right by me and that you told Mr. Barbee I had written full credit for M. Aimee Morot on the drawing itself.

I did that. If you don't remember — pull the drawing out and have a look.

What's all this you told Dorothy about a "Chicken Story" for the LHJ? Maybe Miss IARW wouldn't like such talk, or am I wrong?

Sincerely yours,

FRG

August 15th, 1940

PS — When I have a reply from you anent the above I will write Mr. Barbee a pleasant letter — dam' respectful and polite.

190

A considerable amount of time in preparing this book has been spent in trying to identify and date each of the pictures illustrated. Unfortunately, several have had to be omitted because it has been impossible so far to find any record of their place of publication.

Representative of that group are the two examples reproduced here, which appear to be illustrations for the Old Testament or of historical fiction about that era.

"We're guilty, lording. But it wasn't to be borne, this waiting and starving! You've the right to hang us. We'll climb the stockades and die as men should, if you'll say the word."

THE PIG OF PEN MYNYDD by HENRY JOHN COLYTON
The Saturday Evening Post, July 31, 1943, Page 24

The next to last illustration and, below the line, the last series of pen and ink drawings FRG made for book publication.

Berkeley, Calif.
Aug 20 - 41

My Dear Mr. Gruger —

Almost the first fiction story I ever wrote for the Post — out-and-out fiction, I mean — was graphically illustrated by you, and that's nearly thirty years ago now, God help us!

And now again you've done the pictures for a forthcoming edition of a book of mine and I've just seen them and I take pen in hand to tell you how happy I am that you were the artist unanimously chosen for the said job. Thank you sir!

Personally I'm delighted: the old Gruger truth is there and unmistakably there in every one of the drawings. And if the volume sells I know that a whale of a lot of people will buy it because of your work and not because of mine.

Why, the drawing of "Albert the Headwaiter" even looks as Alfred the original Alfred did. And, Connie Lee might almost have posed for the likeness of him!

With sincere regards and tremendous appreciation.

Yours Gratefully,
Irvin S. Cobb

Jeff Poindexter (Connie Lee) and Judge Priest

F.R. Gruger Chronology

1871	Aug. 2	Born Frederic Rodrigo Gruger in Philadelphia, the son of John Peter Gruger and Rebecca Rodrigo. His father was an amateur sculptor.
1879		Family moves to Lancaster, Pa.
1884		Meets William Arnell, an artist, who introduces him to the work of the Old Masters and illustrators Edwin Austin Abbey, Charles Reinhart and Charles Keene.
1880s		Attends Lancaster High School.
1890	Fall	Enters the Pennsylvania Academy of the Fine Arts. Studies with Thomas Anshutz, Henry J. Thouron, Robert Vonnoh and James P. Kelly.
1891		First work as a newspaper artist, for the Philadelphia *Record* and *The Item*.
	July	Employed by the Philadelphia *Press*, whose art staff soon includes John Sloan, William Glackens, Everett Shinn, George Luks and Edward Davis.
1892	Fall	Meets Robert Henri. Classmates at the Academy include Sloan, Glackens, Shinn, James Preston, Joe Laub and Maxfield Parrish. Begins working full-time as an artist-reporter for the Philadelphia *Public Ledger*.
1893	March	Joins the Charcoal Club, a breakaway from the Academy. Other members include Henri, Sloan, Glackens, Shinn, Davis and Laub.
	Fall	Attends Henri's Tuesday evening talks at 806 Walnut Street.
1895		Establishes a commercial art studio with Davis at 1510 Chestnut Street. Shares studio with Glackens at 1717 Chestnut Street.
	Dec.	Awarded the Sarah J. Field Prize for the best work in the student exhibition at the Academy.
1897	Jan. 26	Marries Florence Felton Gray in Chester, Pa.
	March 4	Covers President McKinley's inauguration for the *Public Ledger*.
1898	Spring	Works for the New York *Herald,* on loan from the *Ledger*.
	Fall	Returns to Philadelphia and the *Ledger*.
	Nov. 5	First illustrations appear in *The Saturday Evening Post*. Birth of daughter Elizabeth Rodrigo Gruger.
1899	Jan. 21	Helps design first modern cover for *The Saturday Evening Post,* assisting Guernsey Moore, J.J. Gould and Preston.
	May 1	First illustrations for *Ainslee's* Magazine. Studio at 1020 Chestnut Street. Friendship with John R. Neill, illustrator for the *Wizard of Oz* stories. Lives at 28 S. 34th Street.
	Oct.	Covers the *America*'s Cup Race for the *Ledger*.
1900	June	First illustrations for *Scribner's* Magazine.
	Aug.	First illustrations for *McClure's* Magazine.
1901		Studio at 729 Walnut Street; home at 3205 Summer Street.
	Sept.	First illustrations for *Success* Magazine.
1902	Jan. 21	Birth of son F.R. Gruger, Jr. Creates illustrations for the novels of Charles Paul de Kock, published by the Quinby Company of Boston. Other illustrators include Sloan, Glackens, Luks and Preston. Lives at 117 Broad Street, Chester.
	May	First illustrations for *Leslie's Popular Magazine*.
1903	April	First illustrations for *The Ladies Home Journal*.
1904	May 29	Birth of daughter Dorothy Gray Gruger.
	June	First illustrations for *The Century Magazine*.
	Summer	Home being built in Avon-by-the-Sea, N.J. Rents a house for the summer at Avon.
1905	April	First illustrations for *Munsey's* Magazine.
	June	First illustrations for *Everybody's* Magazine.
	Summer	Resides in new summer home at 316 Woodland Avenue, Avon. Studio in his home.
	Oct.	First illustrations for *Pearson's* Magazine.
	Nov.	Embarks for Europe, to research illustrations for Anne Warner's *Seeing France with Uncle John,* commissioned by *Century*. Resides at the American Art Association in Paris. Travels through France, Holland and Germany.
1906	Jan.	First illustrations for the *American Illustrated Magazine*. Returns from Europe.
	March	Suffers near-fatal illness. Residence and studio at Avon.
1907		Resides at Avon year 'round.
1908	March	First illustrations for *Youth's Companion* Magazine.
	Oct. 1	First illustrations for *The Delineator*.
	Winter	Resides in Lansdowne, Pa.; studio in Philadelphia.

1909		Resides in Lansdowne; studio in Philadelphia.			becomes one of the most popular offerings; enrollment reaches 140.
1910		Residence and studio in Avon.		May 29	Teaches final session at the Art Students League.
1911	Oct. 11	First illustrations for "Stover at Yale" appear in *McClure's*.		Summer	Residence and studio in Avon.
	Dec.	Vacations with family in Bermuda, residing at "Abergyle" on Spanish Point. Studio on Front Street in Hamilton.	1921	March	Wins First Prize for Black and White Illustration and Design in the Art Directors Club First Annual of Advertising Art.
1912	May	Returns from Bermuda to Avon.		April	First illustrations for *Woman's Home Companion*.
	Dec.	Second winter in Bermuda; residence at "Maycliff."		May	First illustrations for *Cosmopolitan* Magazine.
1913	May	Returns to U.S. from Bermuda.			Rents Riverside Drive apartment to John R. Neill.
	Summer	Residence and studio in Avon.		June	Leaves with family for England, residing at "Darent Hulme," Sevenoaks, Kent.
	Dec.	Sails for Bermuda.		Sept.	Returns to New York.
1914	Jan.	Returns to New York, Occupies the apartment of Julian Street at 138 W. 65th Street.		Dec.	Embarks again for England.
			1922	Jan.	Leaves for Paris and Rome.
	March	First illustrations for *Collier's Weekly*. To Bermuda.		Feb.	First illustrations for *Good Housekeeping* Magazine.
	April	Returns to New York with family. Plan to visit Cornwall, England aborted by the terminal illness of both parents and the outbreak of World War I.			Travels through Southern Italy, Sicily and Malta with Henry Forman, to research illustrations for his book.
	Sept.	First illustrations for *Redbook* Magazine.		March	First illustrations for *MacLean's Magazine*.
	Oct.	First illustrations for *Metropolitan* Magazine.		May	Returns to England; rents "Speldhurst Close" estate at Sevenoaks.
1915		Residence and studio in Avon.		June	To New York.
	Aug.	Listed by *Vanity Fair* as one of "a dozen of the most distinguished illustrators in the world."		July	Embarks for England with Arthur William Brown.
					Grugers travel through France, Germany and Belgium.
1916	Fall	Moves to New York City. Resides at 593 Riverside Drive; shares studio of Arthur William Brown at 233 W. 100th Street.		Sept.	Returns to New York.
					First illustrations for *Hearst's International* Magazine.
1917		Summer in Avon; winter in New York. Produces several illustrations and poster designs for the Division of Pictorial Publicity, to aid in the war effort, together with artists James Montgomery Flagg, Charles Dana Gibson, J.C. Leyendecker and many others.	1923	Feb.	First illustrations for *Harper's Bazaar*. Awarded First Prize in Black and White Illustration, Second Annual of Advertising Art sponsored by the Art Directors Club.
				June	Attends son's graduation from Yale; trip to Bar Harbor, Maine.
1918	Summer	Avon.		Sept.	Shares Arthur William Brown's studio.
	Fall	Returns to New York. Rents studio at 57 W. 57th Street; other artists there include Franklin Booth, Edgar Wittmack, Neysa McMein, Sally Farnum and James Montgomery Flagg.		Nov.	Moves to Beaux Arts Studios building; other occupants include J.C. Leyendecker, Norman Rockwell and Leon Gordon.
		Begins teaching Illustration at the Art Students League.		Dec.	Sails for Europe, joining family already there.
1919		Resides at 593 Riverside Drive; studio at 57 W. 57th Street.			Rents studio at 2 Rue des Italiens, Paris.
	Fall	Son enters Yale.	1924	Feb.	Trip to Milan, Venice, Trieste and Alexandria; travels the Nile to visit King Tut's tomb. Returns to England.
	Winter	Rents house at 99 Broadway, Dobbs Ferry, N.Y.			
1920	March	Gruger's Illustration class at the League			

April	Leaves for New York.
Summer	Beaux Arts Studio (80 W. 40th Street) and Avon.
Oct.	Occupies Leyendecker's studio in the Beaux Arts building.
Nov.	Exhibits at the Anderson Galleries with Henry Raleigh, Wallace Morgan, James Preston and George Wright.
1925		Family rents Paris apartment on Rue Schoelcher, which they maintain for four years.
	Summer	Avon.
	Winter	80 W. 40th Street.
1926	May	Travels to Europe, visiting Capri, Sorrento, Amalfi and Naples.
	Summer	Sells home at Avon.
1927	May	Awarded Gold Medal in Black and White Illustration at the Sixth Annual of the Art Directors Club.
	Summer	Vacations in France. Resides at Rue Schoelcher apartment; travels through Normandy and Brittany.
	Oct.	Trip to Bermuda.
1928	Feb.	First illustrations for *McCall's* Magazine.
	Summer	Resides in Paris apartment; tours chateaux of France.
1929		Writes "Illustration" article for the *Encyclopedia Britannica*.
	Summer	Rents a cottage in Woodstock, N.Y.
	Winter	Moves to Plainfield, N.J.; studio at 138 W. 58th Street, N.Y.
1930	March	First illustrations for *College Humor* Magazine.
	April	Travels to Bermuda with Dudley Summers.
		Relocates studio in the Rubens Studios building, 57th Street and 7th Avenue.
1931		Continues to reside in Plainfield, N.J.; moves studio to downtown Plainfield.
1932		Rents New York studio at 33 W. 67th Street; other occupants of the building include Arthur William Brown, Dean Cornwell, Harry Beckhoff, John Gannam and Gilbert Bundy.
1933	Summer	Moves to newly-built home in Gladstone, Chester Township, N.J.
1936		Relinquishes New York studio; lives and works in Gladstone.
1939	May 1	Article appears in *Time* Magazine referring to Gruger as "the dean of U.S. illustrators."
1943		Began series of 120 comic strip-style illustrations of serialized best-sellers for King Features Syndicate.
	Nov. 6	Final illustrations appear in *The*

		Saturday Evening Post.
1946		Lectures on Composition at Pratt Institute.
1947	Fall	Teaches Composition to war veterans at the Society of Illustrators.
		Elected an Honorary Member of the Society.
1951	Oct.	Included as one of the "Big Four" illustrators in an exhibition at the Society of Illustrators, to mark its 50th anniversary.
1952	Nov.	Embarks on a motor trip to Mexico; taken ill in Texas.
1953	March 21	Dies at Doctors Hospital, New York City, at the age of 82.

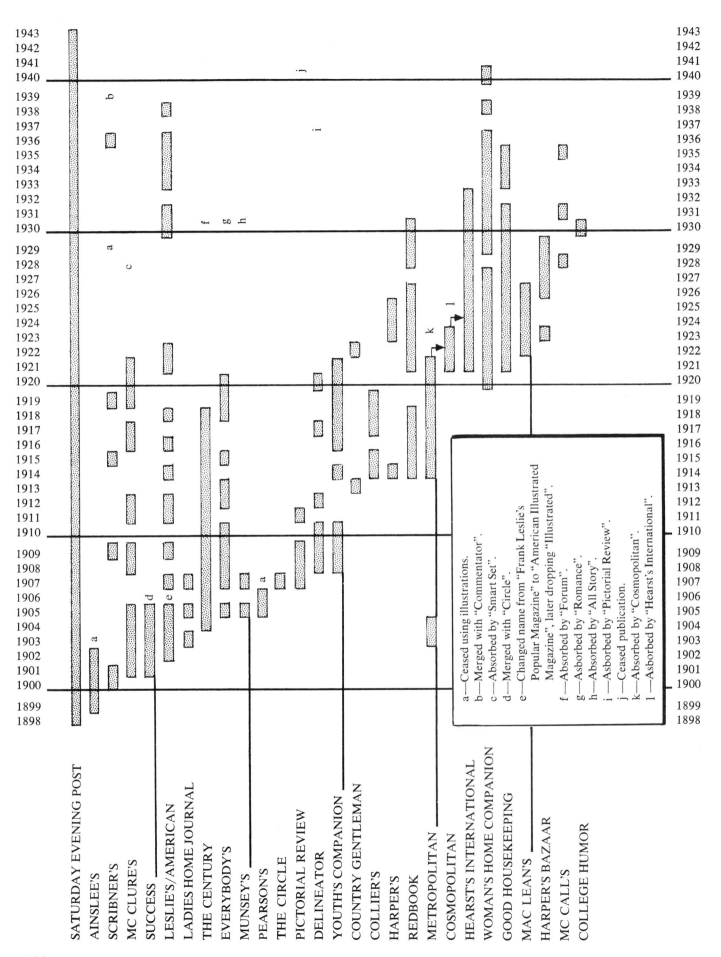

a —Ceased using illustrations.
b —Merged with "Commentator".
c —Absorbed by "Smart Set".
d —Merged with "Circle".
e —Changed name from "Frank Leslie's
　　Popular Magazine" to "American Illustrated
　　Magazine", later dropping "Illustrated".
f —Absorbed by "Forum".
g —Absorbed by "Romance".
h —Absorbed by "All Story".
i —Absorbed by "Pictorial Review".
j —Ceased publication.
k —Absorbed by "Cosmopolitan".
l —Absorbed by "Hearst's International".

SATURDAY EVENING POST
AINSLEE'S
SCRIBNER'S
MC CLURE'S
SUCCESS
LESLIE'S/AMERICAN
LADIES HOME JOURNAL
THE CENTURY
EVERYBODY'S
MUNSEY'S
PEARSON'S
THE CIRCLE
PICTORIAL REVIEW
DELINEATOR
YOUTH'S COMPANION
COUNTRY GENTLEMAN
COLLIER'S
HARPER'S
REDBOOK
METROPOLITAN
COSMOPOLITAN
HEARST'S INTERNATIONAL
WOMAN'S HOME COMPANION
GOOD HOUSEKEEPING
MAC LEAN'S
HARPER'S BAZAAR
MC CALL'S
COLLEGE HUMOR

F.R. GRUGER
RECORD OF MAGAZINE ILLUSTRATION 1898-1943

About 800 of F.R. Gruger's original illustrations are in the possession of F.R. Gruger, Jr. All but 50 have been identified. Research to achieve this brought to light well over 5000 drawings. Extrapolation would suggest that he must have produced over 6000. Some may have been for obscure publications. For instance, in one of his letters he mentions a request from a Masonic magazine, but it has not been possible to find any trace of the publication. Others may have been directly for book publishers, but the pursuit of this lead would be endless. About thirty books with his drawings have been located, but most of these appeared originally as serialized stories in one of the magazines.

In addition to the above he must have made a hundred or more advertising illustrations.

Over and above this vast production, he was able to find time for constant reading, for the pursuit of many hobbies and for months of travel.

These lists give the number of illustrations per story or part. Where no letter follows the number, it stands for half-tones. Of the letters which follow -
p stands for pen drawing
h for a drawing used as a heading (often without caption)
s for a two page spread.

The chart shows the years in which FRG worked for each magazine.

THE SATURDAY EVENING POST

1898

11/5	The Mystery Connected With Mrs. Jessup (1p signed F.R. Gruger in script; others unsigned.)	2, 2p	E. Rentoul Esler

1899

1/7	The General's Belated Christmas (p signed Frederic R. Gruger in script; other unsigned.)	1, 1p	Will N. Harben
1/21	The Taming Of The Bear (COVER) (1p signed FRG; 1, F.R. Gruger; 1, F.R. Gruger in italics; other unsigned.)	1, 3p	Herbert E. Hamblen
2/25	The Joskins Jar (1 signed FRG in script; 1, F.R. Gruger in caps and one Frederic R. Gruger.)	3p	Marshall Steele
3/11	The Hundred And Sixty-sixth Man (COVER)	1, 3p	
4/1	The President And Tom Collins (COVER)	1, 1p	Richard Stillman Powell
4/22	A Sudden Drop In Copper (COVER)	1, 3P	Elizabeth Phipps Train
4/29	Tales Of The Cross Roads (2 of the p were small, decorative spots.)	4p	Julia Truitt Bishop
5/20	Mrs. Parkhurst's Interference	2p	Octave Thanet
7/29	Sitting Up With Mrs. Jenks	1p	Julia Truitt Bishop
9/9	Not Legal Testimony	1, 2p	Octave Thanet
10/7	The Ketcham Pardon	2	William Ellis
10/14	The Schooner That Turned Squatter	1, 2p	M.E. McIntosh
10/28	The Naming Of Snubb	1	Hayden Carruth
12/2	The Millionaire's Christmas Card	2	Barry Pain
12/16	The Desperado: A True Story	1	Cy Warman
	The Diary Of A Weakling	1	Barry Pain
12/30	The Stolen President	1, 1p	W.A. Fraser
	The Cost Of Seeing The Paris Exposition	2P	Vance Thompson

1900

1/6	The Making Of A Railroad Man	1p*	J.T. Harahan
1/13	The "Great" Houses Of New York	3p	Mrs. Burton Harrison
1/27	A Rub Of The Green	1, 1p	Edwin L. Sabin
	Tales Of Men Of Many Trades	1	Charles Battell Loomis
2/17	Tales Of Men Of Many Trades	1	Charles Battell Loomis
2/24	A Watch In The Night	1	Madeline S. Bridges

	The Making Of A Railroad Man	1p*	William J. McQueen
4/7	The making Of A Railroad Man	1p*	J.H. Wicks
6/2	Not A Question Of Evidence	2, 1p	Elizabeth Phipps Train
12/8	Jane's Christmas Slippers	1p**	Hayden Carruth
12/29	The Lively Adventure Of The Widow's Cow	1, 1p***	M. Quad
	Why He Loved Her	2 **	Marten Marteens

* First used as cover for 1/21/99 No. Will be used again in the 7/27/01 No.

** Script

*** Unsigned, Magazine credit.

1901

4/6	Miss James, A Mystery	1, 1p	W.L. Alden
6/8	The Memoires Of Professor Bink	1, 1p*	Hayden Carruth
7/27	American Locomotives And Foreign Buyers	2, 1p	S.R. Calloways
	Ballads Of The Banks, Song Of The Doryman	1,3p**	Holman F. Day
8/10	Tales Of The Department Store	1, 2p**	N.H. Higinbotham
8/24	Ballads Of The Banks	1**	Holman F. Day
9/21	Tales Of Old Turley	1**	Max Adeler
9/28	Tales Of Old Turley	1	Max Adeler
	Ballad Of The Banks, The Awful Wah-Hoo-Woo	1	Holman F. Day
10/5	Letters From A Self-Made Merchant To His Son	4***	George Horace Lorimer
	Tales Of Old Turley	1	Max Adeler
10/12	COVER Theodore Roosevelt, Harvard '80	2*	Owen Wister
10/19	Tales Of Old Turley	1	Max Adeler
10/26	Tales Of Old Turley	1	Max Adeler
	Letters From A Self-Made, etc.	2p	George Horace Lorimer
11/2	Tales Of Old Turley	1**	Max Adeler
11/9	A Letter From Horace Greeley	1	Hayden Carruth
11/16	The White Invasion Of China	2+	Albert J. Beveridge
11/23	The White Invasion Of China	2+	Albert J. Beveridge
2/7	The White Invasion Of China	2++	Albert J. Beveridge
	Christmas At The Windward Light	1+++	Joseph C. Lincoln
	Daniel Borem	7, 1p	Bret Hart

* Signed: Frederic R. Gruger, the second time in script.

** Signed: F.R. Gruger, last four times in script.

*** Unsigned but credited

\+ Also 1 by James Preston

\+ + Also 1p by James Preston

\+ + + Also 2 by James Preston

Note. All of the Beveridge story illustrations, by FRG and JP, were combined into a single composition.

1902

1/11	Letters From A Self-Made, etc.	3	George Horace Lorimer
1/18	COVER (orange and blue) by FRG and JP. A Diplomatic Game For An Empire	1*	Albert J. Beveridge
1/25	The March Of A Nation To The Sea	2	Albert J. Beveridge
	A Business Man's Reading	1	Frank A. Vanderlip
2/8	The Great Natural Healer	4	Max Adeler
2/8	The Coming War Between Russia and Japan	1	Albert J. Beveridge

* Also one by James Preston

2/22	Frictional Electricity	4	Max Adeler
	Letters From A Self-Made, etc.	3	George Horace Lorimer
3/22	Letters From A Self-Made, etc.	3	George Horace Lorimer
4/26	Letters From A Self-Made, etc.	2	George Horace Lorimer
5/17	The David Harum Of The Cabinet	2	Jesse Lynch Williams
5/31	The Agent Of Missouri Station	4	Willis Gibson
6/14	Billy Lorimer - The Serene Boss	3	Forrest Crissey
6/21	A Woman's Washington	2	The Congressman's Wife
6/28	Men And Measures	1	Charles Emory Smith
7/5	Muffles - The Bar-Keep	4	F. Hopkinson Smith
	Safe Now In The Wide, Wide World	1p	Jesse Lynch Williams
7/12	A Scout Of The American Invasion	3	Robert Barr
7/19	The Probation Of Buckle's Ghost	2	Robert Barr
8/2	Letters From A Self-Made, etc.	2	George Horace Lorimer
8/16	Letters From A Self-Made, etc.	2	George Horace Lorimer

Date	Title	Notes	Author
	Miss Barkey	2, 1p	Frank H. Spearman
8/30	Letters From A Self-Made, etc.	2	George Horace Lorimer
9/13	The Admirable Tinker	2,	Edgar Jepson
	Letters From A Self-Made, etc.	2	George Horace Lorimer
9/27	The Admirable Tinker	1	Edgar Jepson
	Letters From A Self-Made, etc.	2	George Horace Lorimer
10/4	The Reception Bill	1	Francis Dana
10/11	Letters From A Self-Made, etc.	3	George Horace Lorimer
	The Admirable Tinker	1	Edgar Jepson
10/18	The Candid Circus Man	2**	Philip L. Allen
10/25	The Romance Of Thomas Skilhew	4	Chester Bailey Fernald
	The Admirable Tinker	2	Edgar Jepson
	College Wit	4p	William Matthews
11/15	A Lodge In The Wilderness	2, 1p	Arthur E. McFarlane
11/22	Veritable Quidors	3	Charles Battell Loomis
12/6	The Player's Christmas	1	Julia Marlowe
12/20	the Amateur	3	Will Payne
		3 portraits	

* One signed •G•

1903

Date	Title	Notes	Author
1/17	A Peculiar People	2	Rebecca Harding Davis
1/24	The Admirable Tinker	2	Edgar Jepson
2/7	The Uninherited Inheritance	2	Elliot Flower
2/14	Putting On The Play	1	Lawrence Marston
2/21	The Law Of Heart's Desire	2	Emerson Hough
	The Admirable Tinker	2	Edgar Jepson
2/28	Americans Of Today And Tomorrow	1h	Albert J. Beveridge
	Our American Snobs	1h	James L. Ford
3/14	The Politicians	1h	William Allen White
	Freaks And Fortunes In Advertising	2	Paul Latzke
3/28	The Heroism Of Surrender Peaslove	1	Joseph C. Lincoln
4/4	The Kidnapping Of Rockvelt	2, 2p	
		1d	Robert Barr
	Soul Sonnets Of A Stenographer	4p	S.E. Kaiser

Date	Title	Notes	Author
4/11	Soul Sonnets Of A Stenographer	3p	S.E. Kaiser
4/18	Soul Sonnets Of A Stenographer	3p	S.E. Kaiser
4/25	Soul Sonnets Of A Stenographer	3p	S.E. Kaiser
	Fortunes And Freaks In Advertising	5p	Paul Latzke
5/2	Men And Women	5p	Anonymous
5/9	The American Nights Entertainment	3	Charles Battell Loomis
	The Lighter Side	5p	Alfred Henry Lewis
5/16	The Lighter Side	6p	Alfred Henry Lewis
	The American Nights Entertainment	2	Charles Battell Loomis
5/23	Men And Women	4p	Anonymous
	The American Nights Entertainment	1, 2p	Charles Battell Loomis
6/6	The Chief Engineer	2	Lloyd Osborne
6/13	Men And Women	5p	Anonymous
7/4	A Non-Union Town	3	I.K. Friedman
7/11	The President's Daughter	3	Frank H. Spearman
7/18	The President's Daughter	3	Frank H. Spearman
7/25	The President's Daughter	3	Frank H. Spearman
8/1	The President's Daughter	3	Frank H. Spearman
8/8	The President's Daughter	3	Frank H. Spearman
8/15	The President's Daughter	3	Frank H. Spearman
	Absent Minded Great Men	2p	William Matthews
8/22	Song Of The Siren	1p	Stanley Waterloo
	The President's Daughter	3	Frank H. Spearman
8/29	The President's Daughter	3	Frank H. Spearman
	Men And Women	2p	Anonymous
9/5	The Daughter Of A Magnate	3	Frank H. Spearman
9/12	The Daughter Of A Magnate	3	Frank H. Spearman
9/26	The Chicago Man	3	Opie Read
10/3	Old Gordon Graham	COVER, 2	George Horace Lorimer
	The Boss	3*	Alfred Henry Lewis
10/24	The Last Chance	2, 2p	Brand Whitlock
10/31	Old Gordon Graham	2	George Horace Lorimer
11/7	The Devious Way	3**	Elliott Flower
12/12	The Business Side Of The Big Unions	2p	I.K. Friedman
	The Steal	3	Wm. Hamilton Osborne

Date	Title	No.	Author
12/9	The Business Side Of The Big Unions	3p	I.K. Friedman

* This was an installment in a serial previously illustrated by Glackens. FRG seems to have modified his style to harmonize with that of Glackens. Glackens resumed in the next installment.

** Signed G on one drawing.

1904

Date	Title	No.	Author
1/2	Andy's Way	3	Elliott Flower
1/19	The Made Up Photograph And The Millionare	2	William Hamilton Osborne
1/16	The Substitute Manager	3	Elliott Flower
1/30	Old Gordon Graham	2	George Horace Lorimer
2/13	Old Gordon Graham	2	George Horace Lorimer
3/12	Old Gordon Graham	3	George Horace Lorimer
4/9	Old Gordon Graham	2	George Horace Lorimer
4/16	The Outsiders	2	Elliott Flower
4/23	The Troublesome Truth	3	Will Payne
5/14	The Buccaneers	3	Henry M. Hyde
5/21	The Buccaneers	3	Henry M. Hyde
	Old Gordon Graham	1	George Horace Lorimer
5/28	The Buccaneers	2p	Henry M. Hyde
6/11	Fifty Fathoms Down	3	Morgan Robertson
6/18	An Unpredicted Trip	2	Charles Battell Loomis
6/25	Where The Money Is Going To	4p	Arthur E. McFarlane
	Old Gordon Graham	3	George Horace Lorimer
7/9	Why America Wins	1p	Eustace Miles, NA
7/16	Old Gordon Graham	2	George Horace Lorimer
7/23	Fun At The Fair	4p	Jesse Lynch Williams
7/30	The Megaphone Of Money	1, 1p	Henry M. Hyde
8/20	Old Gordon Graham	3	George Horace Lorimer
10/29	Graft In Business	5p	Henry M. Hyde
12/3	St. Nicholas Scraggs	5	Henry Wallace Phillips
12/17	The Speculations Of John Steele	1, 5p	Robert Barr

1905

Date	Title	No.	Author
1/7	The Speculations Of John Steele	1, 2p	Robert Barr
1/14	The Works Of Plupy Shute	1	Henry A. Shute
1/28	The Speculations Of John Steele	3	Robert Barr
2/4	A Holiday Touch	2	Charles Battell Loomis
3/11	The Speculations Of John Steele	1, 2p	Robert Barr
3/18	The Jensen Case	4	Will Payne
3/25	The Speculations Of John Steele	1, 2p	Robert Barr
4/29	Lest I Forget	1	J.W. Foley
5/27	The String Of Pearls	3	Will Payne
6/24	In The Hands Of The Law	3	Will Payne
8/19	Patrick Sarsfield, Diplomat	3	Maud L. Radford
9/2	Why Nobody Loves The Umpire	4p	Allen Sangree
9/9	Scribes And Pharisees	3	William Allen White
9/16	The Young Prince	2	William Allen White
9/30	The Society Editor	3	Williams Allen White
10/7	The Joys Of Vulgarity	1	Lillian Bell
10/14	The Coming Of The Leisure Class	3	William Allen White
10/28	As A Breath Into The Wind	3	William Allen White
11/11	The Bolton Girl's Position	3	William Allen White
11/25	Jabez The Third	3	H.S. Cooper
	A Bundle Of Myrrh	5	William Allen White
12/2	Our Loathed but Esteemed Contemporary	3	William Allen White
12/9	A Question Of Climate	2	William Allen White
12/16	By The Rod Of His Wrath	3	William Allen White
12/23	The Casting Out Of Jimmy Meyers	3	William Allen White
12/30	A-Babbled O'Green Fields	2	William Allen White
		1*	

* By Glackens who, in this case appears to have altered his style to harmonize with FRG's.

1906*

Date	Title	No.	Author
1/6	The Tremolo Stop	1, 2p	William Allen White
2/24	Uncle Sam As A Business Man	1, 1p	Will Payne
3/3	Thirty	3	William Allen White
	The Way He Won Her	3	George Hibbard
3/17	Billy Fortune And The Drinkwater Lad	3	W.R. Lighton
	The Woman In The Way	3, 1p	Elliott Flower
4/14	The Back Of The Throne	6	Will Payne
8/25	My Provoking Husband	4	Ernest Poole
9/1	Who's Who And Why	2p	Anonymous
9/15	Shopping In Paris	4**	John Van Vorst
	The Fatal Gun	3	Henry Wallace Phillips
9/29	The Windfall	1	Robert Barr
10/6	Aristippus	3	Kenneth Harris
10/13	Sampson Rock Of Wall Street	COVER	Edwin Lefever
11/10	Letters To Unsuccessful Men	COVER, 6, 2p	

Date	Title		Author
11/17	The Seat Of Judgment	3	Maud L. Radford
11/24	Letters To Unsuccessful Men	4	George Horace Lorimer
12/8	Letters To Unsuccessful Men	1, 2p	George Horace Lorimer
12/15	Letters To Unsuccessful Men	5	George Horace Lorimer
12/29	Letters To Unsuccessful Men	3	George Horace Lorimer

* FRG seriously ill during spring and summer.
** Pencil drawings.

1907

Date	Title		Author
2/2	How Doth The Simple Selling Bee Improve Each Shining Hour	6	Owen Wister
3/30	Confessions Of A Juror	5	Percival Salters
4/6	Jack Spurlock - Prodigal	1	George Horace Lorimer
4/13	Your Humble Servant	4	Meta Richards Hoyt
4/20	Jack Spurlock - Prodigal	5	George Horace Lorimer
4/27	The Jail That Paid Dividends	4	Holman F. Day
5/4	Jack Spurlock - Prodigal	3	George Horace Loimer
5/18	Jack Spurlock - Prodigal	5	George Horace Lorimer
6/1	An Extra Number	4	Eugene Manlove Rhodes
6/22	The Handwriting Of Apollo	3	Wm. Chester Eastbrook
7/6	The Orator Of The Day	3	Brand Whitlock
8/3	The Respectability Shop	3	Will Payne
8/10	The Cook's Mate	4	Morley Roberts
8/24	His Own People	3	Booth Tarkington
8/31	His Own People	3	Booth Tarkington
8/24	The Impossible Mr. Curley	4	Gelett Burgess
9/21	Roosevelt, The Politician	4	Victor Proud
	Jim Bledso's Courtship	4	Mrs. L. H. Harris
9/28	Big Men And Their Salaries	6p	James H. Collins
10/5	Getting Rich Quick	5	Geo. Randolph Chester
	Jack Spurlock - Prodigal	4	George Horace Lorimer
10/12	Getting Rich Quick	3	Geo. Randolph Chester
10/26	Jack Spurlock - Prodigal	4	George Horace Lorimer
11/23	Jack Spurlock - Prodigal	3	George Horace Lorimer

1908

Date	Title		Author
1/18	Selling A Patent	5	Geo. Randolph Chester
1/25	Selling A Patent	4	Geo. Randolph Chester
2/15	Regina's Path Is Crossed	4	Dorothea Deakin
2/22	Jack Spurlock - Prodigal	3	George Horace Lorimer
3/21		COVER	
5/23	Jack Spurlock - Prodigal	4	George Horace Lorimer
6/20	The Eternal Question	3	Bert Leston Taylor
7/25	The Beggar At Your Gate	4	Charles Belmont Davis
	The Franchise	3	Will Payne
8/15	A Venture In The High C's	4	Geo. Randolph Chester
8/22	A Venture In The High C's	1	Geo. Randolph Chester
8/29	Hammering Stone	4	Geo. Randolph Chester
9/5	Hammering Stone	3	Geo. Randolph Chester
9/26	Cleaning Up	7	Geo. Randolph Chester
	The Autobiography Of An Obscure Author	3	
10/3	The Autobiography Of An Obscure Author	6	
10/10	The Autobiography Of An Obscure Author	3	
10/17	The Autobiography Of An Obscure Author	4	
	Friends	3	Myra Kelly
10/24	Warrior, The Untamed	4	Will Irwin
	The Autobiography Of An Obscure Author	4	
10/31	The Autobiography Of An Obscure Author	3	
11/7	Making Friends (Lawrenceville)	4	Owen Johnson
11/14	Easy Money	5	Geo. Randolph Chester

Date	Title	No.	Author
12/5	The Triple Cross	4	Geo. Randolph Chester
	We Have With Us Tonight	4	Samuel G. Blythe
12/19	The Trivial Incident	3	Melville Davisson Post
12/26	Spoiling The Egyptians	3	Geo. Randolph Chester

1909

Date	Title	No.	Author
1/9	Songs In Exile	3	Arthur Stringer
2/27	The Bank Manager	4	Robert Barr
3/6	Having Authority	3	Kenneth Harris
3/13	Robbies Bake-Off	4	Anonymous
4/3	Figgerin' Jim	4	Eleanor Gates
4/24	An Executive Mind	4	Eugene Manlove Rhodes
5/22	The Boy With An Idea	5	Owen Johnson
7/3	The Man With A Country	5	Eugene Manlove Rhodes
7/24	The Mouth Of The Gift Horse	4	Rupert Hughes
	''A Brand From The Burning''	4	Myra Kelly
8/7	The Humming Bird	4	Owen Johnson
10/2	The Losing Game	4	Will Payne
10/16	The Losing Game	3	Will Payne
10/23	The Losing Game	3	Will Payne
10/30	The Losing Game	3	Will Payne
11/6	The Losing Game	3	Will Payne
11/13	The Losing Game	3	Will Payne
	The Serpent's Tooth	3	Emery Pottle
11/20	The Losing Game	3	Will Payne
11/27	The Losing Game	3	Will Payne
	The Escape Of Mr. Trimm	4	Irvin S. Cobb

1910

Date	Title	No.	Author
1/1	The Spartan	4	Geo. Randolph Chester
1/29	Melusine	4	Dorothy Deakin
3/5	What Our National Guard Needs	3	Rupert Hughes
3/12	Easy Money	4	Maximalian Foster
3/19	Easy Money	4	Maximalian Foster
	''What Is There In It For Me''	2*	Samuel G. Blythe
3/26	Easy Money	3	Maximalian Foster
4/2	The RR Prince And His Principality	2*	Edward Hungerford
4/9	The Varmint	4	Owen Johnson
4/16	The Varmint	4	Owen Johnson
4/23	The Varmint	4	Owen Johnson
4/30	The Varmint	4	Owen Johnson
5/7	The Varmint	4	Owen Johnson
5/14	The Varmint	4	Owen Johnson
5/21	The Varmint	4	Owen Johnson
5/28	The Varmint	3	Owen Johnson
6/4	The Varmint	3	Owen Johnson
6/11	The Varmint	3	Owen Johnson
7/2	The Star In Mufti	4	H.H. Bashford
7/23	Keeping The Line Open	3	Edward Hungerford

Date	Title	No.	Author
8/6	Chocolate Duhamel	4	Montague Glass
8/13	Gasoline Goes Up	3	R.W. Hofflund
8/20	The Pirates Of Penzance	5	Mary Roberts Rinehart
8/27	College While You Wait	4	George Fitch
9/24	The gold Spike	4	Calvin Johnson

* Repeats

Date	Title	No.	Author
10/1	The Home Of Garfield And Arthur	3	Colonel W.H. Crook
10/22	The Career Of Farthest East	4	Will Payne
10/29	The Career Of Farthest East	4	Will Payne
11/5	The Career Of Farthest East	4	Will Payne
11/12	The Career of Farthest East	4	Will Payne
11/19	The Career Of Farthest East	4	Will Payne
11/26	The Career of Farthest East	4	Will Payne
12/3	The Career Of Farthest East	4	Will Payne
12/10	The Career Of Farthest East	4	Will Payne
12/24	Tad Sheldon, Second Class Scout	4	John Fleming Wilson

1911

Date	Title	No.	Author
1/14	The Million Dollar Twins	4	H.C. Rowland
2/18	A Break In The Training	3	Allen Sangree
3/11	On A Field Sable	4	H.S. Stabler
4/1	A Message From The Mikado	3	Harry Leon Wilson
4/8	A Number Of Things	4	Eugene Manlove Rhodes
5/6	The Ringer	4	Allen Sangree
5/20	Comrades All -Unknown	4	Calvin Johnson
6/17	In Dutch	4	Allen Sangree
7/1	Artemas Quibble, LLB	4	Arthur Train
7/8	Artemas Quibble, LLB	4	Arthur Train
7/15	Artemas Quibble, LLB	3	Arthur Train
7/22	Artemas Quibble, LLB	2	Arthur Train
7/29	Artemas Quibble, LLB	4	Arthur Train
8/5	Artemas Quibble, LLB	2	Arthur Train
8/12	Artemas Quibble, LLB	3	Arthur Train
8/19	Artemas Quibble, LLB	4	Arthur Train
9/9	The Big Idea	4	Will Payne
	Takis' Career	4	Mary R.S. Andrews
9/16	The Big Idea	4	Will Payne

Date	Title	No.	Author
9/23	The Big Idea	3	Will Payne
	The Agent At Bantam Spur	4	Calvin Johnson
9/30	The Big Idea	3	Will Payne
10/7	The Big Idea	3	Will Payne
	The American Father	2*	W. Hutchinson, AM, MD
10/14	The Big Idea	3	Will Payne
10/21	The Big Idea	3	Will Payne
	Fleecing New Companies	4**	
10/28	The Big Idea	3	Will Payne
12/2	Billy Fortune And The Original Apple	4	W.R. Lighton

*
** No author or illustrator named, but almost surely FRG. A second check leads me to think that only two of the five were by FRG. All were pick-ups from former stories and as usual, signatures have been removed.

1912

Date	Title	No.	Author
1/20	The Grand Cross Of The Crescent	5	Richard Harding Davis
1/27	Billy Fortune And The Young Feeling	4	W.R. Lighton
2/10	The Mob From Massac	4	Irvin S. Cobb
4/13	The Newspaper Game	4	
4/20	The Newspaper Game	4	
4/27	The Newspaper Game	4	
5/4	The Newspaper Game	4	
5/11	The Newspaper Game	3	
6/15	My Lady's Garter	4	Jacques Futrelle
6/22	My Lady's Garter	4	Jacques Futrelle
6/29	My Lady's Garter	4	Jacques Futrelle
7/6	My Lady's Garter	3	Jacques Futrelle
7/13	My Lady's Garter	4	Jacques Futrelle
7/20	My Lady's Garter	4	Jacques Futrelle
7/27	My Lady's Garter	4	Jacques Futrelle
8/3	My Lady's Garter	4	Jacques Futrelle
8/10	My Lady's Garter	4	Jacques Futrelle
10/12	English Standards Of Gentility	4	John Corbin
	His Majesty Bunker Bean	4	Harry Leon Wilson
10/19	His Majesty Bunker Bean	4	Harry Leon Wilson
10/26	His Majesty Bunker Bean	4	Harry Leon Wilson
11/2	His Majesty Bunker Bean	4	Harry Leon Wilson
11/9	His Majesty Bunker Bean	4	Harry Leon Wilson
11/16	His Majesty Bunker Bean	4	Harry Leon Wilson
11/23	His Majesty Bunker Bean	4	Harry Leon Wilson
11/30	The Cub	3	James Hopper
	His Majesty Bunker Bean	4	Harry Leon Wilson
12/7	His Majesty Bunker Bean	3	Harry Leon Wilson
12/14	His Majesty Bunker Bean	3	Harry Leon Wilson

1913

Date	Title	No.	Author
2/1	A Business Administration	4	Geo. Randolph Chester
2/15	A Business Administration	4	Geo. Randolph Chester
3/1	One Touch Of Nature	4	Peter B. Kyne
	A Business Administration	3	Geo. Randolph Chester
3/15	A Business Administration	3	Geo. Randolph Chester
3/30	A Business Administration	3	Geo. Randolph Chester
4/12	A Business Administration	3	Geo. Randolph Chester
4/26	Guilty As Charged	1	Irvin S. Cobb
5/3	The Door Stopper	3	Will Irwin
5/10	Breaking Into New York	3	Anonymous
5/17	Breaking Into New York	3	Anonymous
	Another Of Those Cub Reporter Stories	4	Irvin S. Cobb
5/24	Breaking Into New York	3	Anonymous
8/2	As Proofs Of Holy Writ	4	Edwin Lefevre
	Illustration, Pg. 7, unsigned	1	Anonymous
8/9	As Proofs Of Holy Writ	4	Edwin Lefevre
8/16	As Proofs Of Holy Writ	3	Edwin Lefevre
8/30	Smoke Of Battle	3	Irvin S. Cobb
9/13	Found In The Fog	3	Melville Davisson Post
9/27	Tiberius Tinker -Press Agent	4	Peter B. Kyne
10/11	The Ruined Eye	3	Melville Davisson Post
10/18	The Treasure	3	Kathleen Norris
10/25	The Treasure	4	Kathleen Norris
11/1	The Treasure	4	Kathleen Norris
11/8	An Idle Million	3	Geo. Randolph Chester
11/15	Blood Will Tell	2	Will Irwin
12/6	The Only Child You Know	3**	Anonymous
12/13	The Goldfish	4	Anonymous
12/27	The Goldfish	4	Anonymous

1914

Date	Title		Author
1/10	The Goldfish	4	Anonymous
1/24	The Goldfish	4	Annoymous
2/7	The Goldfish	4	Anonymous
	An Idle Million	3	Geo. Randolph Chester
2/14	Traitors Both	4	Calvin Johnson
2/21	The Goldfish	4	Anonymous
	An Idle Million	3	Geo. Randolph Chester
3/7	Randolph, Where Have You Been?	3	Montague Glass
3/14	A Noncombattant Of Baseball	4*	
4/4	My Son	4	William Carleton
4/11	My Son	3	William Carleton
4/18	My Son	4	William Carleton
4/25	My Son	3	William Carleton
	A King Among Kings	3	Harry Leon Wilson
5/2	My Son	3	William Carleton
5/16	The Head Of The Family	3	Calvin Johnson
6/13	Discords	4	Ida May Evans
6/20	Superman	4	Fanny Hurst
	Bantry	3	Elmore Elliot Peake
7/18	The Smart Aleck	4	Irvin S. Cobb
	Major Miles And The Grim Reaper	4	L.B. Yates
8/15	Horseshoes	3	Ring W. Lardner
	The Good Provider	4	Fanny Hurst
8/22	The Amachure Grafter	4	Will Irwin
8/29	The Melting Of An Ice Trust	4	L.B. Yates
10/17	Major Miles' Chickens	4	L.B. Yates
11/21	The Mine Layer	1**	C.J. Cutcliffe Hyne
12/5	Jermym The Munificent	5	Julian Hinckley
12/26	Ruggles Of Red Gap	4	Harry Leon Wilson

* Reused. Could be FRG or AWB.
** Reused. Definitely FRG

1915

Date	Title		Author
1/2	The Crow's Nest	4	Will Irwin
	Ruggle's Of Red Gap	4	Harry Leon Wilson
1/9	Ruggles Of Red Gap	4	Harry Leon Wilson
1/16	Ruggles Of Red Gap	4	Harry Leon Wilson
	The Gas War	3	Will Payne
1/23	Ruggles Of Red Gap	4	Harry Leon Wilson
1/30	Ruggles Of Red Gap	4	Harry Leon Wilson
2/6	Ruggles Of Red Gap	4	Harry Leon Wilson
2/13	Ruggles Of Red Gap	4	Harry Leon Wilson
2/20	Ruggles Of Red Gap	4	Harry Leon Wilson
2/27	Ruggles Of Red Gap	4	Harry Leon Wilson
3/13	The Old Man	1	Edward Mott Wooley
4/10	A Change Of Pace	4	Wilbur Hall
4/17	Double Stakes	4	W.R. Lighton
4/24	Double Stakes	4	W.R. Lighton
6/26	Something New	4	P.G. Wodehouse

Date	Title		Author
7/3	Something New	3	P.G. Wodehouse
	The Look Of Eagles	3	John Tainter Foote
7/10	Something New	4	P.G. Wodehouse
7/17	Something New	4	P.G. Wodehouse
7/24	Something New	4	P.G. Wodehouse
7/31	Something New	4	P.G. Wodehouse
8/7	Something New	4	P.G. Wodehouse
	Judge Priest Comes Back	4	Irvin S. Cobb
8/14	Something New	4	P.G. Wodeshouse
8/28	Ma Pettingill And The Song Of Songs	4	Harry Leon Wilson
	A Blending Of The Parables	4	Irvin S. Cobb
10/30	Rich Man Poor Man	4	Maximilian Foster
11/6	Rich Man Poor Man	4	Maximilian Foster
11/13	Rich Man Poor Man	4	Maximilian Foster
11/20	Rich Man Poor Man	3	Maximilian Foster
11/27	Rich Man Poor Man	3	Maximilian Foster
12/4	Rich Man Poor Man	3	Maximilian Foster
12/25	Inside News In Wall Street	1	Annoymous

1916

Date	Title		Author
1/15	According To The Code	3	Irvin S. Cobb
1/22	Once A Scotchman, Always	4	Harry Leon Wilson
1/29	Rosy-Light-Of-Dawn	3	Kenneth Harris
3/11	A Chapter From The Life Of An Ant	4	Irvin S. Cobb
3/25	The Old Dominic	4	George Weston
4/15	The Eyes Of The World	4	Irvin S. Cobb
5/20	The Missing Seventeen	4	Edison Marshall
6/24	Cousin Egbert Intervenes	4	Harry Leon Wilson
7/15	Kate; Or, Up From The Depths	4	Harry Leon Wilson
8/5	Pete's Brother-In-Law	4	Harry Leon Wilson
8/26	Little Old New York	4	Harry Leon Wilson
9/9	Sargasso Sea	4	Donn Byrne
9/30	Rosemary Roselle	4	Joseph Hergesheimer
10/7	Paying Guests	2*	Margaretta Tuttle
10/28	To The Last Penny	4	Edwin Lefevre
11/4	To The Last Penny	4	Edwin Lefevre
	The Salesman Who Lasts	1	J.H. Collins
11/11	To The Last Penny	4	Edwin Lefevre
11/18	To The Last Penny	4	Edwin Lefevre
11/25	To The Last Penny	4	Edwin Lefevre
12/2	To The Last Penny	4	Edwin Lefevre
12/9	To The Last Penny	4	Edwin Lefevre
12/16	Joy Riders	4	Joseph Hergesheimer
12/23	Joy Riders	4	Joseph Hergesheimer

1917

Date	Title		Author
11/20	One Every Minute	4	Edwin Lefevre
1/27	One Every Minute	4	Edwin Lefevre
	The Echo	4	Wallace Irwin
2/3	One Every Minute	4	Edwin Lefevre
2/10	One Every Minute	4	Edwin Lefevre
2/17	Cappy Ricks, Wheat Baron	4	Peter B. Kyne

Date	Title	#	Author
2/24	The Customary Two Weeks	4	Freeman Tilden
3/3	The Customary Two Weeks	4	Freeman Tilden
3/10	Cabbages And Other Luxuries	2	Forrest Crissey
4/7	Bears In Wall Street	2	Albert W. Atwood
	The Batallions Of The Hearth	3	Maud Radford Warren
5/19	Tubal Cain	4	Joseph Hergesheimer
	St. Patrick's Day In The Morning	4	Peter B. Kyne
5/26	Tubal Cain	4	Joseph Hergesheimer
6/2	Tubal Cain	4	Joseph Hergesheimer
6/16	The Dollar Bill	4	Maximilian Foster
	Old Red Rambler	4	Wallace Irwin
6/23	The Huge Black One-Eyed Man	4	Kenyon Gambier
6/30	The Huge Black One-Eyed Man	4	Kenyon Gambier
8/16	N. Brown	3	Thane Miller Jones
8/25	The Medal Of M. Moulin	3	George Weston
	Aplied Hydraulics	2	Cipriano Andrade, Jr.
9/8	Benjamin McNeil Murdock	4	Harvey O'Higgins
9/15	Stannerton And Sons	4	Freeman Tilden
10/6	The Firm	4	Cameron Mackenzie
10/13	All Front And No Back	4	Wallace Irvin
10/20	Never Again	2	Curtis Roth
11/17	Five, Six, Pick Up Sticks	1*	Frank Condon
12/1	The Biography Of A Million Dollars	4	George Kibbe Turner
12/8	The Biography Of A Million Dollars	4	George Kibbe Turner
12/15	The Biography Of A Million Dollars	4	George Kibbe Turner
12/22	The Biography Of A Million Dollars	4	George Kibbe Turner
12/29	The Biography Of A Million Dollars	4	George Kibbe Turner

* One reused

1918

Date	Title	#	Author
1/5	The Biography Of A Million Dollars	3	George Kibbe Turner
2/2	Uncle Hyacinth	1*	Alfred Noyes
2/9	The Grand Romantic Manner	3	George Weston
2/23	Samuel Crew's Dilemma	2	Will Payne
3/2	Wars And Rumors	3	Joseph Hergesheimer
3/16	Free	3	Theodore Dreiser
4/6	Shot With Crimson	3	George Barr McCutcheon
4/13	Shot With Crimson	3	George Bar McCutcheon
4/20	Shot With Crimson	3	George Barr McCutcheon
4/27	Shot With Crimson	2	George Barr McCutchon
5/4	Toward Morning	2	I.A.R. Wylie
5/11	Toward Morning	2	I.A.R. Wylie
5/18	Toward Morning	2	I.A.R. Wylie
5/25	Toward Morning	2	I.A.R. Wylie
6/1	Toward Morning	2	I.A.R. Wylie
6/8	Toward Morning	2	I.A.R. Wylie
	Gassed	1	Major S.J.M. Auld
6/15	Toward Morning	2	I.A.R. Wylie
6/22	Toward Morning	2	I.A.R. Wylie
8/1	Open Sesame	3	Frederic Orin Bartlett
8/17	Open Sesame	3	Frederic Orin Bartlett
10/5	Java Head	3	Joseph Hergesheimer
10/12	Java Head	3	Joseph Hergesheimer
10/19	Java Head	4	Joseph Hergesheimer
10/26	Java Head	3	Joseph Hergesheimer
11/2	Java Head	3	Joseph Hergesheimer
11/9	Java Head	3	Joseph Hergesheimer
11/16	The Butterfly	3	Dana Burnet
12/7	Change Of Views	3	Harry Leon Wilson
12/21	Can Happen	2	Harry Leon Wilson

1919

Date	Title	#	Author
1/4	The Taker-Up	2	Harry Leon Wilson
1/11	Curls	2	Harry Leon Wilson
1/18	The Refugees	4	Edith Wharton
1/25	As To Herman Wagner	3	Harry Leon Wilson
2/8	Reprisal	2	Britten Austin
	The Sacred Wolloch	3**	Geo. Randolph Chester
	The Siamese Twin	1**	Frederic I. Anderson
3/1	Order Of Merit	3	Joseph Hergesheimer
3/8	The Hasher	3	Charles Van Loan

* Repeat. Not sure. Possibly A.O. Fisher.
** Unsigned and no by-line. Look very much like FRG.

Date	Title	#	Author
3/8	From Generation To Generation	2*	Grace Ellery Channing
4/5	Red Friday	2	George Kibbe Turner
4/12	Red Friday	3	George Kibbe Turner
4/19	Red Friday	3	George Kibbe Turner
4/26	Demobilizing The American Woman	1**	Corra Harris
5/17	Below Par For A Day	1+	Henry Irwin Dodge
5/31	In High C	1	Maxwell Smith
	Free Air	4	Sinclair Lewis
6/7	Free Air	3	Sinclair Lewis
6/14	Free Air	3	Sinclair Lewis
6/21	Free Air	3	Sinclair Lewis
7/12	The Gibson Upright	4	B. Tarkington and H.L. Wilson
7/19	The Gibson Upright	3	B. Tarkington and H.L. Wilson
7/26	The Gibson Upright	2	B. Tarkington and H.L. Wilson
8/9	Her Son	2	John Peter Tooley
8/23	An Outrage Or Two	3	William Hamilton Osborne
9/20	Wandering Stars	2	Wallace Irwin

Date	Title	No.	Author
9/27	The Avenger	3	Richard Washburton Childs
	The Great Accident	2	Ben Ames Williams
10/4	The Great Accident	3	Ben Ames Williams
10/11	The Great Accident	3	Ben Ames Williams
10/18	The Great Accident	3	Ben Ames Williams
10/25	The Great Accident	3	Ben Ames Williams
11/1	The Great Accident	3	Ben Ames Williams
11/8	The Great Accident	3	Ben Ames Williams
11/15	The Great Accident	3	Ben Ames Williams
11/22	The Chance	2	Herschel S. Hall
	The Trouble Doc	2	Rufus Steele
12/6	White Lines	3	Herschel S. Hall
12/27	The Man From Hell	2	May Edington
	The Metal	3	Herschel S. Hall

  * Unsigned and no by-line. Look very much like FRG.
 ** Repeat, unsigned. Look very much like FRG.
  + Repeats, one signed. Other not sure.

1920

Date	Title	No.	Author
1/5	The Troglodyte	3	Alfred Noyes
1/17	The New Fairyland	2	Harry Leon Wilson
1/24	The Key Man	2	Herschel S. Hall
2/7	Business Neurology	1*	Wilbur Hall
2/28	Court-Martial	2	Alfred Noyes
3/27	The Fate Makers	3	Nina Wilcox Putnam
4/3	The Fate Makers	2	Nina Wilcox Putnam
4/10	The Fate Makers	3	Nina Wilcox Putnam
	At The Dim Gate	1	Elizabeth Jordan

  * Possibly a pick-up with signature removed.

Date	Title	No.	Author
5/1	Bed Rock	3	Hugh Wiley
	Your Check	3	Edward H. Smith
	G.S.L. To Himself	1	Gerald Stanley Lee
5/8	The Wasted Deadline	3	Irvin S. Cobb
5/22	Wherefore Art Thou Romeo	3	Wallace Irwin
6/12	Promoted	3	Herschel S. Hall
6/26	Steel	3	Joseph Hergesheimer
7/3	Steel	3	Joseph Hergesheimer
7/10	Steel	3	Joseph Hergesheimer
7/17	Steel	3	Joseph Hergesheimer
7/24	Steel	3	Joseph Hergesheimer
7/31	Steel	3	Joseph Hergesheimer
8/28	Miss Ashton's House	3	Anthony Wharton
10/2	The Hell Diggers	3	Byron Morgan
10/30	The Last Titan	3	Arthur Stringer
11/27	The Wrong Twin	3	Harry Leon Wilson
12/4	The Wrong Twin	3	Harry Leon Wilson
12/11	The Wrong Twin	3	Harry Leon Wilson
12/18	The Wrong Twin	3	Harry Leon Wilson
12/25	The Wrong Twin	3	Harry Leon Wilson

1921

Date	Title	No.	Author
1/1	The Wrong Twin	3	Harry Leon Wilson
1/8	The Wrong Twin	3	Harry Leon Wilson
1/15	The Wrong Twin	3	Harry Leon Wilson
1/22	The Wrong Twin	2	Harry Leon Wilson
1/29	The Wrong Twin	2	Harry Leon Wilson
3/5	Number One	2	Hugh McNair Kahler
3/19	QED	2	Gerald Mygatt & Garret Smith
4/30	The Commune, Limited	2	Hugh McNair Kahler
5/7	The Biography Of A Small Town	4*	Jay E. House
5/21	The Islanders	3	Josephine Daskam Bacon
5/28	The Islanders	2	Josephine Daskam Bacon
6/4	The Silent House	2	Mary Brecht Pulver
8/6	Manslaughter	3	Alice Duer Miller
8/13	Manslaughter	2	Alice Duer Miller
8/20	Manslaughter	2	Alice Duer Miller
8/27	Manslaughter	2	Alice Duer Miller
9/3	Manslaughter	2	Alice Duer Miller
	The Uses Of Calamity	2	Will Irwin
11/26	Bristol Eyes	2	Appelby Terrill
12/3	Happy Strikes Twelve	2	Will Irwin

  * Three of them portraits.

1922

Date	Title	No.	Author
1/7	Relativity	2	Hugh McNair Kelly
1/21	Gentle Annie	3	Harry Leon Wilson
1/28	The Winter Bell	3	Henry Miller Rideout
2/4	The Winter Bell	3	Henry Miller Rideout
2/11	The Winter Bell	3	Henry Miller Rideout
6/10	J. Pointdexter, Colored	3	Irvin S. Cobb
6/17	J. Pointdexter, Colored	3	Irvin S. Cobb
6/24	J. Pointdexter, Colored	3	Irvin S. Cobb
7/1	J. Pointdexter, Colored	3	Irvin S.Cobb
7/15	"—That Shall He Also Reap"	3	Irvin S. Cobb
7/22	On The Shell	3	Viola Brothers Shore
7/29	The Hero	3	Hugh McNair Kahler
11/4	The Captain Of His Soul	3	J.P. Marquand
11/18	Proxy	2	Percival Gibbon
11/25	The Concierge And The King	3	George Pattullo
12/2	Ma Pettinggill Arbetrates	3	Harry Leon Wilson
12/9	Rough-Heavy Stuff	2	George Pattullo
12/16	Art For Red Gap's Sake	3	Harry Leon Wilson
12/30	Flora And Fauna	3	Harry Leon Wilson
	That Devil, Fanfaron	3	George Pattullo

1923

Date	Title	No.	Author
2/10	Money, Money, Money	3	Harry Leon Wilson
3/10	The Piano	2	Ben Ames Williams
4/14	The English Tutor	3	Percival Gibbon
5/12	Barbry	3	Henry Miller Rideout
	Miss Tanner	3	MayEdington

Date	Title		Author
5/19	Barbry	2	Henry Miller Rideout
5/26	Barbry	3	Henry Miller Rideout
6/2	Barbry	3	Henry Miller Rideout
6/9	Barby	3	Henry Miller Rideout
8/18	Cat's Paw	3	C.E. Scoggins
8/25	Cat's Paw	3	C.E. Scoggins
9/1	My Book And Heart	3	Corra Harris
9/8	My Book And Heart	3	Corra Harris
9/15	My Book And Heart	3	Corra Harris
9/22	My Book And Heart	2	Corra Harris
9/29	My Book And Heart	3	Corra Harris
10/6	My Book And Heart	3	Corra Harris
10/13	My Book And Heart	3	Corra Harris
10/20	My Book And Heart	2	Corra Harris
12/1	Ethical Dative	2	Thomas Beer

1924

Date	Title		Author
1/19	Star Of Destiny	3	Clifford Raymond
6/14	The Pyramid Of Lead	2	Bertram Atkey
6/21	The Pyramid Of Lead	2	Bertram Atkey
6/28	The Pyramid Of Lead	2	Bertram Atkey
	In Right	2	Thomas McMorrow
7/5	The Pyramid Of Lead	2	Bertram Atkey
7/12	The Pyramid Of Lead	2	Bertram Atkey
	What's Politics Among Friends	2	Thomas McMorrow
7/19	The Pyramid Of Lead	2	Bertram Atkey
7/26	Balisand	3	Joseph Hergesheimer
8/2	Balisand	2	Joseph Hergesheimer
8/9	Balisand	2	Joseph Hergesheimer
	the Set-Up	2	Thomas McMorrow
8/16	Balisand	2	Joseph Hergesheimer
8/23	Balisand	2	Joseph Hergesheimer
	After The Fair	2	Thomas McMorrow
8/30	Balisan	2	Joseph Hergesheimer
9/6	Balisand	2	Joseph Hergesheimer
9/20	Tom Gentry Qualifies	2	Thomas McMorrow
10/4	What Becomes Of The Rich Man's Income	1	A.W. Atwood
10/25	The Candidate	2	Thomas McMorrow
11/8	Votes For Women	2	Thomas McMorrow
11/22	Didos: Official Report	2	Horatio Winslow
12/13	Joe Yorick Strives To Please	2	Thomas McMorrow

1925

Date	Title		Author
1/3	Andrew Bride, Of Paris	3	Henry Sydnor Harrison
	And All Things Else	2	Thomas McMorrow
1/10	Andrew Bride, Of Paris	2	Henry Sydnor Harrison
1/17	Andrew Bride, Of Paris	2	Henry Sydnor Harrison
2/14	The Educated Money	2	J.P. Marquand
1/31	The Holdup	2	Stewart Edward White
3/7	Home Folks	3	George Pattullo
3/21	The Foot Of The Class	3	J.P. Marquand
4/11	Blind Goddess	2	George Pattullo
5/9	In Praise Of James Carabine	3	Donn Byrne
	Spoils Of War	2	Hugh Wiley
6/13	Sam In the Suburbs	3	P.G. Wodehouse
6/20	Sam In The Suburbs	2	P.G. Wodehouse
6/27	Sam In The Suburbs	2	P.G. Wodehouse
7/4	Sam In The Suburbs	2	P.G. Wodehouse
7/11	Sam In The Suburbs	2	P.G. Wodehouse
7/18	Sam In The Suburbs	2	P.G. Wodehouse
8/29	Crossed Wires	1	Percival Gibbon
	Eyes Of Heaven	2	Louise Dutton
9/19	Splendid With Swords	2	Wyeth Williams
10/10	Spanish Men's Rest	3	Donn Byrne
10/17	Spanish Men's Rest	2	Donn Byrne
12/26	Man Alone	3	George Agnew Chamberlain

1926

Date	Title		Author
1/2	Man Alone	2	George Agnew Chamberlain
1/9	Man Alone	2	George Agnew Chamberlain
1/16	Man Alone	2	George Agnew Chamberlain
1/23	Man Alone	2	George Agnew Chamberlain
1/23	Paradise on Choct-chee, Florida	2	Thomas McMorrow
1/30	Man Alone	2	George Agnew Chamberlain
2/6	To Let, On Flagler Street	2	Thomas McMorrow
3/6	Land Of Promise	2	Thomas McMorrow
3/27	Sunrise	3	Alice Duer Miller
4/3	Sunrise	2	Alice Duer Miller
4/10	Sunrise	2	Alice Duer Miller
	Where Every Prospect Pleases	2	Thomas McMorrow
4/17	The Old People	3	I.A.R. Wylie
8/7	Replicas For Reality	2	Joseph Hergesheimer
8/21	Fine Metal	2	Joseph Hergesheimer
9/4	The Signet Packet	2	Joseph Hergesheimer
9/11	Grandmother Bernle Learns Hers Letters	2	I.A.R. Wylie
10/2	Collector's Blues	2	Joseph Hergesheimer
10/9	The Derby Rule	2	Donn Byrne
10/16	The Derby Rule	2	Donn Byrne
	A Further Study Of Plants	2	Joseph Hergesheimer
10/30	En Garde	3	Wyeth Williams
	Fiddle Backs	2	Joseph Hergesheimer

Date	Title	#	Author
11/13	Arts Of Hoax	2	Joseph Hergesheimer
11/27	The Primitive Motive	2	Joseph Hergesheimer
12/11	Reality From Replicas	2	Joseph Hergesheimer
12/25	1888	2	Joseph Hergesheimer

1927

Date	Title	#	Author
1/1	1918	2	Joseph Hergesheimer
1/8	The Americans Arrive	3	Alice Duer Miller
1/15	The Americans Arrive	2	Alice Duer Miller
1/22	The Americans Arrive	2	Alice Duer Miller
4/16	Young Nowheres	2	I.A.R. Wylie
4/23	Grandpa	2	Struthers Burt
4/30	Villa Beata	2	Beatrix Demarest Lloyd
5/7	Albany	2	Joseph Hergesheimer
5/21	Natchez	2	Joseph Hergesheimer
6/4	Washington	2	Joseph Hergesheimer
6/18	Lexington	2	Joseph Hergesheimer
7/9	Charleston	2	Joseph Hergesheimer
7/23	New Orleans	2	Joseph Hergesheimer
9/10	Boston	2	Joseph Hergesheimer
9/24	Crusade	4	Donn Byrne
10/1	Crusade	2	Donn Byrne
10/8	Crusade	2	Donn Byrne
10/15	Crusade	2	Donn Byrne
10/29	Pittsburgh	2	Joseph Hergesheimer
11/12	Philadelphia	2	Joseph Hergesheimer

1928

Date	Title	#	Author
1/14	Snob's Progress	2	Day Edgar
2/4	A Pretty Little Property	2	C.E. Montague
3/3	Escape, Extra Narrow	2	Day Edgar
3/31	Behind That Curtain	3	Earl Derr Biggers
4/7	Behind That Curtain	2	Earl Derr Biggers
4/14	Behind That Curtain	2	Earl Derr Biggers
4/21	Behind That Curtain	2	Earl Derr Biggers
4/28	Behind That Curtain	2	Earl Derr Biggers
5/5	Behind That Curtain	2	Earl Derr Biggers
	After Holbein	2	Edith Wharton
5/26	The Desert's Dusty Face, The Firm's Bachelor	2	Dorothy Black
6/9	The Desert's Dusty Face, The Firm's Boats	2	Dorothy Black
6/23	The Desert's Dusty Face, The Three Musketeers	2	Dorothy Black
7/21	The Desert's Dusty Face	2	Dorothy Black

1929

Date	Title	#	Author
2/9	He'll Come Home	3	Roland Pertwee
2/16	He'll Come Home	2	Roland Pertwee
2/23	He'll Come Home	2	Roland Pertwee
3/2	He'll Come Home	2	Roland Pertwee
	A Man To Avoid	3	Alice Duer Miller
3/9	A Man To Avoid	2	Alice Duer Miller
	He'll Come Home	2	Roland Pertwee
3/16	He'll Come Home	2	Roland Pertwee
	A Man To Avoid	2	Alice Duer Miller
3/23	A Man To Avoid	2	Alice Duer Miller
4/6	In Heaven A Little Window	2	Eleanor Mercein
5/18	The Black Camel	3	Earl Derr Biggers
5/25	The Black Camel	2	Earl Derr Biggers
6/1	The Black Camel	2	Earl Derr Biggers
6/8	The Black Camel	2	Earl Derr Biggers
6/15	The Black Camel	2	Earl Derr Biggers
6/22	The Black Camel	2	Earl Derr Biggers
7/27	Pappy Blue Boy	2	Colonel Givens
9/21	Impromptu	3	Harold McGrath
9/28	Impromptu	2	Harold McGrath
10/5	Impromptu	2	Harold McGrath
10/26	El U E El Dos	2	Eleanor Mercein
11/23	The Limestone Tree, Les Kaintocks	3	Joseph Hergesheimer
12/7	The Limestone Tree, The Craven Image	2	Joseph Hergesheimer

1930

Date	Title	#	Author
1/18	The Limestone Tree, Dark Memory	2	Joseph Hergesheimer
2/1	The Limestone Tree, The Rose Arbor	2	Joseph Hergesheimer
2/22	The Limestone Tree, The Purse Race	2	Joseph Hergesheimer
3/29	The Limestone Tree, The Lincoln Gun	2	Joseph Hergesheimer
4/26	The Limestone Tree, The Rebel Trace	2	Joseph Hergesheimer
5/31	The Limestone Tree, Ladies In Nashville	2	Joseph Hergesheimer
6/28	The Limestone Tree, The Stainless Heart	2	Joseph Hergesheimer
7/12	The Limestone Tree, The Long Hunter	2	Joseph Hergesheimer
8/9	The Champion From Far Away	2	Ben Hecht
12/13	Tumble-Down Dick	2	Richard M. Hallet
	The House Of Dawn	3	C.E. Scoggins
12/20	The House Of Dawn	2	C.E. Scoggins
12/27	The House Of Dawn	2	C.E. Scoggins

1931

Date	Title	#	Author
1/3	The House Of Dawn	2	C.E. Scoggins
1/10	The House Of Dawn	2	C.E. Scoggins
1/17	The House Of Dawn	2	C.E. Scoggins
2/14	Fine Apparel	2	Joseph Hergesheimer
4/25	Pomegranate Seed	2	Edith Wharton
8/8	Upstairs	4	J.P. Marquand
9/5	Escapade	2	Leonard H. Nason
9/12	Conjurers Of The North	2	Richard M. Hallet
10/10	The Castle Of Hohenems	4	Dornford Yates
10/17	The Castle Of Hohenems	2	Dornford Yates
10/24	The Castle Of Hohenems	2	Dornford Yates
10/31	The Castle Of Hohenems	2	Dornford Yates

Date	Title	No.	Author
11/7	The Castle Of Hohenems	2	Dornford Yates

1932

Date	Title	No.	Author
1/9	Son Of Mithra	2	Horatio Winslow
3/12	Sold South	2	J.P. Marquand
4/16	Jine The Cavalry	2	J.P. Marquand
6/11	Jack Still	2	J.P. Marquand
6/18	Black Wolf	2*	Walter D. Edmonds
8/6	Through Bertelot's Fence	2**	Guy Gilpatrick
8/13	Far Away	2	J.P. Marquand
9/10	Piamissimo	2	Phil Strong
10/8	High Tide	2	J.P. Marquand

* Full Color

** One two color; one, three color

1933

Date	Title	No.	Author
1/21	Rodney	2s	Leonard H. Nason
	Throw Him Down McCloskey	2	Richard Mathews Hallet
2/11	The Quiet Man	2	Maurice Walsh
4/8	Slava	2s	Eleanor Mercein
4/8	The Last of The Romans	2	Richard M. Hallet
4/22	"Gilla-Horse!"	2	Guy Gilpatrick
5/13	Expedition Eugenic	2	Lucy Stone Terrill
6/17	The Portcullis Room	3	Valentine Williams
6/24	The Portcullis Room	2	Valentine Williams
7/1	The Portcullis Room	2	Valentine Williams
7/8	The Portcullis Room	2	Valentine Williams
7/15	The Portcullis Room	2	Valentine Williams
7/22	The Portcullis Room	2	Valentine Williams
7/29	The Portcullis Room	2	Valentine Williams
8/5	The Portcullis Room	2	Valentine Williams
9/9	The Foolscap Rose, The Hired Girl	3	Joseph Hergesheimer
9/23	The Foolscap Rose, The Journeyman	3	Joseph Hergesheimer
10/7	The Foolscap Rose, The Master	2	Joseph Hergesheimer
	Courtship Of My Cousin Doone	3	Walter D. Edmonds
10/14	Courtship Of My Cousin Doone	2	Walter D. Edmonds
10/21	Honor Of The Country	3	Walter D. Edmonds

1934

Date	Title	No.	Author
2/3	The Foolscap Rose Unfolding: Three Views Of Amasa Kinzer - I	2	Joseph Hergesheimer
2/10	- II	2	Joseph Hergesheimer
2/17	- III	2	Joseph Hergesheimer
	The House Of Dawn	3	C.E. Scoggins
2/24	The House Of Dawn	2	C.E. Scoggins
	The First Race Of Blue Dandy	3	Walter D. Edmonds
3/3	The First Race Of Blue Dandy	3	Walter D. Edmonds
	The House Of Dawn	2	C.E. Scoggins
3/10	The House Of Dawn	2	C.E. Scoggins
3/17	The House Of Dawn	2	C.E. Scoggins
3/24	The House Of Dawn	1*	C.E. Scoggins
5/12	The Foolscap Rose, Unfolded: The Old Ladies	2	Joseph Hergesheimer
5/19	The Banker	3	Joseph Hergesheimer
5/26	The Vernal Rose	2	Joseph Hergesheimer
6/2	Caviar To Candida	3	Walter D. Edmonds
7/14	The Crystal Chandalier	2	Joseph Hergesheimer
8/4	Killers In The Valley	3	Walter D. Edmonds
9/8	The White Nosed Colt	2	Walter D. Edmonds
9/29	Ambuscade	2	William Faulkner
10/13	Retreat	2	William Faulkner
10/20	Then Came The Captain's Daughter	3	Maurice Walsh
11/3	Raid	2	William Faulkner
12/8	Ming Yellow	3	J.P. Marquand
12/15	Ming Yellow	2	J.P. Marquand
12/22	Ming Yellow	2	J.P. Marquand
12/29	Ming Yellow	2	J.P. Marquand

* Also 4 fragments repeated

1935

Date	Title	No.	Author
1/5	Ming Yellow	2	J.P. Marquand
1/12	Ming Yellow	1*	J.P. Marquand
3/30	No Hero	3	J.P. Marquand
4/6	No Hero	2	J.P. Marquand
4/13	No Hero	2	J.P. Marquand
4/20	No Hero	2	J.P. Marquand
4/27	No Hero	2	J.P. Marquand
	Chambelona	2	Josph Hergesheimer
5/4	Chambelona	2	Joseph Hergesheimer
	No Hero	1	J.P. Marquand
6/1	Smoke Over The Prairie	3	Conrad Richter
7/20	Legacy	2	Thornton Martin
8/3	Judge	2	Walter D. Edmonds
10/12	Early Settlers	3	Carlin Reed
11/9	Murder In Mesopotamia	3	Agatha Christie
11/16	Murder In Mespotamia	3	Agatha Christie
11/23	Murder In Mesopotamia	2	Agatha Christie
11/30	Murder In Mesopotamia	3	Agatha Christie
12/7	Murder In Mesopotamia	4	Agatha Christie
12/14	Murder In Mesopotamia	2	Agatha Christie

1936

Date	Title	No.	Author
1/4	The Great Day	2	Hugh McNair Kahler
2/8	Thank You, Mr. Moto	3	J.P.Marquand
2/15	Thank You, Mr. Moto	2	J.P. Marquand
2/22	Thank You, Mr. Moto	2	J.P. Marquand
2/29	Thank You, Mr. Moto	2	J.P. Marquand

Date	Title		Author
3/7	Thank You, Mr. Moto	2	J.P. Marquand
3/14	Thank You, Mr. Moto	1	J.P. Marquand
3/21	Hang It On The Horn	3	J.P. Marquand
4/18	No One Ever Would	2	J.P. Marquand
5/9	Indians At McKlennars	3	Walter D. Edmonds
6/13	Contrabando	3	Carl Detzer
6/20	Contrabando	2	Carl Detzer
	Put Those Things Away	2	J.P. Marquand
6/27	Contrabando	2	Carl Detzer
7/4	Contrabando	2	Carl Detzer
7/11	Contrabando	2	Carl Detzer
7/18	Contrabando	2	Carl Detzer
7/25	Contrabando	1	Carl Detzer
9/12	Fiddling Fool	2	Ben Ames Williams
	Think Fast, Mr. Moto	3	J.P. Marquand
9/19	Think Fast, Mr. Moto	3	J.P. Marquand
9/26	Think Fast, Mr. Moto	2	J.P. Marquand
10/3	Think Fast, Mr. Moto	2	J.P. Marquand
10/10	Think Fast, Mr. Moto	2	J.P. Marquand
10/17	Think Fast, Mr. Moto	1	J.P. Marquand
10/24	The Devil And Daniel Webster	2	Stephen Vincent Benet
11/14	The Unvanquished	2s	William Faulkner
12/5	Troy Weight	1	J.P. Marquand
1937			
2/13	The Captives	2	Walter D. Edmonds
	Child's Play	2	James Gould Cozzens
3/30	Caty Breen	2	Walter D. Edmonds
4/3	Delia Borst	2	Walter D. Edmonds
4/17	Squaw	3	Walter D. Edmonds
5/1	Skanasunk	2	Walter D. Edmonds
5/15	Dygartsbush	2	Walter D. Edmonds
6/26	The Brotherhood	2	Allan Swinton
7/17	The Spanish Gun	2	Walter D. Edmonds
9/11	The Child By Tiger	3	Thomas Wolf
9/18	Johnny Pie And The Fool Killer	4	Stephen Vincent Benet
10/23	The Dream	2	Agatha Christie
1938			
1/22	Dakota's Coming	3	McKinley Kantor
3/12	The Woman With Kind Hands	3	McKinley Kantor
4/16	Elder Brother	2	Hugh McNair Kahler
7/2	Mr. Moto Is So Sorry	3	J.P. Marquand
7/9	Mr. Moto Is So Sorry	2	J.P. Marquand
7/16	Mr. Moto Is So Sorry	2	J.P. Marquand
7/23	Mr. Moto Is So Sorry	2	J.P. Marquand
7/30	Mr. Moto Is So Sorry	2	J.P. Marquand
8/6	Mr. Moto Is So Sorry	2	J.P. Marquand
8/13	Mr. Moto Is So Sorry	1	J.P. Marquand
9/17	The Die Hard	2	Stephen Vincent Benet
1939			
2/11	I Will Do My Best	2	McKinley Kantor
2/25	The Pipe Major Of Little Sorrowful	2	Glen Allen
4/15	The Witch Doctor Of Rosy Ridge	4	McKinley Kantor
5/20	The Bobbycock Trout	3	Glen Allen
9/16	The Soldier's Peaches	2	Stuart Cloete
1940			
2/24	My Grandmother's Leg	3	Ben Ames Williams
3/2	My Grandmother's Leg	1	Ben Ames Williams
4/27	Lands Sake	2	I.A.R. Wylie
5/18	Freedom's A Hard Bought Thing	3	Stephen Vincent Benet
6/20	"March On", He Said	2	J.P. Marquand
6/20	Far Enough	2	Stuart Cloete
7/27	A Hunting We Will Go	1	I.A.R. Wylie
8/10	Blind McNair	3	Thomas H. Raddell
9/7	You Were My Friend	2	Naomi Lane Babson
	Crashaw On Strategy	2s	William Arthur Breyfogle
11/2	Walk To Glory	2	Louis Kaye
11/30	The Sunflower Kid	3	Brendon Gill
1941			
5/31	The Tall Men	3	William Faulkner
6/21	Uncle Sharkey And The Walking Match	2	Edward W. O'Brien
8/2	Nothing To Hinder	2	Carl D. Lane
11/15	Give Me Steam	2	Carl D. Lane
12/13	The Far Away Look	2	Edward W. O'Brien
1942			
9/12	The Swamp	2s	Robert Murphy
1943			
7/31	The Pig Of Pen Mynydd	2	Henry John Colyton
11/6	The People's Choice	1	Edward W. O'Brien

AINSLEE'S MAGAZINE

Date	Title		Author
1899			
May	The Happiest Day Of His Life	4	Lloyd Osborne

July	COVER		
	The Pardon Of Thomas Whalen	6	Brand Whitlock
Aug	Her Atonement	5	John Luther Long
Nov	A Secret Of State	5	Brand Whitlock
1900			
Feb	The Vindication Of Henderson Of Greene	5	Brand Whitlock
April	Greenfield's First Campaign Fund	4	Brand Whitlock
Aug	That About Laura Hornblower	4, 1p	Eugene Wood
Oct	The Colonel's Last Campaign	3. 2p	Brand Whitlock
1901			
Jan	The Marquis' Couch	4	Rafael Sabatini
March	The Lottery Ticket	3	Rafael Sabatini
July	Reform In The First	3, 1p	Brand Whitlock
Aug	The Ghosts Of The Brig	4	Colin McKay
Sept	The Republic's Seal	4	Rafael Sabatini
Nov	The Fortunes Of Lal Faversham 1. The Loadad Dice	3	Rafael Sabatini
Dec	2. Of What Befel At Balienochy	4	Rafael Sabatini
1902			
Jan	3. After The Worcester Field	3	Rafael Sabatini
Feb	4. The Chancellor's Daughter	4	Rafael Sabatini
March	5. Carolus and Caroline	1, 3p	Rafael Sabatini
April	6. In The Eleventh Hour	2, 2p	Rafael Sabatini
July	The Cutting Out Of The "Heavenly Home"	4	Norman Duncan
Sept	Malachi Nolan	2, 1p	Brand Whitlock

Signatures were script, sometimes just initials

A policy change on the part of the magazine resulted in the elimination of illustrations after October, 1902.

LESLIE'S POPULAR MONTHLY MAGAZINE

1902			
May	Hope Of Glory	1, 3p*	Harvey J. O'Higgins
	In The Presence Of The Enemy	1, 3p*	Frederic T. Hill
1903			
May	A Dogged Chase	5p**	Frederick Walworth
July	Marmaduke Dulcimer, Codicil Forger	5p	Henry A. Hering
	A Few Real Boys, The School	12p	Henry A. Shute
Aug	A Few Real Boys, The Fight	7p	Henry A. Shute
Sept	A Few Real Boys, The Fishing Trip	5p	Henry A. Shute
Nov	A Few Real Boys, The Majesty Of The Law	5p	Henry A. Shute
Dec	A Few Real Boys, Christmas Festivities	6p	Henry A. Shute
1904			
Jan	A Few Real Boys, The Country Fair -The Present And The Past	5p	Henry A. Shute
Feb	The Crimson Cord	6p	Ellis Parker Butler
March	The Squire's Shrewd Move	2p	George S. Wasson
	The Downfall Of Pembroke	3p	Henry C. Rowland
April	The Adventures Of The Fifth Street Church	3p	Ellis Parker Butler
June	One Hour Late	3p	Edith G. McLeod
July	A Fortune In Hot Air	3p	Ellis Parker Butler
Aug	The Chloride Holdup	3p	Harry Irving Green
Sept	Jimmy Hicks' Patent	3p	John F. Wilson
1905			
Jan	Mr. Rick's Go-Carts	1p	Henry Sydnor Harrison
March	The Appeasing Of Khali	3p	Frederick Walworth
April	Matthew	3p	E.F. Sterns
June	The Americano At Cerdos	3p	George Allan England
Aug	Common Business Honesty	3p	Arthur S. Pier
Oct	Plupy's Lecture	5p	Henry A. Shute
Nov	Plupy's Debating Club	3p	Henry A. Shute

The magazine's name changed to:

AMERICAN ILLUSTRATED MAGAZINE

1906			
Jan	The "Antiquers"	4p	Joseph C. Lincoln
March	Swan Carlson's Wooing	4p	Lynn D. Follett
July	How The Prince Saw America	3p	Susan K. Glaspell
1909			
Jan	Groping Children	5	James Oppenheim
April	Grover Cleveland	5	Jesse Lynch Williams
1911			
Oct	The Turn Of The Coin	3	D.H. Haines
	Advertisement by McClure's for the forthcoming serial, "Stover At Yale", Pg. 20		
1912			
Nov	A Little Flier In Appendicitis	3	"An Initiate"
	Darcey Klaw	3+	E. Albert Apple

Announcement of change in the magazine's format.

1914

June	Saved By Proxy	3	Earl Derr Biggers

1916

April	The Septagon	1	Jack Lait
May	One Touch Of Art	2	Jack Lait

1918

March	Wanted - A Younger and More Practical Man.	2	William Dudley Pelley
May	Through Thick And Thin	3	William Dudley Pelley
June	The One White Sheep In A Family Of Black Ones	2	William Dudley Pelley

AMERICAN ILLUSTRATED MAGAZINE

1918

July	What Put "Pep" Into John Stevens	2	William Dudley Pelley
Oct	Why The Judge Felt Safe	2	William Dudley Pelley

1921

June	He Couldn't Stand Prosperity	2s	Harriet Abbott
July	The Man Who Wasn't Wanted	2	Nellie Gardner White

1930

Feb	The Pirate Who Wanted To Be King	2s	Herbert Ravenal Sass
April	The King's Minion	4s +	Rafael Sabatini
May	The King's Minion	3	Rafael Sabatini
June	The King's Minion	3	Rafael Sabatini
July	The King's Minion	2	Rafael Sabatini
Aug	The King's Minion	2	Rafael Sabatini
Sept	The King's Minion	2	Rafael Sabatini
Oct	The King's Minion	2	Rafael Sabatini

1931

May	Between Men	3	Faraday Keene

1933

Feb	Sailor's Knot	3	Peter B. Kyne
April	The Road To Honor	2s	Karl Detzer
Sept	The Man Who Liked Toys	3s	Leslie Charteris

1934

Dec	The Leader	1 + +	Katherine Haviland Taylor

1935

May	Security	1	Walter Lippman

1936

Aug	Local Color	1	R.G. Kirk
Nov	Gratitude	2s	Henry and Syliva Lieferant

1938

April	Blank Interlude	1	H. Thompson Rich

* Script signatures: F.R. Gruger and Frederic R. Gruger
** Unsigned
 s Spread

+ One three-color
· + + Super

THE CENTURY

1904

June	The Sectional House	5p	Ellis Parker Butler
Nov.	An Impossible Possibility	4p	Elliot Flower

1905

Feb	Keegan's Coup At Ka	8p	Edw. W. Townsend
July	A Nevada Samaritan	5	Phillip V. Mighels
Nov	The Selma Protective Association	4p	Carroll Watson Rankin

1906

April	The Off-Day Of An Automobile	7p	Phillip V. Mighels
	The Yarn Of Captain Bill	4p	Ellis Parker Butler
June	Seeing France With Uncle John*	4, 3p	Anne Warner
July	An Economic Revel	1p	Charles A. Seldon

1907

May	The Renegation Of Hogg	5p	Herman Whitaker
Aug	The Non-Resistance of Amos**	5, 2p	Reginald W. Kauffman
Sept	The Mind Reader	2, 4p	S. Weir Mitchell, MD

1908

Feb	The Quest Of Aunt Nancy	4p	Elizabeth Jordan
April	Advertisement of book "Seeing England With Uncle John" by Anne Warner. One pen illustration and statement "Funny illustrations by Gruger."		
Oct	The Unpledged Man	4p	Elliott Flower

1909

June	The Cakes Of Judgment	4p	Victor Rousseau
Nov	Millington's Motor Mystery	2p	Ellis Parker Butler

1910

Jan	The Vacillations of Peter "Poet"	6p	Herman Whitaker
March	The Man Who Was Someone Else	5	Ellis Parker Butler
May	Cartoon, humorous, page 157	1p	
	The Cirkelatin' Whalans	6p	Edith Livingston Smith
June	The Women He Might Have Married	5p	Deborah Joy
Nov	Jerry's Pachyderm	5p	Ellis Parker Butler

1911

Jan	The Belsnickel Mothering On Perilous	1	Elsie Singmaster
	II The Pure Scholar	1p	Lucy Furman
Feb	III The Fightingest Boy	1p	Lucy Furman

* Believe FRG made his first trip abroad in connection with this assignment. Due to his serious illness after his return, the serial was completed by May Wilson Preston.

** Believe this may be the story for which FRG made a trip into the Amish country with a doctor and impersonating another doctor, starting from experienced "professional" adventures.

+ Excellently reproduced on coated stock with yellowish-green tint.

++ Editor of "The Century".

CIRCLE MAGAZINE

COLLEGE HUMOR

This magazine had a rather singular career. The first number was dated 1920-1921 and was named Spring; the next two appeared in 1922 and were called Autumn and Winter. The 1922 Winter number was also the first number in 1923 which had, in addition, Spring, Summer, Autumn and Christmas numbers. Volume 3 contained four season and a Christmas number. Up to this point C.H. was a pulp magazine - very poor paper and rather poor printing. From this point on the quality gradually improved until in the late twenties it rated as a slick paper magazine. Beginning with 1925 there were monthly numbers divided into two volumes per year. Arthur William Brown's and James Montgomery Flagg's illustrations began to appear and remained the most frequently used until the demise of the magazine in the late thirties. Raleigh was used several times, FRG twice and Mowat once. The character of work of the last two quite obviously did not fit this magazine.

COLLIER'S WEEKLY MAGAZINE

7/13	The Flying Fish	3	Arthur Somers Roche
7/20	The Flying Fish	3	Arthur Somers Roche
7/27	The Flying Fish	2	Arthur Somers Roche
8/3	The Flying Fish	2*	Arthur Somers Roche
8/10	The Flying Fish	3	Arthur Somers Roche
8/17	The Flying Fish	3	Arthur Somers Roche
8/24	The Flying Fish	2	Arthur Somers Roche
8/31	The Flying Fish	3	Arthur Somers Roche
9/7	The Flying Fish	2	Arthur Somers Roche
9/14	The Flying Fish	2	Arthur Somers Roche

The following illustrations were made in collaboration with Arthur William Brown. Usually they were unsigned, but occasionally a drawing would be signed by one or the other. The by-line read; "Illustrated by F.R. Gruger and Arthur William Brown."

1918	From Baseball To Boches, First Inning		H.C. Witwer
	Second Inning		H.C. Witwer
	Third Inning		H.C. Witwer
3/16	Fourth Inning	1	H.C. Witwer
4/13	Fifth Inning	1	H.C. Witwer
5/11	Sixth Inning	2	H.C. Witwer
6/15	Seventh Inning (FRG, pg 13; AWB, pg 14)	2	H.C. Witwer
7/13	Eighth Inning (FRG, pg 12; AWB, pg 13)	2	H.C. Witwer
7/27	Ninth Inning	2	H.C. Witwer
8/31	Tenth Inning	2	H.C. Witwer
9/21	Eleventh Inning (AWB only)	2	H.C. Witwer
10/12	Twelfth Inning	2	H.C. Witwer
11/2	Plain Water	2	H.C. Witwer
12/7	A Midsummer Night's Scream	2	H.C. Witwer
1919			
2/1	Somewhere In Harlem	2	H.C. Witwer
3/1	Harmony	2	H.C. Witwer
3/29	As You Were	2	H.C. Witwer

Arthur William Brown illustrated several more stories by H.C. Witwer alone, after which neither illustrator appeared again in Collier's.

* This is the subject at the New Britain Museum which they named "Serious Business", appropriately enough. This picture was at the head of the part and carried no caption.

COSMOPOLITAN MAGAZINE

1921			
May	Roulette	4	Fanny Hurst
Aug	Kelly Of Charles Street	3	Royal Brown

1922			
April	Elements	2, 1s	Stephen Vincent Benet
July	A Law Unto Ourselves	2, 1s	Rita Weyman
1923			
Jan	The Old Boy	3	Gouverneur Morris
Feb	The Last Witch	2, 1s	H. Tarkington Jameson*
March	The Poisoner	2, 1s	Arthur Train
May	Isabel	2, 1s	Inez Haynes Irwin
July	The Eighth Wonder	2, 1s	A.S.M. Hutchinson
Aug	Derrick's Return	2	Gouverneur Morris
Nov	As Hard As Nails	2	Royal Brown

In 1924 the Cosmopolitan Magazine absorbed the Metropolitan Magazine

1924			
Feb	Cornflower Cassi's Concert	2, 1s	Peter B. Kyne
March	The Luncheon	1	W. Somerset Maughn
Aug	The Woman Who Tried To Dodge Life	2, 1s	Belle Burns Gromer
Sept	Youth Has Its Fling	2, 1s	Sir Philip Gibbs
Oct	The Raveled Sleeve	2s	Stephen Vincent Benet
Dec	Heaven	1, 2s	Basil King
1925			
Feb	Diamond Cut Diamond	3	J.S. Flectcher

In March, 1925 the Cosmopolitan Magazine was absorbed by Hearst's International and became HEARST'S INTERNATIONAL COSMOPOLITAN.

1926			
Oct	The Virgin Warrior	2**	Blasco Ibanez
Nov	The Slave Of Seven Women	2	Blasco Ibanez
1927			
Feb	Another Lady Bountiful	1s	Zona Gale
May	Three Lumps Of Sugar	1s	Amory Hare
June	The Hermit's Love Story	1, 1s	George Moore
Oct	H.R.H.	2	Robert Hichens
1928			
April	Murder	1, 1s	Robert Hichens
May	A Slip Of The Knife	1, 1s	Robert Hichens
1929			
April	Five And Ten	4	Fanny Hurst
May	Five And Ten	2s	Fanny Hurst
June	Five And Ten	1, 1s	Fanny Hurst
July	Five And Ten	2	Fanny Hurst
Aug	Five And Ten	2	Fanny Hurst
Sept	Five And Ten	1s	Fanny Hurst
1930			
April	The Bracelet	3	Robert Hichens
May	The Bracelet	3	Robert Hichens
June	The Bracelet	2	Robert Hichens
July	The Bracelet	1, 1s	Robert Hichens
Aug	The Bracelet	3	Robert Hichens

Sept	The Bracelet	5	Robert Hichens
Oct	The Bracelet	1	Robert Hichens

HEARST'S INTERNATIONAL
COSMOPOLITAN

Nov	Great Day In The Morning	4	Irvin S. Cobb
Dec	"Ole Miss"	3	Irvin S. Cobb
1931			
Feb	Arise And Shine	4	Irvin S. Cobb
April	The Sun Shines Bright	2	Irvin S. Cobb
May	Br'er Rabbit, He Lay Low	4	Irvin S. Cobb
June	A Colonel Of Kentucky	4	Irvin S. Cobb
Aug	Judge Priest Goes Fishing	3	Irvin S. Cobb
Oct	An Incident Of The Noble Experiment	4	Irvin S. Cobb
Nov	"Aged Local Vets Hold Final Rally"	3	Irvin S. Cobb
1932			
May	One Way To Stop Panics	2	Irvin S. Cobb

  * Sister of Booth Tarkington
  ** Given to the New Britain Museum of Art, Sanford Low Collection
  s All spreads are half tones.
  All of the 1931 Cobb stories are about Judge Priest.

COUNTRY GENTLEMAN

1913			
June 7,	How One Jones Got Even	3	Henry Irving Dodge
1921	In Honor Of A Saint	1	Shirley L. Seifert

THE DELINEATOR

1908			
Oct	The Sin	4	Annie H. Donnell
Nov	Mrs. Peevy's Signature	4	Hugh Pendexter
Dec	For Unto Us	1*	Harriet Monroe
1909			
June	The Seven Stages Of The Stage	8	Louise Closser Hale
1910			
May	Finer Clay	3	Kate Jordan
1912			
June	Boleslas	2	Ellis Parker Butler
July	Help! Help! Help!	1	Harris Dickson
Nov	The Woman	1**	Charles Marcus Horton
1917			
July	AH-LEE-Bung	1, 1p	Wallace Irwin
1920			
May	The Man Who Was Tired Of His Wife	2	Lucille Van Slyke
June	The Man Who Was Tired Of His Wife	2	Lucille Van Slyke
1927	Pretty Pagan	1	Bernice Brown

1929			
March	Cousin Captain	2	Marion & Webb Waldron
April	Jane's First Lame Duck	2	John Galsworthy
Sept	Prelude	2	Eliz. Sanaxy Holding
Oct	Landlady	3	William Corcoran
Dec	Christmas Ballad	1	Theodosia Garrison
1930			
Feb	Treasures Of Vasco Gomez	2	Stephen Vincent Benet

  * This picture is credited to Frederic Roderigo, pg 991
  ** Reproduced as a wood engraving. Caption: From behind the stone wall, and dragging a shotgun, went a shawl, a wrapper and a hank of hair.

May	Thief Of Salvation	1	Anna Brand
Dec	The Emperor's Aide De Camp	2	Sir Philip Gibbs
1931			
Feb	Bands Playing	2	I.A.R. Wylie
July	Field Of Honor	3	Margaret Sangster
1932			
April	Waiting Room	1s	Margaret Sangster

EVERYBODY'S MAGAZINE

1905			
June	The Law Breakers	5p	Robert Grant
Dec	One Christmas Day In The Morning	5p	Grace S. Richmond
1907			
Aug	A Phyrric Victory	4p	Dorothy Canfield
Nov	The Heroism Of Mr. Peglow	3p	E.J. Roth
1908			
July	Mr. Trimble's Speech	3p	E.J. Roth
Oct	The Anecdote	4p	Kenneth Harris
1909			
Jan	The Seer And The Servant	6p	Joseph C. Lincoln
1910			
March	An Unframed Picture	7p	Dorothy Canfield
1912			
June	The Acid Test	6	Lloyd Osborne
1913			
July	The Championship	6	Gouverneur Morris
1915			
Aug	The Family Tree	3	Richard M. Hallett
1918			
Dec	Ethel Louvander's Husband	3*	Ida M. Evans
1919			
Feb	The Duel	3	Donald H. Haines
Aug	The Orchid	3	Dora Burnet
1920			
June	Simple Simon And The Fourth Dimension	1	Ruth Sawyer
July	The Little God Of Hunches	2	Arthur Crabb

Dec	The Pirate Of Park Avenue	2	Lucian Cary

* Very poor paper and reproduction.
  This magazine deteriorated markedly after 1920.

GOOD HOUSEKEEPING MAGAZINE

1922			
Feb	Tale Of Triona	2	William J. Locke
March	Tale Of Triona	2	William J. Locke
April	Tale Of Triona	2	William J. Locke
May	Tale Of Triona	2	William J. Locke
June	Tale Of Triona	2	William J. Locke
July	Tale Of Triona	2	William J. Locke
Aug	Tale Of Triona	2	William J. Locke
Sept	Tale Of Triona	2	William J. Locke
Dec	The Magic Promise	2	Katherine Holland Brown
1923			
Aug	Eyes Of The Blind	2	Adela Rogers St. John
Sept	A Hollywood Love Story	2	Adela Rogers St. John
1924			
Jan	Rendezvous	2	Fanny Heaslip Lea
July	Mrs. Hartigan	3	Mary Synon
Dec	Mrs. Margrove Finds Her Children	2	I.A.R. Wylie
1925			
March	Lured Toward Beauty	3	Henry James Forman
1926			
April	True Thomas	1, 1s	Steven Vincent Benet
1927			
Dec	A Princess Passes	2	Jay Gelzer
1928			
April	The Fire Of Youth	2	Margaret E. Sangster
1929			
April	The Hem Of His Garment	2	Margaret E. Sangster
Nov	What Is Man	1	William Lyons Phelps
1930			
April	The Crowded Room	2	Margaret E. Sangster
May	The Wisdom Of Folly	1	William Lyons Phelps
Nov	Because Of Thy Great Bounty	1	Grace Knoll Crowell
1931			
Sept	That Good Part	1	Margaret E. Sangster
Nov	The Beauty Of Holiness	1	William Lyons Phelps
1933			
Nov	The Foghorn	2	Gertrude Atherton
1934			
March	Walk With Me Lad	1	Ann Shannon Monroe
1935			
April	Not Made With Hands	1	Sara Henderson Hay

HARPER'S MAGAZINE

1914			
Oct	Cousin Paul	4	Victor Rousseau
1923			
July	Knights And Sights Of Malta	5, 1*	Henry James Forman
Aug	Golden Cities Of Sicily	5, 1*	Henry James Forman
Sept	The Land Of The Lotus Eaters	6	Henry James Forman
Oct	The Country Of The Sybarites	5, 1*	Henry James Forman
1924			
Jan	The Journey	3, 1*	Laura Spencer Porter

* Magazine frontespiece, full color.

HARPER'S BAZAAR

1923			
Feb	''Sir Willie Of The Valley''	2	Stephen Vincent Benet
April	Keats Shadd	2	Richard Washburn Child
May	Hereafter	2, 1s	Gouverneur Morris
June	It Can't Be Done	2, 1s	Phyllis Duganne
1926			
Sept	The Thunderer	3	E. Barrington
Oct	The Thunderer	2	E. Barrington
Nov	The Thunderer	2	E. Barrington
Dec	The Thunderer	2	E. Barrington
1927			
Jan	The Thunderer	2	E. Barrington
Aug	The Dumbell	2	Frances F. Williams
Sept	A Birthday Cake For Lionel	1	Elinor Wylie
Nov	Not To Be Opened	1	Lloyd Osborne
Dec	Not To Be Opened	2	Lloyd Osborne
1928			
Jan	Not To Be Opened	2	Lloyd Osborne
Feb	Not To Be Opened	2	Lloyd Osborne
Mar	Not To Be Opened	2	Lloyd Osborne
Oct	Ecstasy	2	Hugh Walpole
Nov	Sudden Money	1s	Sir Philip Gibbs
Dec	Sudden Money	1s	Sir Philip Gibbs
1929			
Nov	Mr. Walcot Goes Home	2	Francis Brett Young

HEARST'S INTERNATIONAL

1922			
Sept	The Gioconda Smile	2, 1s	Aldous Huxley
1923			
May	Diamonds	3, 2s	Grace Sartwell Mason
Nov	During Dinner	2, 1s	Arnold Bennett

1924

Month	Title		Author
July	The Ardent Bigamist	2, 1s	W. Somerset Maugham
Aug	On Drinking Today	1	Ray Long
Sept	The Goose Woman	3, 1s	Rex Beach
Oct	The Goose Woman	2	Rex Beach

Hearst's International took over the Cosmopolitan Magazine in March, 1925 and it was renamed "Hearst's International Cosmopolitan". See *Cosmopolitan Magazine* for further work.

THE LADIES HOME JOURNAL

1903			
April	Josia Allen's Easter Ode	1	Josiah Allen's Wife
1905			
Feb	"Mirry"	2	Charles Battel Loomis
1907			
Oct	The Letters of Jennie Allen	4	Grace Donworth
Nov	The Letters Of Jennie Allen	4	Grace Donworth
Dec	The Letters Of Jennie Allen	4	Grace Donworth
1914			
Nov	The Store That Steals Your Money	1	J. George Frederick
1916			
Jan	The Fatal Kink In Algernon	3	P.G. Wodehouse
March	The Girl Who Didn't Care	2	George Weston
April	Dominie Dean	2	Ellis Parker Butler and James B. Dare
May	Dominie Dean	1	Elis Parker Butler and James B. Dare
June	Dominie Dean	1	Ellis Parker Butler and James B. Dare
Aug	The Faith Of A Woman	1	James Oppenheim
Oct	Junior, Of The Bathtub	3	Edna Tucker Muth
1917			
May	The Apple Tree Girl	3	George Weston
June	The Apple Tree Girl	3	George Weston
Oct	The Godson Of Jeannette Contreau	2	Francis Wm. Sullivan
1919			
April	The Bungalo In Bayside	3	George F. Worts
June	The Cat That Got The Bird	2	Bruno Les
Sept	Harold Child, Bachelor	2	Arthur Crabb
Nov	Romance And Mary Lou	1	Natalie Dew

MAC LEAN'S MAGAZINE (Canadian)

1922			
3/15	Judgement	2	Ben Ames Williams
8/1	A Guest Of Tradition	2	Jos. Lister Rutledge
12/15	Different Drummers	1	Marjorie Bowen
1923			
12/15	Lighted Windows	1	
1924			
5/15	The Failure	1	Archie P. McKishnie
8/15	The Madonna Of The Trenches	1	Rudyard Kipling

MAC LEAN'S MAGAZINE (Continued)

1925			
6/1	The Burton Murder Case	3	Harvey O'Higgins
6/15	The Case Of The Forged Letter	2	Harvey O'Higgins
7/15	James Illinois Bell	1	Harvey O'Higgins
1926			
3/15	Moon Lady	1	Isabel E. Mackay

McCALL'S MAGAZINE

1923			
April	Her Grace	2	Frances Noyes Hart
June	The King's Adviser	2	Frances Noyes Hart
1928			
Feb	The Little Yellow House	3	Beatrice B. Morgan
March	The Little Yellow House	3	Beatrice B. Morgan
April	The Little Yellow House	2	Beatrice B. Morgan
	Are Women Fit To Judge Guilty	1s	Louis E. Bisch
May	The Little Yellow House	2	Beatrice B. Morgan
Dec	Four Soldiers From Four Countries	1	Remarque, Sherriff, Barbousse, Thomason
1931			
July	Famous Masters On Demand	1	John Tasker Howard
1935			
Sept	Cup Brimming Over	1, 1s	Margaret W. Jackson
Nov	A Hard Woman	1s	Nelia Gardner White
Dec	The Misses Meekins	2	Ellis Parker Butler

McCLURE'S MAGAZINE

1900			
Aug	The Shallow Spirit Of Judgment	5p*	Edith Wyatt
1900			
Oct	Trade Winds	3p*	Edith Wyatt
1901			
April	Deepwater Politics	6	May McHenry
1902			
May	A Night With Whispering Smith	10p	Frank H. Spearman
1903			
June	"49 Message"	5p*	Charles B. DeCamp

217

Date	Title	Pages	Author
Dec	The Pimienta Pancakes	6p	O. Henry
1904			
March	A Kind Of Hero	5p	W.H. Boardman
1905			
July	Tommy Cutts	6p	R.W. Child
1908			
Feb	Mrs. McClanahan, The Chinese Laundry and Beller	6	Mary Heaton Vorse
1909			
Jan	Veronica And The Angelinos	6p	Casper Day
1910			
Nov	Molly	5p	George Pattullo
1911			
Oct	Trajedies	6p	Estelle Sturgis
	Stover At Yale	5	Owen Johnson
Nov	Stover At Yale	5	Owen Johnson
Dec	Stover At Yale	4	Owen Johnson
1912			
Jan	Stover At Yale	5	Owne Johnson
Feb	Stover At Yale	3p	Owen Johnson
March	Stover At Yale	4, 2p	Owen Johnson
April	Stover At Yale	4p	Owen Johnson
May	Stover At Yale	3p	Owen Johnson
1912			
June	A Pousse Cafe Promotion	4	Harris Murton Lyon
1916			
July	"Somewhere In-"	4	Foster Emerson Brown
1917			
May	Victims Of The Law	4	C.P. Connolly
1919			
Jan	The Nice Present	4	Bruno Lessing
April	Good Time Evans	3	Louise Closser Hale
Sept	The Edgar Jennings Case	3	Wm. Hamilton Osborne
1920			
Feb	The Maternal Feminine	3	Edan Ferber
April	You've Got To Be Selfish	1s	Edna Ferber
May	Rainy Week	3	Eleanor Howell Abbott
June	Rainy Week	3	Eleanor Howell Abbott
July	Rainy Week	2	Eleanor Howell Abbott
Aug	Rainy Week	2	Eleanor Howell Abbott
Sept	Rainy Week	1	Eleanor Howell Abbott
Feb	Time Out For Granberry	3	Samuel Merwin
1921			
March	The Valiant	3	Halworthy Hall

* Script Signature

METROPOLITAN MAGAZINE

Date	Title	Pages	Author
1903			
Nov	The Whole Truth		

Date	Title	Pages	Author
	About Stephen Locke	3p	Harrison Rhodes
1904			
Jan	A Leaf In The Current - The Diary Of A Private Secretary	1p	Jane Wade
Feb	A Leaf In The Current	3p	Jane Wade
March	A Leaf In The Current	3p	Jane Wade
April	A Leaf In The Current	3p	Jane Wade
May	A Leaf In The Current	3p	Jane Wade
June	A Leaf In The Current	2p	Jane Wade
July	A Leaf In The Current	1p	Jane Wade
Aug	A Leaf In The Current	2p	Jane Wade
Sept	A Leaf In The Current	3p	Jane Wade
1914			
Oct	Angela's Business	2	Henry Sydnor Harrison
Nov	Angela's Business	2	Henry Sydnor Harrison
Dec	Angela's Business	2	Henry Sydnor Harrison
1915			
Jan	Angela's Business	2	Henry Sydnor Harrison
Feb	Angela's Business	2	Henry Sydnor Harrison
March	Angela's Business	2	Henry Sydnor Harrison
April	Angela's Business	1	Henry Sydnor Harrison
May	Angela's Business	2	Henry Sydnor Harrison
June	Angela's Business	1	Henry Sydnor Harrison
1916			
Jan	Through A Glass Darkly	3	Fanny Hurst
July	Star Light, Star Bright	3	Ruth Sapinsky
Nov	Yetta Flumbum	3	Ruth Sapinsky
1917			
Aug	People And Things	3	Mable Dunham Thayer
Nov	Dorothy For The Day	4	Henry Kitchell Webster
Dec	The Accidental	4	Henry Kitchell Webster
1918			
Jan	The Harbor	4	Henry Kitchell Webster
March	A Girl Named Mary	3	Juliet Wilbor Tompkins
April	A Girl Named Mary	3, 1s	Juliet Wilbor Tompkins
May	A Girl Named Mary	2	Juliet Wilbor Tompkins

June	A Girl Named Mary	2		Juliet Wilbor Tompkins
July	A Girl Named Mary	2		Juliet Wilbor Tompkins
1919				
May	The Black Book	3		Henry C. Rowland
1920				
March	Mother O'Mine	2		Edgar Wallace
May	Salvage	2		Mary Hastings Bradley
1921				
Feb	My Own People	2		Anzia Yezierska

The Metropolitan Magazine was absorbed by the Cosmopolitan Magazine in 1924.

MUNSEY'S MAGAZINE

1905			
April	A Police Court Romeo	6p	Chas. M. Williams
Aug	A Walapi Cupid	5p	Wm. Chester Eastbrook
1907			
April	The Mulcahey's Biddy	4p	E.J. Roth

PEARSON'S MAGAZINE

1905			
Oct	George Harlis, Suburbabite	5p	Charles Battell Loomiss
Nov	George Harlis, Suburbanite	4p	Charles Battell Loomis
Dec	George Harlis, Suburbanite	4p	Charles Battell Loomis
1906			
Jan	George Harlis, Suburbanite	2p	Charles Battell Loomis

Pearson's Magazine carried illustrations through March, 1912. The policy of the magazine was changed and announced in a statement by Arthur W. Little, President, in the April, 1912 issue. He explained that illustration would be eliminated (to cut costs) made necessary by the elimination of advertising (to maintain editorial independence). Subsequently very cheap paper (about like newsprint) with occasional simple woodcut story headings was used.

PICTORIAL REVIEW MAGAZINE

1916			
Nov	In The Valley Of The Sorceress (Also one vignette HT by John R. Neill.)	1	Sax Rohmer
1917			
June	Ex-Fighting Billy	2	Irvin S. Cobb
1918			
Feb	The Hidden Shame	3	George Pattullo

1920			
May	Mr. Rundel's Exit	2	Wallace Irwin
1935			
May	Head Of The House	2	Gordon Malherbe Hillman

REDBOOK

1914			
Sept	The Hare Of March	2	Justin Huntley McCarthy
Nov	Hempsey Burke	3	Frank N. Westcott
Dec	Hempsey Burke	2	Frank N. Westcott
1915			
Jan	Hempsey Burke	2	Frank N. Westcott
Feb	Hemnpsey Burke	2	Frank N. Westcott
March	Hempsey Burke	2	Frank N. Westcott
April	Hempsey Burke	2	Frank N. Westcott
1916			
May	The Frame-Up	3	Harris Dickson
1917			
Nov	The Family Honor	3	Peter Clark Macfarlane
1918			
Jan	The Fighting Blood Of The Kehoes	3	Anne O'Hagan
May	The Doll	3	
Aug	The Magic Of Mohammed Din	3	F. Britten Austin
Oct	Jimmy Makes Up His Mind	3	Anne E. Watton
1921			
Aug	The Forgotten Goddess	4	Burton Kline
1922			
May	Inhibiting Wattles	3	Maxwell Struthers Burt
June	Her Own Life	3	Wallace Irwin
July	A Girl Of The Films	4	Rob Wagner
Aug	A Girl Of The Films	3	Rob Wagner
Sept	A Girl Of The Films	3	Rob Wagner
Oct	A Girl Of The Films	3	Rob Wagner
Nov	A Girl Of The Films	3	Rob Wagner
Dec	A Girl Of The Films	3	Rob Wagner
1923			
April	A Touch Of Eternity	3	Wallace Irwin
June	The Blue Image	3	Melville Davisson Post
July	The Blue Image	1	Melville Davisson Post
Aug	The Blue Image	2	Melville Davisson Post
1924			
March	The Bridge Of Beauty	3	George Weston
April	The Closed House	3	Grace Startwell Mason
June	Pepper's Ghost	2	Maxwell Struthers Burt
Sept	The Vanished Duke	3	F. Britten Austin
Oct	The Fourth Degree	3	F. Britten Austin
Dec	One Venetian Night	3	Rita Weiman
Dec	A Paris Frock	3	F. Britten Austin
1925			
Jan	The Great Mallet Case	3	F. Britten Austin

Feb	Street Of The Malcontents	3	Cyril Hume
	Diamond Cut Diamond	2	F. Britten Austin
March	The Burton Murder	3	Harvey O'Higgins
April	The Forged Letter	2	Harvey O'Higgins
June	James Illinois Bell	2	Harvey O'Higgins
Sept	Stop Thief	3	Harvey O'Higgins
Nov	The Famous Parson Case	3	Harvey O'Higgins
1926			
Jan	The Rich Boy	3	F. Scott Fitzgerald
Dec	Dinner Is Served	3	Rita Weyman
1928			
July	The News Reel	2	Frederick I. Anderson
Sept	Candleshine	2	Stephen Vincent Benet
1929			
Jan	Forty-Fives Don't Roar	2	Frederick H. Brennan
July	The Murder In The Storm	3	Rufus King
Aug	The Murder In The Storm	3	Rufus King
Sept	The Murder In The Storm	3	Rufus King
Oct	The Murder In The Storm	3	Rufus King
1930			
March	The Murder On The Ship	3	Rufus King
1930			
April	The Murder On The Ship	4	Rufus King
May	The Murder On The Ship	6	Rufus King
June	The Murder On The Ship	5	Rufus King

SCRIBNER'S MAGAZINE

1900			
June	How A President Is Elected	1	A. Maurice Low
1909			
Oct	Something	4p	Juliet W. Tompkins
1915			
Dec	Her Own Sort	5	Chas. Belmont Davis
1919			
Jan	Lady Gaunt	3	Major Wolcott LeClear Beard
1937			
Feb	Pro Arte	3	Allan Seager

SUCCESS MAGAZINE

1901			
Sept	Attorney Swift And Counselor Easy	2	R. Gray
Dec	Greeley's Ambition Culminated In His Hopeless Presidential Struggle	1	Col. A.K. McClure

Drawn by F.R. Gruger from a description furnished by Colonel McClure.

1902			
Jan	On pages 20 and 21 there are two vertical, decorative panels. They do not look particularly like FRG's work, but he was experimenting a lot at this time. They are signed with a G which he is known to have used.		
March	Graduate No. 1	1	Daniel E. Sickles
June	Garlan And Company	2	David Graham Phillips
Sept	Down Wren's Wrinkle	3	Alva Milton Kerr
Dec	The Stuff That Stands	3	Cy Warman
1903			
Jan	Orion Dombay, Grocer	3*	J. George Frederick
March	T. Nolan, Jr. And The Franchise	7p	Wm. Hamilton Osborne
May	The Whip Hand	6**	Samuel Merwin
June	The Whip Hand	3, 1p	Samuel Merwin
July	The Whip Hand	1, 3p+	Samuel Merwin
Aug	The Whip Hand	1, 2p	Samuel Merwin
Sept	The Whip Hand	2, 1p	Samuel Merwin
Oct	The Whip Hand	4	Samuel Merwin
1904			
Feb	An Artist In Publicity	4	Howard Fielding
March	With Plenary Power	1, 1p	Howard Fielding
March	Guthrie Of "The Times"	5	Jos. A. Altsheler
April	Guthrie Of "The Times"	3	Jos. A. Altsheler
May	Guthrie Of "The Times"	3	Jos. A. Altsheler
June	Guthrie Of "The Times"	3	Jos. A. Altsheler
July	Guthrie Of "The Times"	3	Jos. A. Altsheler
Aug	Guthrie Of "The Times"	3	Jos. A. Altsheler
Dec	The Wrath Of The Diamond Syndicate	1, 2p	H.S. Cooper
1905			
Jan	The Wrath Of The Diamond Syndicate	1, 2p	H.S. Cooper
April	A Mouse For A Monarch	2	Holman Day
May	A Mouse For A Monarch	2	Holman Day
July	Inspector Val's Adventures		Alfred Henry Lears
Oct	Nate Well's Love Affair	1, 1p	William R. Lighton

From October 1905 till the magazine was absorbed by "Circle Magazine" in 1911, FRG did no further work for "Success". The absence of any work by him in 1906 would logically be explained by his trip abroad followed by his extended illness and recuperation, but it was unusual that the relationship was not resumed. The only other comparable lapse was with the Metropolitan Magazine, but in this case the relationship was resumed after eight years.

*Frederic Gruger
**First by-line
+ F.R. Gruger

'Publication of Success Magazine was resumed in the Twenties.

WOMAN'S HOME COMPANION

1921			
April	"Oh, Moon Of My Delight"	3	Alice Garland Steele
1922			
July	Golden Beads And Poppy Seeds	2	James Francis Dwyer
Aug	Golden Beads And Poppy Seeds	2	James Francis Dwyer
Nov	Pines O'Maine	2	James Francis Dwyer
Dec	Pines O'Maine	3	James Francis Dwyer
1923			
Jan	Norlon Bars A Cage	2	Alan Sullivan
1924			
May	The Splendid Life	2	Percival Gibbon
1925			
March	A Working Man's Wife	2	Sheila Kaye Smith
Sept	One Of My Oldest Friends	2	F. Scott Fitzgerald
1926			
Jan	So The Soldier Went To War	2	May Eddington
April	Show Boat	3*	Edna Ferber
May	Show Boat	2	Edna Ferber
June	Show Boat	2	Edna Ferber
1927			
Aug	Bugles In The Night	3	Barry Benefield
Sept	Bugles In The Night	3	Barry Benefield
Oct	Bugles In The Night	1	Barry Benefield
Dec	One Pound Of Sugar	3	Maxwell Aley
1928			
Aug	The Father	3*	Katherine Holland Brown
Sept	The Father	2	Katherine Holland Brown
Oct	The Father	2	Katherine Holland Brown
Nov	The Father	3	Katherine Holland Brown
Dec	The Father	2	Katherine Holland Brown
1931			
Oct	What The Reason Was	3	Eleanor Howell Abbott
Nov	What The Reason Was	2	Eleanor Howell Abbott
Dec	What The Reason Was	2	Eleanor Howell Abbott
1932			
March	The 3:40 Bus	2	Leona Dalyrimple
1933			
Aug	Salt Of The Sea	2	S.B.H. Hurst
1934			
Nov	When The Curtain Fell	1	Paul Deresco Augsburg
1935			
Sept	The Whole Of The Story	2	Phyllis Bentley
1936			
Jan	Binney Gets A Holiday	2	Laurie Hillyer
July	Miss Watson Strikes Out	2	Doris Peel
1937			
July	The Missing Character	7	Phyllis Bentley
1938			
March	Brass Buttons	2	Thomas Walsh
1941			
April	The Silver Ship	1	Elizabeth Goudge

* Of which two were full color.

THE YOUTH'S COMPANION

1908			
3/26	Helping The Burton Girls	1	F.E.C. Robbins
5/21	The Calico Cat	2	Charles Miner Thompson
5/28	The Calico Cat	1	Charles Miner Thompson
6/4	The Calico Cat	2	Charles Miner Thompson
6/11	The Calico Cat	2	Charles Miner Thompson
6/18	The Calico Cat	2	Charles Miner Thompson
6/25	The Calico Cat	1	Charles Miner Thompson
7/2	The Calico Cat	2	Charles Miner Thompson
1909			
4/29	The Passing Of A Singer	1	F.E.C. Robbins
7/29	A Bag Of Dried Apples	1	Charles T. White
1910			
2/10	An Army Mule	2, 1p*	Charles Miner Thompson
2/17	An Army Mule	1	Charles Miner Thompson
2/24	An Army Mule	1	Charles Miner Thompson
3/3	An Army Mule	1	Charles Miner Thompson
3/10	An Army Mule	2*	Charles Miner Thompson
3/17	An Army Mule	2*	Charles Miner Thompson
3/25	An Army Mule	2*	Charles Miner Thompson
1914			
12/24	Miss Susan And Phoebe	1	Helen Ward Banks
1916			
5/25	A Late Transplanting	1	Elsie Singmaster

10/12,	When Grandpop Voted	1	Elsie Singmaster
10/26	The Maker Of Governors	1	Elizabeth Scott Child
1917			
4/5	Mrs. Pepper Passes	1	Helen Ward Banks
1918			
5/16	The Thankful Spicers	1	Agnes Mary Brownell
5/23	The Thankful Spicers	1	Agnes Mary Brownell
6/13	The Thankful Spicers	1	Agnes Mary Brownell
6/27	The Thankful Spicers	1	Agnes Mary Brownell
7/4	The Thankful Spicers	1	Agnes Mary Brownell
7/25	The Thankful Spicers	1	Agnes Mary Brownell
8/8	The Thankful Spicers	1	Agnes Mary Brownell
8/22	The Thankful Spicers	1	Agnes Mary Brownell
1919			
12/11	Christmas Guests	2	Edith Barnard Delano
1920			
12/16	Suzanne	1	Edith Barnard Delano
12/23	Suzanne	1	Edith Barnard Delano
12/30	Suzanne	1	Edith Barnard Delano
1921			
1/6	Suzanne	1	Edith Barnard Delano
1/13	Suzanne	1	Edith Barnard Delano
1/20	Suzanne	1	Edith Barnard Delano
1/27	Suzanne	1	Edith Barnard Delano
2/3	Suzanne	1	Edith Barnard Delano
2/10	Suzanne	1	Edith Barnard Delano
2/17	Suzanne	1	Edith Barnard Delano

* One a spot. The pen drawing was a heading.

AUTHORS
OF STORIES ILLUSTRATED BY
F. R. GRUGER

Practically every well known author of fiction of the period - 1898 to 1943 - appears in these lists

Men	343
Women	119
	462

KEY to REFERENCE SYMBOLS used to identify the MAGAZINES

Individual parts of a serial are counted the same as a short story - each as an appearance. Figures after a symbol indicate the number of appearances in that particular magazine; except in the case of The SEP when the number follows the year.

A	American	PR	Pictorial Review
Ain	Ainslee's	R	Redbook
C	The Century	S	Scribner's
Cir	Circle	WHC	Woman's Home
CH	College Humor		Companion
Col	Collier's		
Cos	Cosmopolitan		
CG	Country Gentleman		
D	Delineator		
E	Everybody's		
GH	Good Housekeeping		
H	Harper's		
HB	Harper's Bazaar		
HI	Hearst's International		
L	Leslie's		
M	Metropolitan		
McC	McCall's		
McCl	McClure's		
Mun	Munsey's		
P	Pearson's		
SEP	The Saturday Evening Post (followed by two-digit year)		

-A-

Abbott, Eleanor Howell	McCl-5, WHC-3
Abbott, Harriet	A
Adeler, Max	SEP '01-5, SEP '02-2
Alden, W. L.	SEP '01
Aley, Maxwell	WHC
Allen, Glen	SEP '39-2
Allen, Josia's wife	LHJ
Allen, Philip L.	SEP '02
Altsheler, Joseph A.	Suc-6
Anderson, Frederick I.	R, SEP '19
Andrade, Cipriano, Jr.	SEP '17
Andrews, Mary R. S.	SEP '11
Apple, Arthur	A
Aswell, James	CH
Atherton, Gertrude	GH
Atkey, Bertram	SEP '24-5
Atwood, A. W.	SEP '17, SEP '24

Augsburg, Paul Deresco	WHC
Austin, F. Britten	R-6, SEP '19

-B-

Babson, Naomi Lane	SEP '40
Bacon, Josephine Daskam	SEP '21-2
Banks, Helen Ward	Y-2
Barbousse, Henri	McC
Barr, Robert	SEP '02-2, '03, '04, '05-4, '06, '09
Barrington, E.	HB-5
Bartlett, Frederic Orin	SEP '18-2
Bashford, H. H.	SEP '10
Beach, Rex	HI-2
Beard, Wolcott LeClear, Major	S
Beer, Thomas	SEP '23
Bell, William	SEP '05
Benefield, Barry	WHC-3
Benet, Stephen Vincent	Cos-2, D, GH, HB, R, SEP '36, '37, '38, '40
Bennet, Arnold	HI
Bentley, Phyllis	WHC-2
Beveridge, Albert J.	SEP '01-3, '02-3, '03
Biggers, Earl Derr	A, SEP '28-6, '29-6
Bisch, Louis E., MD, PhD	McC
Bishop, Julia Truil	SEP '99-2
Black, Dorothy	SEP '28-4
Blythe, Samuel G.	SEP '08, '10
Boardman, W. H.	McCL
Bowen, Marjorie	Macl
Bradley, Mary Hastings	M
Brand, Anna	D
Brennan, Frederick H.	R
Breyfogle, William Arthur	SEP '40
Bridges, Madeline S.	SEP '00
Brown, Bernice	D
Brown, Foster Emerson	McCl
Brown, Katherine Holland	GH, WHC-4
Brown, Royal	Cos-2
Brownell, Agnes Mary	Y-8
Burgess, Gelett	SEP '07
Burnet, Dana	SEP '18
Burnet, Dora	E
Burt, Maxwell Struthers	R-2, SEP '27
Butler, Ellis Parker	L-3, C-7, D, LHJ-3, McC
Byrne, Donn	SEP '16, '25-3, '26-2, '27-4

-C-

Calloways, S. R.	SEP '01
Canfield, Dorothy	E-2
Carleton, William	SEP '14-5
Carruth, Hayden	SEP '99, '00, '01-2
Chamberlain, George Agnew	SEP '25, '26-5

223

Channing, Grace Ellery	SEP '19
Charteris, Leslie	A
Chester, George Randolph	SEP '07-2, '08-10, '09, '13-6, '14-2, '19
Child, Elizabeth Scott	Y
Child, Richard Washburn	HB, McCl, SEP '19, H
Christie, Agatha	SEP '35-6, SEP '37
Cloete, Stuart	SEP '39, '49
Cobb, Irvin S.	SEP '09, '12-6, '13-3, '14, '15-2, '16-3, '20, '22-5, PR, Cos-10
Collins, James H.	SEP '07
Colyton, Henry John	SEP '43
Condon, Frank	SEP '17
Connolly, C. P.	McCl
Cooper, H. S.	SEP '05, Suc-2
Corbin, John	SEP '12
Corcoran, William	D
Cory, Lucian	E
Cozzens, James Gould	SEP '37
Cragg, Arthur	E, LHJ
Crissey, Forrest	SEP '02
Crook, W. H., Colonel	SEP '10
Crowell, Grace Knoll	GH

-D-

Dalyrimple, Leona	WHC
Dana, Francis	SEP '02
Dare, James B.	LHJ-3
Davies, Maria Thompson	C
Davis, Charles Belmont	S, SEP '08
Davis, Rebecca Harding	SEP '03
Davis, Richard Harding	SEP '12
Day, Casper	McCl
Day, Holman F.	SEP '01, '07, Suc-2
Deakin, Dorothea	SEP '08, SEP '10
DeCamp, Charles B.	McCl
Delano, Edith Barnard	Y-11
Detzer, Karl	A, SEP '36-7
Dew, Natalie	LHJ
Dickson, Harris	D, R
Dodge, Henry Irwin	CG, SEP '19
Donnell, Annie H.	D
Donworth, Grace	LHJ-3
Dreiser, Theodore	SEP '18
Duganne, Phyllis	HB
Duncan, Norman	Ain
Dutton, Louise	SEP '25
Dwyer, James Francis	WHC-4

-E-

Eastbrook William Chester	Mun, SEP '07
Edgar, Day	SEP '28-2
Edington, May	WHC, SEP '19, '23
Edmonds, W. D.	SEP '32, '33-3, '34-5, '35, '36, '37-7
Edwards, Harry Stillwell	C
Ellis, William	SEP '19
England, George Allan	L

Esler, E. Rentoul	SEP '98
Evans, Ida M.	E. SEP '14

-F-

Faulkner, William	SEP '34-3, '36, '41
Ferber, Edna	WHC-3, McCl-2
Fernald, Chester Bailey	SEP '02
Fielding, Howard	Suc-2
Fitch, George	SEP '10
Fitzgerald, F. Scott	R, WHC
Fletcher, J. S.	Cos
Flower, Elliot	C-3, SEP '03-2, '04-3
Foley, J. W.	SEP '05
Follett, Lynn D.	A
Foote, John Tainter	SEP '15
Ford, James L.	SEP '03
Forman, Henry James	Col, GH, H-4
Foster, Maxamilian	SEP '10-3, '15-6, '17
Fraser, W. A.	SEP '99
Frederick, J. George	LHJ, Suc
Friedman, I. K.	SEP '03-3
Furman, Lucy	C-7
Futrelle, Jacques	SEP '12-9

-G-

Gale, Zona	Cos
Galsworthy, John	D
Gambier, Kenyon	SEP '17-2
Garrett, Garet	SEP '20
Garrison, Theodosia	D
Gates, Eleanor	SEP '09
Gatlin, Dana	C
Gelzer, Jay	GH
Gibbon, Percival	WHC, SEP '22, '23, '25
Gibbs, Sir Philip	Cos, D, HB-2
Gibson, Willis	SEP '02
Gill, Brendon	SEP '40
Gilpatrick, Guy	SEP '32, '33
Givens, Colonel	SEP '29
Glaspell, Susan K.	A
Glass, Montague	SEP '10, '14
Goudge, Elizabeth	
Grant, Robert	E
Gray, R.	Suc
Green, Harry Irving	L
Gromer, Belle Burns	Cos

-H-

Haines, Donald H.	E, A
Hale, Louise Closser	D, McCl
Hall, Halworthy	McCl
Hall, Wilbur	SEP '19-3, '20-2
Hallet, Richard M.	E, SEP '30, '31, '33
Hamblen, Herbert E.	SEP '99
Hanby, William	C
Harahan, J. T.	SEP '00
Harben, Will N.	SEP '99

Hare, Anthony	Cos
Harris, Cora	SEP '19-2, '23-8
Harris, Kennith	E, SEP '06, '09, '16
Harris, L. H., Mrs.	SEP '07
Harrison, Henry Sydnor	L, M-8, SEP '25-3
Harrison, Burton, Mrs.	SEP '00
Harte, Bret	SEP '01
Hay, Sara Henderson	GH
Hecht, Ben	SEP '30
Henry, O.	McCl
Hergesheimer, Joseph	SEP '16-3, '17-3, '18-7, '19, '20-6, '24-7, '26-10, '27-10, '29-2, '30-8, '31, '33-3, '34-7, '35-2
Hering, Henry A.	L
Hibbard, George	SEP '06
Hichens, Robert	Cos-10
Higinbotham, H. N.	SEP '01
Hill, Frederic T.	L
Hillman, Gordon Malherbe	PR

-L-

Lait, Jack	A-2
Lane, Carl D.	SEP '41-2
Lardner, Ring W.	SEP 14
Latzke, Paul	SEP '03-2
Lea, Fanny Heaslip	GH
Lears, Alfred Henry	Suc
Lee, Gerald Stanley	SEP '20
Lefevre, Edwin	SEP '06, '13-3, '16-7, '17-4
Lessing, Bruno	LHJ, McCl
Lewis, Alfred Henry	SEP '03-2
Lewis, Sinclair	SEP '19-4
Lieferant, Henry and ˜Sylvia	A
Lighton, William L.	SEP '06, '11, '12, '15-2
Lincoln, Joseph C.	A, E, SEP '01, '03
Lippman, Walter	A
Lloyd, Beatrix Demarest	SEP '27
Locke, William J.	GH-8
Long, John Luther	Ain
Long, Ray	HI
Loomis, Charles Battell	Pear-4, LHJ, SEP '00-2, '02, '03-3, '04, '05
Lorimer, George Horace	SEP '01-2, '02-9, '03-2, '04-8
Low, A. Maurice	S
Lyon, Harris Merton	McCl

-Mc-

McCarthy, Justin Huntley	R
McClure, A. K., Colonel	Suc
McCutcheon, George Barr	SEP '18-4
McFarlane, Arthur E.	SEP '02, '04
McGrath, Harold	SEP '29-3
McHenry, May	McCl

McIntosh, M. E.	SEP '99
McKay, Colin	Ain
McKishnie, Archie P.	MacL
McLeod, Edith G.	L
McMorrow, Thomas	SEP '24-8, '25, '26-4
McQueen, William J.	SEP '00

-M-

Macfarlane, Peter Clark	R
Mackay, Isabel Ecclestons	MacL
Mackenzie, Cameron	SEP '17
Marlowe, Julia	SEP '02
Marquand, J. P.	SEP '22, '25-2, '31, '32-5 '34-4, '35-8, '36-16, '38-7, '40
Marshall, Edison	
Marston, Lawrence	SEP '03
Marteens, Marten	SEP '00
Martin, George Maddin	C
Martin, Thornton	SEP '35
Mason, Grace Sartwell	HI, R
Matthews, William	SEP '02, '03
Maughn, W. Somerset	Cos, HI
Mercein, Eleanor	SEP '29-2, '33
Merwin, Samuel	McCl, Suc-6
Mighels, Philip V.	C-2
Miles, Eustace	SEP '04
Miller, Alice Duer	SEP '21-5, '26-3, '27-3, '29-4
Mitchell, S. Weir, MD	C
Monroe, Ann Shannon	GH
Monroe, Harriet	D
Moore, George	Cos-2
Montague, C. E.	SEP '28
Morgan, Beatrice Burton	McC-4
Morgan, Byron	SEP '20
Morris, Gouverneur	Cos-2, E, HB
Murphy, Ralph	SEP '42
Muth, Edna Tucker	LHJ
Mygatt, Gerald	SEP '21

-N-

Nason, Leonard H.	SEP '31, SEP '33
Norris, Kathleen	SEP '13-3
Noyes, Alfred	SEP '18, '20-2

-O-

O'Brien, Edward W.	SEP '40, '41, '43
O'Hagan, Anne	R
O'Higgins, Harvey J.	L, C-3, R-5, SEP '17, MacL-3
Oppenheim, James	A, LHJ
Osborne, Lloyd	Ain, SEP '03, E, HB-5
Osborne, William Hamilton	Ain, SEP '03, '04, '19,

McCl, Col

-P-

Pain, Barry	SEP '99-2
Pattullo, George	PR, SEP
Payne, Will	'02, '04, '05-3, '06-2, '07, '08, '09-8, '10-8, '11-8, '15, '18 '22-3, '25-2
Peake, Elmore Eliot	SEP '14
Peel, Doris	WHC
Pelley, William Dudley	A-5
Pendexter, Hugh	D
Pertwee, Roland	SEP '29-6
Phelps, William Lyons	GH-3
Phillips, David Graham	Suc
Phillips, Henry Wallace	SEP '04, '06
Pier, Arthur S.	L
Pier, Florida	C
Pierce, Fredrick	Col
Poole, Ernest	SEP '06
Porter, Laura Spencer	H
Post, Melville Davisson	SEP '08, '13-2, R-3
Pottle, Emery	SEP '09
Powell, Richard Stillman	SEP '99
Proud, Victor	SEP '07
Pulver, Henry Brecht	SEP '21
Putnam, Nina Wilcox	SEP '20-3
Weyman, Rita	R
Weyman, Stanley	Cos
Wharton, Anthony	SEP '20
Wharton, Edith	SEP '19, '28, '31
Whitaker, Herman	C-2
White, Charles T.	Y
White, Nellie Gardner	A, McC
White, Stewart Edward	SEP '25
White, William Allen	SEP '03, '05-12, '06-2
Whitlock, Brand	Ain-7, SEP '03, '07
Whitman, Stephen	C-7
Wicks, J. H.	SEP '00
Williams, Ben Ames	SEP '19-8, '23, '36, '40-2, MacL
Williams, Charles Mitchell	Mun
Williams, Frances Fenwick	HB
Williams, Jesse Lynd	A, SEP '02-2, '04
Williams, Valentine	SEP '33-8
Williams, Wyeth	SEP '25, '26
Wiley, Hugh	SEP '20, '25
Wilson, Harry Leon	SEP '11, '12-10, '14-2, '15-10, '16-5, '18-2, '19-6, '20-6, '21-4, '22-4, '23
Wilson, John Fleming	L, SEP '10
Winslow, Horatio	SEP '24, '32
Wister, Owen	SEP '01, '07, H
Witwer, A. C.	Col-18
Wodehouse, P. G.	LHJ, SEP '15-7, '25-6

Wolf, Thomas	SEP '37
Wood, Eugene	Ain
Wooley, Edward Mott	SEP '15
Worts, George F.	LHJ
Wyatt, Edith	McCl-2
Wylie, Elinor	HB
Wylie, I. A. R.	D, SEP '18-8, '26-2, '40-2, GH

-XYZ-

Yates, Danford	SEP '31-5
Yates L. B.	SEP '14-3
Yezierska, Anzia	M
Young, Francis Brett	HB

Selected Bibliography

Unpublished Material

Bolton, Theodore, "American Book Illustrators." Collection of the New York Public Library, 1941.

—————, "Index to American Illustrators." Collection of the New York Public Library, undated.

Brown, Arthur William, "Fifty Years with Artists, Models and Authors," undated. Collection of William Zerbo.

Bullard, III, Edgar John, "John Sloan and the Philadelphia Realists as Illustrators, 1890-1920." Doctoral dissertation, University of California at Los Angeles, 1968.

Denney, Sandra Lee, "Thomas Anshutz: His Life, Art and Teachings." Masters thesis, University of Delaware, 1969.

Grafly, Charles. Diaries. Collection of Dorothy Grafly.

Gruger, Florence. Diary. Collection of F.R. Gruger, Jr.

Gruger, F.R. Correspondence. Collection of F.R. Gruger, Jr.

Luks, George B. Scrapbooks. Collection of Carolyn Luks.

Shinn, Everett. Autobiography. Collection of Charles T. Henry.

Sloan, John. Notes. Collection of Helen Farr Sloan, Delaware Art Museum, Wilmington.

Ward, Roswell, Biographical Notes about F.R. Gruger, 1944. Collection of F.R. Gruger, Jr., 1944.

Weitenkamp, Frank, "The American Illustrator." Collection of the New York Public Library, 1955.

Books and Periodicals

Adams, Herbert, "The War's Influence on Art," *The Forum.* New York, January, 1919.

Armstrong, Regina, "Representative Young Illustrators," *The Art Interchange,* Vol. XLIII, No. 5, November, 1899.

"Artists of the Philadelphia Press," *Philadelphia Museum Bulletin,* Vol. XLI, No. 207, November, 1945, pp. 1-15.

Benjamin, S.G.W., "American Art Since the Centennial," *The New Princeton Review,* 1887.

Bolton, Theodore, *American Book Illustrators.* New York, R.R. Bowker Co., 1938.

Brown, Arthur William, "Frederic Rodrigo Gruger," *Society of Illustrators Bulletin,* April-May, 1953, p. 9.

—————, "Recollections of a Great Illustrator, F.R. Gruger," *Society of Illustrators Bulletin,* March, 1964, p. 2.

—————, "Then and Now," *Society of Illustrators Summer Bulletin,* 1962, p. 2.

Brown, Dee, *The Year of the Century: 1876.* New York, Charles Scribner's Sons, 1966.

Buckley, Charles E., foreword, *William Glackens in Retrospect.* St. Louis, City Art Museum of St. Louis, 1966.

Buechner, Tomas S., *Norman Rockwell: A Sixty Year Retrospective.* New York, Harry N. Abrams, Inc., 1972.

Butterfield, Roger, ed., *The Saturday Evening Post Treasury.* New York, Simon and Schuster, 1954.

Cameron, Duncan F., intro., *A Century of American Illustration.* Brooklyn, N.Y., The Brooklyn Museum, 1972.

Chapman, Altona A., "Lady Artists in Philadelphia," *Philadelphia Press,* January 24, 1892, p. 24.

"Contributions to the International Exposition, Philadelphia, 1876," *Art Journal,* 1876, pp. 153-4, 249.

Deford, Frank, *There She Is: The LIfe and Times of Miss America.* New York, Viking Press, 1971.

Division of Pictorial Publicity: Souvenir menu of a banquet held in New York, February 14, 1919. A History of the Division of Pictorial Publicity. New York, 1919.

Downey, Fairfax, *Portrait of an Era as Drawn by C.D. Gibson.* New York, Charles Scribner's Sons, 1936.

duBois, Guy Pene, intro., *Five American Illustrators.* New York, The Anderson Galleries, 1924.

du Pont, Eleuthere I., foreword, *The Life and Times of John Sloan.* Wilmington, The Wilmington Society of the Fine Arts, 1961.

Egner, Arthur F., foreword, *Catalog of an Exhibition of the Work of George Benjamin Luks.* Newark, N.J., The Newark Museum, 1934.

Elzea, Rowland, intor., *An Album of Brandywine Tradition Artists.* New York, Great American Editions, 1971.

—————, *The Golden Age of American Illustration, 1880-1914.* Wilmington, Delaware Art Museum, 1972.

Flagg, James Montgomery, *Roses and Buckshot.* New York,

G.P. Putnam's Sons, 1946.

Fraser, Jr., Joseph T., foreword, *The One Hundred and Fiftieth Anniversary Exhibition.* Philadelphia, The Pennsylvania Academy of the Fine Arts, 1955.

"F.R. Gruger," *American Artists.* Philadelphia, Gatchel & Manning, Inc., March, 1939.

Gallatin, Albert Eugene, "Art and the War," *Allied War Salon.* New York, 1918.

————, *Suggestions for Artists Desiring to Apply Their Knowledge to War Work.* New York, The Mayor's Committee on National Defense, 1918.

————, *Art and the Great War.* New York, E.P. Dutton & Co., 1919.

Glackens, Ira, intro., *George Luks.* Utica, N.Y., Munson-Williams-Proctor Institute, 1973.

————, *William Glackens and the Ashcan Group: The Emergence of Realism in American Art.* New York, Crown Publishers, Inc., 1957.

Gottesman, Rita S., "Early Commercial Art," *Art in America,* December, 1955.

Guptill, Arthur L., *Drawing with Pen and Ink.* New York, The Pencil Points Press, Inc., 1928.

Henderson, Helen W., *The Pennsylvania Academy of the Fine Arts and Other Collections in Philadelphia.* Boston, L.C. Page & Co., 1911.

Homer, William Innes, *Robert Henri and his Circle.* Ithaca, N.Y., Cornell University Press, 1969.

Landgren, Marchal E., *Years of Art: The Story of The Art Students League of New York.* N.Y., Robert M. McBride & Co., 1940.

Lee, Alfred McClung, *The Daily Newspaper in America.* New York, The MacMillan Co., 1937.

"Life begins at 50: The Society of Illustrators Celebrates its Golden Anniversary and Looks Forward to Another 50 Years," *American Artist,* vol. 15, no. 7, September, 1951, pp. 32-4, 83-4.

Little, Stuart W., "Are Illustrators Obsolete?" *Saturday Review,* July 10, 1971, pp. 40-4.

Ludwig, Coy, *Maxfield Parrish.* New York, Watson-Guptill, 1973.

Mannix, Daniel P., "The Father of the Wizard of Oz," *American Heritage,* Vol. XVI, No. 1, December, 1964, pp. 36-47, 108-9.

Massey, James C., *Frank H. Furness and his Centennial Sensation: The Pennsylvania Academy of the Fine Arts Building.* Philadelphia, Pennsylvania Academy of the Fine Arts, undated.

McDougall, Walt, "Old Days on the World," *American Mercury,* January, 1925.

Mellquist, Jerome, *The Emergence of an American Art.* New York, Charles Scribner's Sons, 1942.

Meyer, Susan E., *James Montgomery Flagg.* New York, Watson-Guptill, 1974.

Morse, Peter, *John Sloan's Prints.* New Haven, Yale University Press, 1969.

"Notable Sales Recalled by the Brilliant Annuals of the American-Anderson Galleries," *The Art News,* June 11, 1932, pp. 3, 11.

"Pasting Things Together," *Art Students League News,* Vol. 5, No. 3, March 15, 1952, p. 6.

Perlman, Bennard B., *The Immortal Eight: American Painting from Eakins to the Armory Show,* 1870-1913. New York, Exposition Press, 1962.

Peterson, Theodore, *Magazines of the Twentieth Century.* Urbana, Ill., University of Illinois Press, 1964.

Phillips, Duncan, "Art and the War," *The American Magazine of Art,* June, 1918.

Pyle, Howard: Diversity in Depth. Wilmington, Delaware Art Museum, 1973.

Reed, Walt, *The Illustrator in America 1900-1960's.* New York, Reinhold, 1966.

Renwick, Stephen Lee, "F.R. Gruger: A Milestone in the Tradition of American Illustration," *American Artist,* Vol. 7, No. 8, October, 1943, pp. 14-7, 32B.

Saint John, Bruce, *John Sloan.* New York, Praeger, 1971.

Schau, Michael, *J.C. Leyendecker.* New York, Watson-Guptill, 1974.

Scott, David W., and Bullard, E. John, *John Sloan, 1871-1951.* Washington, D.C., National Gallery of Art, 1971.

Shestack, Alan, intro., *Edwin Austin Abbey.* New Haven, Yale University Art Gallery, 1973.

Sloan, John, *Gist of Art.* New York, American Artists Group, 1939.

Smith, Katherine L., "Newspaper Art," *The Art Interchange,* Vol. XLIV, No. 3, March, 1900, pp. 52-3.

Stout, Wesley, "Yes, We Read The Story," *The Saturday Evening Post,* June 25, 1932, pp. 8-9, 34, 36, 38, 40.

Street, Julian, "Our Fighting Posters," *McClure's Magazine,* July, 1918.

Taylor, Carol, "Seeing Himself as Others See Him, Fellow Illustrators Pay Tribute to Arthur William Brown," *New York World-Telegram,* May 20, 1961.

"The News of Art Circles: Plans and Purposes of the Recently Organized Charcoal Club," *The Times—Philadelphia,* April 8, 1893.

The Well-Knowns as seen by James Montgomery Flagg. New York, George H. Doran Co., 1914.

"U.S. Illustrators," *Time* Magazine, May 1, 1939, pp. 49-50.

THE FOOLSCAP ROSE UNFOLDED, THE BANKER, by JOSEPH HERGESHEIMER, *The Saturday Evening Post,* May 19, 1934, Page 18

Index